R (PETE) Parcells

General Equilibrium Analysis

General Equilibrium Analysis

A Micro-economic text

MELVYN B. KRAUSS

Associate Professor of Economics
Stanford University

HARRY G. JOHNSON

Professor of Economics
University of Chicago

Aldine Publishing Company, *Chicago*

ABOUT THE AUTHORS

Melvyn B. Krauss is Associate Professor of Economics at Stanford University. Harry G. Johnson is Charles F. Grey Distinguished Service Professor of Economics at the University of Chicago. Both have published numerous journal articles applying general equilibrium analysis to micro-economics, international trade, public finance, and related fields.

Published 1975 by
Aldine Publishing Company
529 South Wabash Avenue
Chicago, Illinois 60605

ISBN 0-202-06069-1 clothbound edition
Library of Congress Catalog Number 74-18213
First published 1974 by George Allen & Unwin Ltd
Printed in the United States of America

PREFACE

This book represents what we believe to be a very different approach to the teaching of micro-economic theory than that normally followed, and one that we hope will be of greater long-run value to the serious student of economics. In place of the usual textbook development of the subject as traditionally conceived through topics of increasing complexity and analytical difficulty, using partial equilibrium techniques of analysis, we have concentrated on the exposition and application of a more logically integrated set of tools that we have found of great use in the analysis of problems arising not only in traditional micro-economics but also in a number of fields of economics that have customarily been hived off into separate specialized advanced courses. These specialized courses typically build on the introductory micro-economics course but tend both to mingle theory with institutional detail and the re-exposition of set pieces of traditional analysis, and to introduce rigorous theory on an eclectic and *ad hoc* basis. By contrast this text is organized around the unified set of analytical concepts and techniques generically described as 'the two-sector model of general equilibrium', and deals with those problems in a range of fields of economics for which the techniques are appropriate. The basis is thus laid for a more coherent integration of the general micro-economics course with advanced more specialized courses.

The two-sector model is the simplest possible model of general equilibrium that is capable of being expounded without large-scale prior preparation in mathematics. Mathematics has become increasingly necessary to professional economists. But the differential calculus form of it usually employed in micro-economics is incapable of dealing with certain kinds of problems, involving non-infinitesimal changes; moreover, some students find it easier to learn mathematics after they have come to appreciate the need for and usefulness of it than before they confront its economic applications. The main loss, from the viewpoint of theory, from confining attention to the two-sector model is that it rules out consideration of problems involving complementarity among goods in consumption and factors in production; but the possibility of complementarity is frequently

7

reduced to trivial importance for the convenience of the mathematical model-builders.

The book begins with an introduction describing the assumptions of the model, showing how the two sectors are built up from the behaviour of the individual micro-units comprising them and how they fit into the general concept of 'the circular flow of income', and discussing the vexed and controversial question of the basis, if any, on which welfare judgments about the effects of economic changes can be arrived at in a capitalist economy. The next chapter analyses in detail the general equilibrium model of the production side of the economy and the requirements of equilibrium in commodity and factor markets. Subsequent chapters deal with the evaluation of changes in factor endowment, demand preferences and technical progress by means of the two-sector model; and the theory of government, which includes both the newly-emerging theory of government expenditure, or public goods, and the theory of government tax and/or subsidy programmes—changes in budgetary scale, tax substitution and expenditure substitution. The model is then extended to an open economy—the so-called 'two by two by two'—to consider both the normative effect of international trade and the possible determinants of international trade, with special attention being given to the relationship between commodity trade and factor mobility. The subsequent theory of tariffs is a logical extension of the theory of international trade, considering the effects of tariffs on the economic welfare of both the individual micro-units comprising the community and the 'aggregate' community itself; an analysis which is extended into the more generalized 'theory of distortions', which considers the 'best' policies for a welfare-oriented government to follow under the assumption that obstacles, or distortions, prevent the economy from attaining a position of full Pareto optimality. Finally, the two-sector model is opened out into a dynamic model of economic growth with attention focusing on the requirements for the economy to maximize consumption per head on its long-run equilibrium growth path, and the effect of international trade on the growth path itself.

The express purpose of the exposition is not to deal in detail with every problem that anyone has ever raised or considered in every field of economics covered, but to deal with the central problems in such a way that the careful student should be able to work out the solutions to other problems not dealt with explicitly. For this purpose, we offer from time to time in passing some tips on the analogies between the problems analysed and related problems not analysed but analysable with the techniques developed in the book. (Analysis of some of these problems should enable the student to test his comprehension of the techniques themselves, as distinct from the answers arrived at by applying them to particular cases.)

As is customary, we must, and gladly do, end this preface by expressing our indebtedness not only to colleagues, both institutional and professional, who have both themselves written on the subjects covered, and discussed them with us, but also to our regular students at The London School of Economics, The University of Chicago, McMaster University, The Europa Institute, The Johns Hopkins Bologna Center, and to students encountered in seminars and lectures at many other universities, whose difficulties and questions have contributed greatly to the clarification and simplification of our methods of expounding detailed points. We should also like to express our particular gratitude to Irene Krauss, who has been both a patient and understanding passive spectator of our efforts to achieve close intellectual collaboration in a series of short and hectic meetings in a variety of scattered locations, and an extremely accurate typist of what to her was a foreign language; and to Lois Rodgers, who has been understandably less patient but equally devoted to getting the typescript ready for the press.

Harry G. Johnson
The University of Chicago

Melvyn B. Krauss
Stanford University

CONTENTS

CHAPTER 1

Assumptions and
Introductory Concepts

Economic analysis is concerned with the understanding of how the economic system works and what the effects of various kinds of social, economic, and policy changes are likely to be. Every citizen has ideas of his own on these matters; what distinguishes the economist is the consistent application of a body of logical principles and methods of empirical verification developed and tested by the work of generations of economic scholars. The development of scientific economics has necessarily required heavy reliance on the main principle of all scientific enquiry: the use of logical abstraction to reduce a problem to its essentials and permit concentration on those essentials to be untrammelled by peripheral detail.

For most of its contemporary history, economics has performed the necessary abstraction by assuming that it is a legitimate approximation to isolate a single market from the complex network of markets, ignoring 'feedbacks' from that market to other markets and thence back into the market under analysis, and analysing the market under study in terms of the familiar 'partial equilibrium' concepts of demand and supply. These concepts can take one a very long way towards understanding of how the economic system works— but not the whole way; and it is often difficult to determine the borderline between conditions under which partial equilibrium analysis contains the usable predominance of truth, and conditions under which the 'feedbacks' dominate the results. Consequently, economists have increasingly come to the belief that a 'general equilibrium' analysis—i.e. an analysis which concerns itself with the equilibrium of the whole system, and not of just a sub-sector of it—is necessary both for scientific dependability and for checking the reliability of the results of partial equilibrium analysis.

The purpose of this book is to develop from its foundations the simplest kind of general equilibrium analysis, the so-called 'two-by-two-by-two' model of general equilibrium (two goods produced, two factors required to produce each good, two individuals with different shares in the ownership of the economy's factors and therefore with different income prospects); and to apply that model to a number of problems of general interest in such fields as public finance and tax incidence, the distribution of income among persons, and the effects of international trade and of commercial policy measures on economic welfare and income distribution. Our main purpose, however, is not to provide ceremonially adequate answers to set questions, but to show the reader how a fairly simple set of technical economic tools, once mastered, can be applied to an unexpectedly wide range of economic problems with fruitful results.

I. METHOD OF ANALYSIS

There is a generally accepted distinction between two methods of economic analysis: the 'static' and the 'dynamic'. The central concept in static analysis is that of equilibrium, defined as the position which if attained will be maintained under *ceteris paribus* conditions (no change in the 'givens' of the system). There are two analytically distinguishable components of static analysis; that of statics proper, which is exclusively concerned with the position of equilibrium under *ceteris paribus* conditions, and that of comparative statics where attention focuses on the comparison of two or more different equilibrium positions. Comparative statics involves studying the consequences for the static equilibrium of the system of changing one or more of the 'givens' of strict static analysis. It is a method of studying dynamic change in the system, which proceeds by reducing dynamic change to once-over shifts in the 'givens'. Dynamic analysis, on the other hand, is concerned on the one hand with the stability of pure static equilibrium—i.e. if there were a chance departure from static equilibrium, are there forces that would drive the system over time back to the initial equilibrium or would it instead be driven to some alternative equilibrium position?—and on the other hand with the time-path of adjustment of the system to a lasting change in the 'givens' of the system—will the system approach the new static equilibrium in a steady asymptotic fashion, or with oscillations, and if there are oscillations will they fade out gradually over time or will they increase in amplitude so that the economy never actually reaches a new stationary equilibrium? A still more ambitious dynamic economics, developed in the past quarter century or so, assumes that the 'givens' (e.g. population size, available technology) change at a steady rate over time, and is concerned with whether the economy will settle down to a steady-state growth path determined by the exogenously-given rate of change of the variables taken as given in pure and comparative static analysis.

The two-by-two-by-two model presented in this book is in the field of pure and comparative statics. However, there is an initial problem about static equilibrium which overlaps into the field of economic dynamics. This is the question of whether the static equilibrium of the system is unique, or whether multiple equilibria are possible. The overlap with dynamics arises from the consideration that if the equilibrium is not unique, one has to distinguish between 'stable' and 'unstable' equilibria, i.e. between equilibria that would be self-sustaining against random shocks and equilibria that would be destroyed, and replaced by another equilibrium, in case of disturbance by any random shock. In order to analyse this question, one needs a theoretical specification of how the system adjusts to disequilibrium, i.e. a theory of the dynamic motion of the system when it is disturbed. The simplest and most generally accepted theory, though by no means the only possible one, is the 'Walrasian' or 'Hicksian' theory that if there is excess demand for a commodity at a particular price competition will tend to drive that price upwards, and vice versa if there is excess supply at a particular price. This permits one to say that an equilibrium position will be 'stable' if a small fall in price will produce an excess of quantity demanded over quantity supplied and vice versa for a small increase in price; and conversely an equilibrium will be 'unstable' if a small fall in price produces an excess of quantity supplied over quantity demanded and vice versa for a small increase in price. By extension, a small change in the 'givens' of the system will produce a predictable change in the characteristics of equilibrium of the system if that equilibrium is 'stable'; but if the initial equilibrium is 'unstable', one cannot tell what the effects of a disturbance will be.

The point may be illustrated in terms of the familiar demand and supply curve apparatus. If the demand curve is always downward-sloping to the right, and the supply curve always upward-sloping to the right, the two curves can intersect only once, and in a stable equilibrium position; and any change in demand or supply conditions will produce predictable changes in the equilibrium price and the quantity supplied and demanded. But there is the possibility that demand or supply curves are not 'well-behaved', and that consequently they intersect more than once, producing a case of 'multiple equilibrium'.

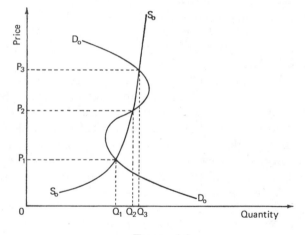

FIGURE 1.1

The standard case of this possibility is illustrated in Figure 1.1, where as price falls over a certain range quantity demanded also falls. The common explanation of this possibility involves the so-called 'Giffen good', i.e. an inferior good in the sense that as people's real income or purchasing power rises they will consume less of the good, but with the added condition that the 'income effect' on real income or purchasing power of a fall in the price of the good—which leads people to demand less of the inferior good—is stronger than the 'substitution effect' of the reduction in the price of the good

16

relative to other goods—which should lead people to substitute this now-cheaper good for other goods. The 'Giffen good' possibility is rather far-fetched, since with both high prices and negligible consumption and large consumption at very low prices the income effect cannot be large enough to outweigh the substitution effect (a point illustrated by the slope of the demand curve in Figure 1.1). However, as we shall show later, in a general equilibrium context a change in the price of a commodity will involve a change in the distribution of income among factor owners, and differences in preferences among the latter may result in an association of a price reduction with a reduction in quantity demanded even though the good in question is not inferior in anyone's consumption. (The reader should note in passing that if the suppliers of a good consume some of it themselves, a rise in its price could lead them to produce more of it but to supply less of it to the market, again creating the possibility of more than one intersection of the demand and supply curves. This possibility figured largely in the accepted theory of development planning in the 1950s, according to which taxation of farm production would increase the marketed supply of farm products; but the weight of the empirical evidence is that marketed farm production is an increasing function of the market price of the product.)

In Figure 1.1, D_0D_0 is the demand curve and S_0S_0 the supply curve. Three intersections of the curves are depicted, with equilibrium prices, P_1, P_2 and P_3, and equilibrium quantities Q_1, Q_2, Q_3. So long as we can assume that at a high enough price nothing will be demanded, and that at a low enough price nothing will be supplied, there must be an odd number (three, five, seven, etc.) of intersections of the two curves. Furthermore, as is evident from the diagram, the odd-numbered intersections (first, third, fifth, etc.) will be stable equilibria on the definition adopted above, while the even-numbered intersections (second, fourth, etc.) will be unstable equilibria. In other words, an unstable equilibrium point will always be bordered on both sides by stable equilibrium points. One might therefore assume that only stable equilibrium points will ever be observed in reality—specifically, we would never observe the combination P_2Q_2. However, the possibility exists that a random disturbance of equilibrium could move the system from the equilibrium position P_1Q_1 to the equilibrium position P_3Q_3 or vice versa.

This possibility becomes still more awkward if we move from pure statics to comparative statics. Consider, say, a shift of the demand curve due to a change in the givens of the system. Suppose P_3 is our initial equilibrium point, and for some reason the demand curve shifts leftwards. For successive small changes, equilibrium price and quantity will both fall by small amounts. But eventually the demand curve will become tangent to the supply curve, we will have an unstable instead of a stable equilibrium, and the system will have to make a discontinuous jump from the P_2P_3 range down to a price-quantity combination below P_1Q_1. (The tangency case can be thought of as still involving three equilibrium points, of which two are identical with respect to price-quantity combination but one is stable for upwards price movements and the other unstable for downwards price movements.)

The possibility of multiple equilibria, including unstable equilibrium positions, is clearly awkward for economic analysis. If the economy may make discontinuous 'jumps' from one equilibrium neighbourhood to another, instead of sticking to a unique equilibrium position determined by the 'givens' of the system and moving to a uniquely-determined new equilibrium when the 'givens' change, nothing can be said reliably about either the characteristics of equilibrium or the effects of changes in the 'givens'. Unfortunately, it is not possible to rule out the possibility of multiple equilibrium on *a priori* grounds; one simply has to assume it away, in order to get on with the business of analysis. Fortunately, though, the conditions required to make multiple equilibrium possible can be shown to be empirically implausible—as with the 'Giffen good' and 'income redistribution' cases discussed above—so that analysis can safely be conducted on the assumption of a unique stable equilibrium position.

This assumption has a great simplifying virtue. If we can assume that equilibrium is stable, and specifically that an excess of quantity demanded over quantity supplied at a given price necessarily requires an increase in that price to restore equilibrium, we can conduct our qualitative comparative-statics analysis of the effects of changes in the 'givens' of the system by asking what effects these changes would produce on the net balance of quantities demanded and supplied at the initial equilibrium prices. If the net effect is an excess demand in a particular market, price in that market must rise, and vice versa. And since the prices of goods and of factors are related, we can use results for the goods market to predict results for the factor market, and vice versa.

This brings us to an important general point about the model developed in this book, which is that its main interest lies in the connection between commodity prices and factor prices, i.e. incomes of factor owners. In a two-commodity model, there can be only one relative commodity price; and, by Walras's law, if that price clears one commodity market (establishes equilibrium in that market) it must simultaneously clear the other. Partial equilibrium analysis conducted in terms of demand curves and supply curves is therefore capable, if used with some sophistication, of analysing equilibrium in the commodity markets. The virtue of general equilibrium analysis in the model under consideration is that it links commodity prices, factor prices, and income distribution together in the determination of the general equilibrium of commodity and factor prices.

II. TYPES OF PROBLEMS: WELFARE ECONOMICS

The two-sector model of general equilibrium (like the partial equilibrium model) is useful in analysing two distinct types of questions. These are:

1. *Positive questions*

These are objective questions, concerned primarily with cause and effect. They are exemplified by scientific investigation, either qualitative as in this book or quantitative as in econometric studies, of the effects of changes in the 'givens' of the hypothetical and simplified economic system constructed by the theorist on the equilibrium values of the prices and quantities of traded goods and the prices of factors and the quantities of them used in different lines of production. Where factor supplies are assumed to depend on the prices received for them by their owners, the equilibrium quantities of factors supplied also become part of the positive problems of general equilibrium.

2. *Normative questions*

These questions are concerned with whether the economic unit or class of units under consideration is, in some sense that we shall see requires careful specification, made 'better off' or 'worse off' by some kind of change in the 'givens' of the system—a 'parametric' change. (What is meant by the term 'economic unit or class of units' is discussed further below.) Among the 'givens' must be included not only such elements as consumer preferences and the technology available to households and firms, but government policies, since included among the normative questions are questions about whether government policies (specifically, taxes or subsidies on particular types of production or consumption) could increase the welfare of 'the community' governed beyond what it would be under *laissez-faire*, or alternatively whether such policies (specifically, income-distribution policies) could increase the welfare derived by the community from a given stock of factors of production and a given technology assumed to be used always with maximum efficiency. (Note, for future reference, that this statement implies a particular view of the function of government that is only one of several possible, and also that contrary to the facts of observation it allows government no independent role in the provision of want-satisfying goods and services.)

Normative questions may arise on either the production side or the consumption side of the economy. On the production side, a problem as long-standing as economics itself has been the effects of monopoly and similar arrangements both in reducing potential production and in redistributing income in a direction usually considered socially undesirable (but not always condemned: the use of monopoly powers by trade unions is generally condoned under the superficial impression that it produces socially desirable re-distribution effects). A more recently-developed problem is that of 'externalities' in production which may be defined as cases in which a firm or industry produces by-products for which, if they are beneficial to other firms or to consumers, it cannot charge, or, if they are harmful to other firms or consumers, it does not have to pay compensation. It has recently been shown by R. H. Coase that such externalities would be 'internalized' by a well-defined system of property and contract rights reinforced by an efficient system of litigation. In any case, the analysis of this book will be simplified by assuming the absence of externalities and a competitive system of production, so that all normative problems appear on the consumption side of the economy.

'Externalities' also appear on the consumption side, in two forms. One is 'objective' externalities, for example, where my neighbour's bonfire dirties the clothes on my washing-line or his loud playing of rock music on his hi-fi set prevents me from concentrating on listening to my Mozart records or reading the great philosophers. (Many such cases, however, are subject to legal rights or other regulations.) The other is 'subjective' externalities, for example where his failure to keep his lawn and garden trim or his habit of wearing patched old clothes around his home offends my sense of respectable behaviour. Externalities of both types are excluded by assumption: either they are assumed not to exist, or (in line with the modern welfare economics discussed below) they are assumed to be offset by the imposition of marginal taxes and subsidies by government. Simplification of the problem by abstraction from externalities means that the welfare levels of individuals or households (deemed to constitute a single consuming unit, despite the ubiquitous evidence of conflicts within families over how the household income should be spent) can be assumed to depend simply and solely on the goods and services consumed by the individual or the household.

This simplification permits the adoption of a very simple and presumably general acceptable principle—the so-called 'Pareto principle' of welfare economics—for determining whether a community of people (a term used to include both individuals, and individuals grouped into households) can be said to have been made better off by an economic change. The principle is that the community is deemed to be better off (its welfare has improved) if no one has been made worse off and at least one member of the community has been made better off as a result. Conversely, welfare is deemed to have deteriorated if no one has been made better off and at least one person has been made worse off as a result of the change.

Much of the earlier welfare analysis of the problems dealt with in this book has been conducted explicitly or implicitly on Paretian lines, through the postulation of a set of 'community indifference curves' exactly analogous to the indifference curves that represent the preferences of the individual consumer but presumed to represent a community preference system. This procedure is an analytically justifiable abstraction for the examination of certain types of problems, provided its limitations are understood. However, the ineluctable fact is that, in a competitive economy, almost any type of economic change is likely to benefit some individuals or classes of individuals and damage others, either because tastes differ among individuals or because participations in factor ownership differ or for both reasons. There are various ways, all unsatisfactory, of dodging this problem, by making assumptions which isolate income distribution from changes in commodity and factor prices. One such assumption is the existence of a paternalistic or dictatorial state, which applies its own (unique) set of preferences to the determination of the production pattern and allocates output among its citizens according to its own criteria of merit, regardless of individual preferences. Another is the existence of a socialist state, in which incomes are distributed by the state (or redistributed through income taxes and subsidies on private incomes) so as to achieve at all times a socially desired distribution of income. In this case, individual preferences can be aggregated into a collective preference function, since the weights attached to individual preferences are independent of the individual's earned income as determined by the prices of the factors he owns. However, there is a catch to this procedure: the socialist society must be assumed to maintain a given distribution of individual utility levels, not of individual incomes measured objectively in terms of some numéraire (a particular commodity, or 'money'), because if individual tastes differ and relative prices change while the income distribution in terms of numéraire remains constant, the distribution of utility levels will change (only smokers gain from a fall in the price of cigarettes).

Each of these two assumptions solves the problem by jettisoning the assumption of a competitive capitalist economy. A third assumption, designed to conform at least superficially to the essence of capitalism, is to assume that people possess exactly the same absolute quantities of the factors of production and have identical preference maps, so that each is affected in exactly the same way by any change in the 'givens'. On this approach, the collectivity is merely a multiplication of the 'representative man' beloved of Marshall and Pigou, and all the interesting features of capitalism are assumed away. A more sophisticated but still unsatisfactory version of this approach is to assume that individuals possess factors in the same ratios (but not absolute quantities), and that their indifference curve systems are identical and homothetic (i.e. whatever their numéraire incomes, at any given set of price ratios they will purchase goods in the same ratios); with this assumption, a high-income individual acts simply as if he consisted of a number of low-income individuals.

A fourth assumption, designed to reconcile the facts of competitive capitalism as it now exists—i.e. a broadly competitive system in which nevertheless government redistributes incomes among persons and groups by progressive tax and expenditure policies—with the Pareto criterion is to assume that those who lose from economic change have to be compensated by those who gain. If there is anything left over, there is a gain in social welfare, and vice versa. (Note the parallel between this criterion and the assumption of a socialist state; the difference is that the 'compensation test' simply takes the initial income distribution as given, without assuming that it is fixed by collective decision to maximize social welfare.) Such compensations have to be made in the form of 'lump-sum' taxes and subsidies, to avoid distorting the efficiency of resource allocation in production and commodity allocation in consumption, a stipulation whose impracticality itself casts doubt on the usefulness of the assumption. A more important objection is that in practice compensations for damages due to change are not made on the scale and with the exactitude posited—though they are made in a rough and ready way through such structural aspects of economic policy as progressive tax and expenditure policy and social security, and through special legislation designed to recompense groups identifiably and severely damaged by identifiable changes in the parameters of the system or in economic policy itself.

Recognition of the fact that compensation for the adverse effects of change is normally not paid led economists into the attempt to develop welfare criteria on the basis of whether compensation *could* be paid after a change or not, in the form of various 'compensation tests'. (Clearly, such tests cannot apply to governmental policies of income redistribution, only to changes in other government policies or in the 'givens' of the system: the classical welfare economics case has been the repeal of the British corn laws—tariffs on grain imports —in the early nineteenth century). These compensation tests run into two major difficulties: first, because the compensations are not in fact paid, they may be self-contradictory in the comparison of the situations before and after a change, or contradictory with each other, since the before-and-after-change situations may involve major differences in utility distribution. Second, the choice of any particular initial position as a standard from which to measure a welfare change involves an implicit ethical judgment in favour of the utility distribution corresponding to that position. These difficulties have led to the proposition that the compensation test must be met for all conceivable distributions of utility (note that on this stipulation all compensation tests are consistent with themselves and each other). But even if this condition is fulfilled, it cannot be said that welfare has *actually* improved; all that can be said is that potential welfare has improved, in the sense that regardless of how one evaluates the individual utility levels from a welfare point of view, if one's evaluation were implemented both before and after the change via lump-sum transfers and subsidies (or even by methods that involved some distortions in allocation, provided the effects of these were taken into account in the evaluation), the change would increase actual welfare according to one's evaluation.

The 'compensation test' and 'potential welfare' approach was developed in the 1930s to 1950s period, in response to Lionel Robbins's refutation (*The Nature and Significance of Economic Science*) of the earlier utilitarian belief that social welfare could be regarded simply as the sum of individual utility levels, his grounds being that this procedure rested on making interpersonal comparisons of utility and that this could not be done on a purely scientific basis but required value judgments. That approach also reflected an historical epoch in which economists tended to believe that the competitive system functioned both inefficiently and inequitably (note that these are not the same thing) and espoused an idealistic Benthamistic view of government as designed to correct such inefficiencies and inequities, without crediting existing governments with whatever efforts they were already making in this regard. A more tolerant view, in line with the contemporary existence of the welfare state, would be that government attempts to achieve efficiency and equity within the feasible limits of rough justice available to it, and that the economist's role is to point out unexpected implications of changes in 'givens' and policies rather than to insist on impossibly pure ethical standards for the judgment of welfare effects.

An alternative approach to social welfare evaluation, developed in the same period and identified with the name of Abram Bergson, posits a 'social welfare function' arrived at by some socio-political-ethical process, according to which the changes in individual utilities consequent on changes in 'givens' or policies are to be judged. Such a function is written as $W = W(U_1, U_2, U_3, \ldots, U_n)$, where the Us are the individual utilities achieved in a given state of society. The technology and individual tastes of the society define a 'utility frontier' such that the utility level of one individual is maximized subject to the maintenance of fixed levels of utility for the others, and social welfare maximization involves tangency of a contour of the social welfare function with this frontier. However, society may not be on the frontier, or may not be at the optimum point, and there may be no feasible way of getting there; and the same may be true for a change of situation. In such cases, the social welfare function permits evaluation of the welfare effects of changes, whether they occur from or to Pareto-optimal conditions in production and consumption or not. The problem, however, is to construct a scientifically acceptable social welfare function. Kenneth Arrow's 'impossibility theorem' shows that this cannot be done in general on the basis of democratic voting procedures.

All of the above are 'aggregative' approaches to the normative questions of social welfare, in the sense of attempting to devise means of arriving at conclusions about the welfare effects of economic changes on communities composed of differentially circumstanced individuals. At various points in this book we shall make use of the community indifference curve approach, and at others we shall employ the 'potential welfare' compensation test approach. Our main concern, however, is with the alternative 'disaggregated' approach, according to which the community is divided into sufficiently approximately homogeneous groups and the effects of changes on the separate utility levels of these groups is analysed. In the extreme, there could be as many groups as there are individuals and/or households, and the welfare effects on each member of society analysed; but subdivision into two groups is sufficient to reveal and handle the main analytical problems while avoiding cumbersome complexity. The two groups must be distinguished by economically relevant criteria. The two obvious lines of division are between people of differing tastes (which includes people with the same non-homothetic preferences maps but enjoying different income levels), and people with different relative and/or absolute shares in factor ownership (differences in absolute but not relative factor shares have to be combined with differences in tastes in the sense just defined to produce an economically relevant difference). Generally, we shall assume that differences in tastes and relative factor ownership go together. As regards differences in relative factor shares, a difference should be noted between the international trade theory tradition, which following the English classical tradition identifies groups with ownership of a single factor ('labour' or 'capital') and the public finance tradition, which assumes that groups own some of both factors, but in different proportions. It should also be noted that the analysis can easily be extended to other lines of economically relevant divisions in society, such as those between 'rich' and 'poor', males and females, or whites and blacks, in so far as these lines of division are identifiable with differences in tastes and/or relative and absolute factor ownership.

III. THE FRAMEWORK OF GENERAL EQUILIBRIUM ANALYSIS: THE CIRCULAR FLOW OF INCOME

The basic framework of general equilibrium analysis is the sub-division of economic units into two types: the firm which produces goods; and the household which consumes them. The firm is assumed to maximize profits, and under competitive conditions will either earn only 'normal' profits or zero profits, depending on whether the firm is identified with the ownership of its equity capital, as in the Marshallian tradition, or with entrepreneurship alone, as in the Continental European tradition. The household is assumed to maximize its utility subject to its income or budget constraint. Its income is derived from the sale of the services of the fact ors it owns (including equity capital) to the firms that employ them.

The essential exchange in the model is that of factor services for commodities between firms and households—a single barter transaction. However, it is both more realistic and more convenient to conceive of firms and households as making exchanges in two markets, a commodity market and a factor market, through the intermediation of some kind of medium of exchange or generalized purchasing power or numéraire in terms of which the values of other goods are expressed. (It is theoretically safest not to think of this medium of exchange as 'money', since the analysis of this book is concerned with the real equilibrium of the system and not with monetary problems; however, a monetary model can be restored to operating like a real model if it is assumed that the money price and wage level always adjusts to maintain full employment of resources and equilibrium between the demand for and supply of real balances.)

This general relationship is shown in the central part of Figure 1.2, which depicts what is known as 'the circular flow of income', and where the direction of the arrow-heads indicates sales and the opposite direction purchases.

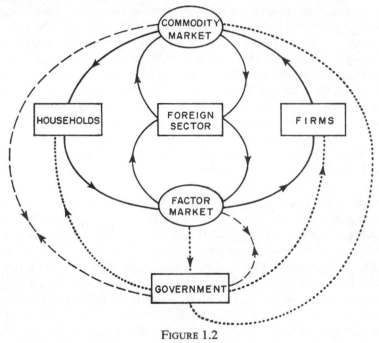

FIGURE 1.2

The diagram is strictly aggregative, that is, all commodities and all factors are lumped together. The general equilibrium problem is to determine the prices of the commodities and of the factors that will ensure equality of the amounts of each offered by one of the group of economic units and demanded by the other (e.g. factors offered by households and demanded by firms). The middle section extends the diagram to allow for an outside world (foreign sector) to which the economy may sell and from which it may buy goods

27

(for simplicity, trade in intermediate goods that serve as factors of production is ignored); or to which the economy may export and from which it may import original factors of production. The bottom section extends the diagram to include a government sector. The dashed lines indicate that the government may influence the resource allocation pattern of the economy through the use of taxes and subsidies on particular or general uses of commodities and/or factors or on particular or general sales of commodities or factors; hence the arrowheads go in both directions. If the government existed purely to redistribute income among citizens, the net balance of taxes and subsidies would be zero. The dotted lines represent the use of commodities and factors purchased by the government in order to render services and commodities to households and firms; such purchases must be paid for by net taxation (net borrowing is also possible, but this raises a problem of the accumulation of government debt and interest payments on it which is better avoided).

As already mentioned, the general equilibrium problem is to determine the prices of goods and factors that will ensure equilibrium between demands and supplies. (The Keynesian problem is parallel but different: as usually employed, the Keynesian approach aggregates output into a single composite good, assumes prices to be fixed, and is concerned with the determination of the level of output at which aggregate demand is just equal to aggregate supply.) To tackle this problem analytically it is necessary to specify the number of commodities and the number of factors into which the economy is to be aggregated. This requires a balancing of two considerations. One is that the model should be complex enough to capture essential relationships, specifically the substitutability between goods in consumption and factors in production. The other is that it should be simple enough both for easy exposition and to satisfy the scientific principle of enabling fairly powerful propositions (predictions) to be arrived at on the basis of the least possible number of restrictive assumptions. These considerations suggest the two-by-two-by-two model—two commodities, two factors, and two groups of factor owners—employed in this book. The main loss involved in confinement of the model to two rather than three or more goods and factors is sacrifice of the possibility of complementarity between two goods in consumption or factors in production, since if there are only two goods or two factors they must be substitutes. However, economists dealing with multi-product and multi-factor systems generally rule complementarity into insignificance anyway because of the mathematical difficulties it would otherwise cause. The two-good two-factor assumption also makes the possibility of inferiority of a good in consumption or a factor in production (less bought as total expenditure by households or firms rises, prices being constant) empirically implausible, so that we shall normally assume that neither good or factor is inferior. (This possibility is also ruled out theoretically in production by the assumption of constant returns to scale, and in consumption by the assumption of homotheticity.)

The terms 'commodity' and 'factor' have been used in the foregoing as if their meaning were perfectly obvious. But it is not. 'Commodities' can be thought of as physical objects providing bundles of want-satisfying or utility-yielding characteristics which are what the consumer fundamentally demands; alternatively they can be thought of as indirectly embodying particular bundles of factor services, with the consumer exchanging the factor services he commands through ownership for a more utility-yielding collection of factor services. For most of this book, however, we shall follow the convention of treating commodities as physical objects produced and sold in the market-place because consumers derive utility from them.

'Factors' raise a different problem. Analytically, one wants to treat them as original resources either in fixed supply or available according to a given supply curve related to the factor's relative price. In fact, all observable factors are created out of nature's bounty (or niggardliness) by some form of investment of resources accumulated by man. Labour, even of the lowest skill, requires up-bringing and some degree of education; land resources are created by such investments as transport facilities, fertilization, and irrigation; and machinery and structures are created by investment of current factor services in forms that yield different factor services in a flow over future time.

The household can nevertheless be thought of as receiving rents for the current services of the factors it owns, under the various descriptions of wages, rents, interest, and profits, the certainty of the rents receivable in future varying with the nature of the factor in question and the length and security of the contractual arrangements for rental. However, to make the problem of analysis manageable, it is necessary to assume that the multiplicity of existing factors can be reduced to a small number of classes (specifically two, in the model expounded in this book) and that within each class the units are sufficiently 'malleable' for them to be re-allocated among industries to the extent required to equalize their rental rates in all uses.

The question of the produced nature of capital goods and its implications has been raised and emphasized, with virtually exclusive reference to capital equipment, in recent years by the neo-Cambridge School (especially Joan Robinson and Nicholas Kaldor), though in the context of production rather than consumption. Specifically they argue that the concept of the production function used on the production side of the model expounded in this book, that is, the concept of a technical functional relationship between inputs of factors and the output of a commodity, is a nonsense because capital is a produced and not an original factor of production, and the value of any physical specification of it depends on knowing the rate of interest in order to cumulate the past costs of investment in creating it or discount its future prospective returns. This criticism does not, however, seem to us cogent in the context of the analysis of this book, for two reasons. First, it is the physical embodiment of capital that enters the production process, not its value; the value is relevant to processes of accumulation via savings from current resources. Second, if one is seriously concerned about such problems, one would abandon the simple production function concept in favour of a model—probably mathematically much more complex— that incorporated assumptions relevant to those problems. The problems of the nature of capital are not the problems that we are specifically interested in here, so that we feel entitled to abstract from them—as we abstract from other such problems—while warning the reader that at present the subject is one of considerable controversy among specialists.

IV. THE THEORY OF INDIVIDUAL CONSUMPTION CHOICE

As is well known from the techniques used to illustrate elementary economic principles, the preference system of an individual—and by extension of a homogeneous group of individuals—can be represented by a map of indifference curves between two goods. Each indifference curve of the preference function defines a locus of commodity bundles, made up of two commodities X and Y, that yield the (aggregate) household equal amounts of utility or satisfaction. These curves are drawn from northwest to southeast, reflecting the assumption that households are satiated with neither good—that is, that the marginal utilities of both goods are positive—and are convex to the origin reflecting the assumption, traditional to static analysis, of diminishing marginal rate of substitution between the goods—that is, that the marginal utility of one good falls relatively to that of the other as the quantity of the first is increased and of the second decreased. The curves are drawn also never to intersect either axis; this reflects the assumption that some of each good is indispensable if the consumer is to enjoy a given level of utility. Non-indispensability ensures that some of both goods will be consumed for any given consumer income and set of relative prices, convexity that the consumer's equilibrium consumption bundle will be unique and the equilibrium stable under the same conditions. Given one such arbitrarily determined indifference curve as a reference, U_2 in Figure 1.3, an entire preference map can be defined such that indifference curves lying northeast of U_2, such as U_3, represent higher levels of consumer satisfaction, while indifference curves lying southwest of U_2, such as U_1, represent lower levels of consumer satisfaction in comparison with the reference curve. Logical transitivity requires that these indifference curves do not cross. The utility ordering of the preference function is a further consequence of the assumption that goods yield positive marginal utility to the consumer.

If households, as consumers, are not assumed to be constrained in their consumption behaviour either because of unlimited resource or free goods, the theory of consumer choice predicts that they would consume quantities of both goods to the point where the marginal utilities of the respective goods would be zero, at least if it is assumed that the objective of consumer behaviour is maximization of utility. But consumer behaviour is constrained by two analytically distinguishable forces summarized in the so-called budget constraint; the constraint imposed on the consumer by the limited resources or income at his disposal at any given moment of time, and that imposed on him by the terms of commodity exchange. The theory of consumer demand postulates that given the various combinations of commodities made available to him by his budget constraint, the consumer makes a rational, as opposed to an arbitrary choice, in that he picks that particular combination of commodities which yields him the highest possible level of satisfaction. Consumer choice can be said to be rational because it is related to a specific though unstated ultimate objective. This objective, whose proxy in the analysis is the term satisfaction or utility, is unstated in order to give the theory of consumer choice the widest possible applicability.

The theory of consumer choice is illustrated in Figure 1.3 where the consumers' preference function is given as U_1, U_2, U_3, . . ., his income is OM, specified in terms of the numéraire commodity Y, and the price ratio between X and Y is expressed by the slope of the

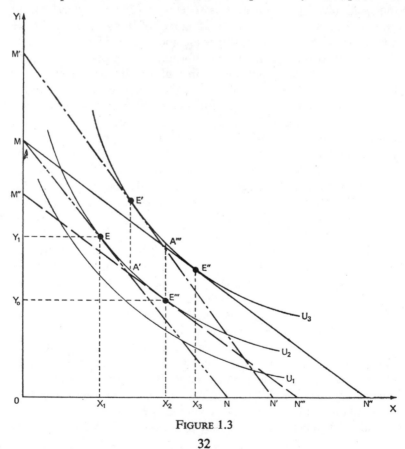

FIGURE 1.3

budget constraint line MN, the slope relative to the X-axis being the number of units of Y required to purchase a unit of X and vice versa. The budget constraint is drawn as a straight line, reflecting constant commodity prices, on the assumption that households, *qua* consumers, are perfectly competitive (that is, they have no monopsony power over the prices of the goods they buy). The corresponding assumption that households also are perfectly competitive in their role of factor sellers, in conjunction with the assumption of full employment of the factors of production, allows us to fix numéraire income and thus concentrate on the problem of consumer choice with respect to the purchase of commodities.

All points on the budget constraint MN are available or open to the consumer and all yield him satisfaction, but there is one unique point given at E in the Figure where the utility of the consumer is maximized. At point E, consistent with demand X_1 of X and Y_1 of Y, the budget line is tangent to the indifference curve; hence the slope of the budget line, the relative commodity price ratio, is equal to the slope of the indifference curve, the marginal rate of substitution between X and Y in consumption, at this point. Utility maximization accordingly is characterized by this equality provided that the indifference curves are convex to the origin. (If they were concave, we would get a 'corner solution' involving the consumer 'jump' from consumption of one good to that of the other.)

As mentioned above, the budget constraint of the consumer consists of two analytically separate components: the real income component, defined in terms of a numéraire commodity, and the price ratio component; and it is useful to trace the effect on consumer behaviour of changing each of these components of the budget constraint in turn. Given relative commodity prices, the effect of increasing numéraire income from OM to OM' is reflected by the parallel outward (from the origin) movement of the budget constraint from MN to $M'N'$, which in conjunction with the consumer's preference function determines the new equilibrium point E', involving more of both commodities being purchased (due to the exclusion of 'inferior' goods). The theory of consumer demand therefore predicts that under *ceteris paribus* conditions an increase in real income, defined in terms of a numéraire commodity (which in this case implies an increase in real income defined in terms of utility as well), will result in an increased demand for all commodities, provided that the demand function is stipulated to exclude inferior goods—that is, goods of which less is demanded as income rises. The function that relates the quantities of commodities demanded to real income on the assumption that tastes and relative prices are constant is known as the Engel curve.

The problem of taking the effect of a change in the commodity price ratio under *ceteris paribus* conditions is somewhat more complex because of a controversy as to what such *ceteris paribus* should consist in. Specifically, the problem is whether real income defined in terms of a numéraire good should be held constant, in which case real income defined in utility terms must change upon a change in relative prices, or whether real income defined in utility terms should be held constant, in which case numéraire income must change (this was not a problem in the previous experiment). Consider the case illustrated in Figure 1.3 where numéraire income is held constant and the relative price of X falls so that the budget constrait line rotates in a counter-clockwise direction around the point M from MN to MN''. The demand for commodity X increases from X_1 to X_3 upon the change, but real income defined in utility terms increases as well, from the level indicated by U_2 to that indicated by U_3. To keep real income, defined in utility terms, constant at U_2 upon the change in prices, an amount of numéraire income—in this case equal to MM''—must be taken away from the consumer so as to leave him at the same utility level with the new price ratio as he achieved at the initial one. The result is an increase in the quantity demand of X, from X_1 to X_2, and a decrease in the quantity demanded of Y, from Y_1 to Y_0, as relative prices change from that given by the slope of MN to that given by the slope of $M''N'''$ (the price of X falls).

The question of which procedure is preferable, holding numéraire income or real income defined in utility terms constant as relative prices change, has two separate aspects. The first is which definition of real income, the utility definition or that in terms of a numéraire good, is held to possess more economic meaning. For the individual consumer, assumed to be constrained by a parametric income fixed in terms of general purchasing power and to face parametric prices, the numéraire definition of income obviously makes sense. However, as Friedman argued in his reinterpretation of the Marshallian demand curve, in a general equilibrium context there can be no net increase in real income for the community as a whole, since a fall in the price of a good produces equal and opposite income effects for buyers and sellers. Hence Friedman and others prefer to derive the price-quantity demanded relationship from a constant utility level, the resulting demand curve being known as the 'compensated demand curve'.

The second aspect of the question is methodological rather than substantive. First, Friedman's procedure has the advantage that the demand curve for an individual consumer or any aggregate of consumers must slope downwards from left to right, whereas on the other approach inferior goods with weak substitution effects may produce a demand curve sloping the opposite way over part of its range and produces an unstable equilibrium (see section (1)). This stability argument is less persuasive, however, for as we shall see later, in the general equilibrium model shifts of real income from one factor-owner to another consequent on relative price changes may produce the same problems of multiple and unstable equilibrium, even if inferior goods are excluded, as inferior goods can produce on the alternative approach. Second, and more important since the 'numéraire income' approach has dominated the textbooks ever since the publication of Hicks's *Value and Capital*, the total effect of a fall in price has invariably been partitioned into a 'real income effect'—the increase in utility level made possible by a price fall or the decrease made necessary by a price rise—and a 'substitution effect' along a given indifference curve. The substitution effect necessarily increases consumption of the good whose relative price has fallen, whereas the (positive) income effect of a price fall will increase or decrease consumption of that good according as the good in non-inferior or inferior in demand, and vice versa for the (negative) income effect of a price rise. The substitution effect can moreover be expressed as the compensated elasticity of demand. Hence the issue is merely one of choosing how to formalize the analysis of effects on whose existence economists are agreed.

It may be noted in passing that there has been some controversy over how exactly 'compensation' is to be defined. The obvious theoretical answer is that compensation should maintain a constant level of utility; though here, for non-infinitesimal price changes, it may make a difference whether the income effect or the substitution effect is evaluated first, i.e. whether, in terms of Figure 1.3, we

35

consider the move from E to E'' as consisting of a move from E to E''' (substitution effect) and then to E'' (income effect) or one from E to E' (income effect) and then to E'' (substitution effect). An objection has been raised to this solution, on the grounds that utility is non-observable and (at least at present) non-calculable, and the alternative proposed of defining compensation as consisting in taking away or adding just sufficient numéraire income to enable the consumer to purchase the same bundle of commodities as he initially purchased before the price change (the so-called Slutzky technique). As the reader can easily see by mentally pivoting the budget line MN about the point E in Figure 1.3, such compensation will in fact allow the consumer to reach a (slightly) higher utility level by substituting the cheaper commodity for the dearer one, hence crediting some of the income effect to the substitution effect. For infinitesimally small changes, however, the difference is negligible.

The derivation of the total effect of a price change and its partitioning into income and substitution effects are exercises in positive economics, designed to aid in the tasks of qualitative analysis of changes and quantitative prediction and measurement. From the point of view of normative economics, the total effect and its partitioning are irrelevant; what matters is the income or utility that results from the fall in the price of X. This cannot be measured directly, since utility is an ordinal and not a cardinal magnitude (U_3 is greater than U_2 and U_2 than U_1 but we cannot say whether $U_3 - U_2$ is greater or less than $U_2 - U_1$); the only way we could measure it directly would be to impose an arbitrary scale of numbers on U_1, U_2, U_3, and we have no observational basis for doing so. The utility gain can, however, be measured indirectly, by finding a change in some observable magnitude that would produce the same effect on utility as the price change. Many ways of doing so have been devised, beginning with Marshall's concept of 'consumer's surplus'. The two most common are due to Hicks, and entail hypothetical changes in numéraire income at constant prices. These are the 'compensating variation'—the reduction in numéraire income that would leave the consumer no better off after the price change than he was before it—represented in Figure 1.3 by MM''; and the 'equivalent variation'—the increase in numéraire income that would make the consumer as well off in the absence of the price change as he would be with his initial numéraire income and the fall in the price of X—represented in Figure 1.3 by MM'. The equivalent variation must be greater than the compensating variation (MM' greater than MM''), as a consequence of non-inferiority and diminishing marginal rate of substitution; which implies that as the quantity of X shifts towards the left (decreases) the vertical distance between any two indifference curves must increase. In Figure 1.3, A''' is vertically above E''' on U_3, and A' vertically below E' on U_2. The distance $E'''A'''$ must exceed the compensating variation MM'', $E'''A'''$ must be less than $A'E'$, and the latter must be less than the equivalent variation MM'.

V. COMMUNITY PREFERENCE AND THE AGGREGATION PROBLEM

The previous section analysed the behaviour of the individual consumer and the effects on his equilibrium position of changes in his numéraire income and the price ratio confronting him by representing his preferences in terms of a set of indifference curves with certain properties and assuming him to seek to reach the highest possible level of utility subject to the budget constraint imposed on him. The technique permitted the derivation of both positive propositions about the effects of changes on his consumption *behaviour* and normative propositions about the effects of changes on his *welfare*.

It would obviously be convenient if the community as a whole—assumed to consist of individuals of varying tastes and incomes—could be treated in the same way, for both positive and normative analysis, by positing a set of community indifference curves possessing the same properties of convexity, uniqueness, non-intersection and indexing outwards from the origin by rising levels of utility. Unfortunately, this is not in general possible, except on assumptions so restrictive as to make the analysis irrelevant if not necessarily uninteresting.

To demonstrate the problem, it is sufficient to assume two individuals, A and B, each with a given income and facing the same market price ratio between commodities X and Y, but with different preference systems. It simplifies the analysis, besides strengthening the argument, to assume that these preference systems are homothetic in that the ratio of the goods consumed are an exclusive function of relative prices and tastes, since this rules out effects of differences in income levels on consumption patterns. In Figure 1.4, OA is A's numéraire income, OB is B's numéraire income, and O, $A + B$ is total community income. At the price ratio represented by the slope of the three budget lines, A's equilibrium consumption point is C_A on U_O^A, B's is C_B on U_O^B and the community's consumption point, arrived at by vector addition of C_A and C_B, is C_{A+B}. By changing the relative price ratio and at the same time making the compensations required to keep A on U_O^A and B on U_O^B, and using vector addition, a locus of aggregate consumption points that would keep both A and B at the same levels of utility as they enjoyed at C_A and C_B can be traced out. This is depicted in the diagram by $U_O{}^{U_O^A, U_O^B}$. It is obvious that this locus must have the same convexity-to-the-origin property as the individual indifference curves. It is also obvious, and can be proven by vector addition, that an increase in the utility level assigned to either individual with the other being held constant, or both individuals, will produce a new $U^{UA, UB}$ curve lying entirely outside-right of the initial one; and by construction any point on this new community indifference curve will satisfy the Pareto criterion for an improvement of welfare as compared with any point on the initial one. In other words, it would appear that a set of community indifference curves can be constructed that will have the same properties as individual indifference curve systems and indicate changes in the community's consumption behaviour and actual welfare.

This conclusion, however, is false, because it depends on two assumptions: the first is the arbitrary choice of U_O^A and U_O^B as the starting point of the construction, the second is the assumption that all changes from that starting point fulfil the conditions of Pareto optimality. To demonstrate the falsity, assume that instead of incomes OA and OB each individual receives half the total community income, $O, \frac{A+B}{2}$, moving A's consumption point northeast to C'_A and B's southwest to C'_B. By vector addition of the new individual consumption points, the community's consumption point must move southeast along the community budget line $A + B$, $A' + B'$, to C'_{A+B}. Through this point can be constructed a new community indifference curve $U_O{}^{UA, UB}_+$, the zero subscript indicating that the curve is defined for the initial community budget line and the superscripts the new fixed utility levels corresponding to the new distribution of community income. The new community indifference curve must intersect the old one (as shown in the diagram), except in the special case where OC_A and OC_B coincide, i.e. the two individuals have identical as well as homothetic indifference curves. By extension, the community indifference curve constructed for a change from the initial utility levels, U_o^A and U_o^B, which increases total community income but reduces the utility level of one of the individuals may intersect the initial community indifference curve $U_O{}^{U_o^A, U_o^B}$.

The important point is that a community indifference curve system analogous to the individual indifference curve system in the sense that the individual curves are unique and non-intersecting and

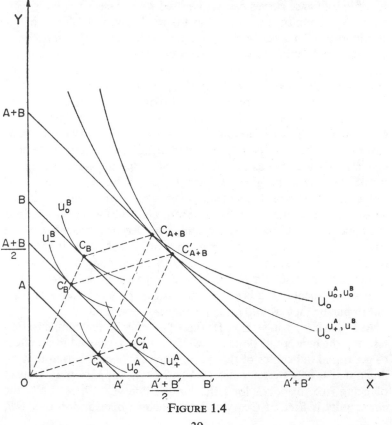

FIGURE 1.4

can be used to represent the behaviour of the community in response to varying community numéraire income and relative price situations, cannot be constructed, because it will not in general be invariant with respect to the distribution of income (utility) among the individual members of the community. The exceptional case of identical homothetic indifference curves essentially makes the individual members of the community identical, in the sense that a high income individual behaves like a multiple of a low income individual, and hence reduces the community to a multiple of the 'representative individual'.

Even in this exceptional case, which permits a unique set of indifference curves with the normal properties of individual indifference curves to express the *behaviour* of the community, that set of indifference curves cannot be used to represent *welfare* effects on the community, because to evaluate the welfare effects of redistribution of a given income requires interpersonal comparisons of individual utilities, whose validity cannot be established on scientific grounds. (Of course it would be possible in certain cases to apply scientific methods to determine whether the community had a consensus on how income should be distributed, and what that consensus and its implications were.) The only value judgment that would permit the set of unique behavioural community indifference curves derived on the assumption of identical homothetic preference systems to serve also as an indicator of economic welfare changes would be that a marginal dollar of income has the same social welfare value whether it accrues to or is taken from a million-dollar-a-year man or a one-dollar-a-year man, i.e. that the socially judged marginal utility of income is the same for everyone regardless of the size of his income. This assumption would make the distribution of income irrelevant to welfare; only the total community income would matter. It should be mentioned in passing that some sophisticated arguments have been produced to support this assumption; but to pursue them would take the analysis too far afield.

As noted earlier in section II, the techniques of the compensation test and the concept of potential welfare were developed in an effort to get round difficulties of this kind. The problems involved may be illustrated briefly by reference to Figure 1.4. Suppose that, instead of being free to move along the budget line $A + B$, $A' + B'$, the community is fixed at C_{A+B} with the income distribution OA, OB, and has the choice of moving to C'_{A+B}. Since C'_{A+B} lies towards the origin from $U_O{}^{UA,\,UB}_O$, it is Pareto inferior to C_{A+B} from the point of view of the initial utility distribution U_O^A, U_O^B and will be rejected. But the same test applied with the income distribution corresponding to C'_{A+B} and the community indifference curve $U_O{}^{UA,\,UB}_-$ would show C_{A+B} to be Pareto-inferior to C'_{A+B} and lead to the choice of C_{A+B} being rejected. The test is therefore self-contradictory, because the weights attached to the individual utility functions shift with the points under comparison. Moreover, the test is only a test of potential welfare improvement or worsening, so long as the test does not stipulate that compensation actually be paid or attempted. Finally, the test is ethically biased by the choice of a particular distribution of income (utility) as its standard of reference.

The only completely ethically neutral procedure available would be to construct the $U_O{}^{UA,\,UB}$ curves for all possible distributions of individual utilities possible with the given community budget constraint $A + B$, $A' + B'$ ranging from $U_A = O$ to $U_B = O$; take the inside envelope of these curves (which would contain a straight-line segment corresponding with $A + B$, $A' + B'$ marked off by the tangency points of A's and B's indifference curve systems with the community budget line) as the dividing line for changes producing potential welfare losses, because for any consumption point between the inside envelope and the origin one individual at least would not be compensated for the change according to any distribution of welfare chosen; and take the outside envelope of the curves as constituting the dividing line for potential welfare gains, since the consumption bundle corresponding to any point northeast of the outside envelope would be redistributed so as to make no one worse off and at least one better off as a result of the change. This test at least achieves ethical neutrality, but at the expense of leaving a possibly large grey area of indeterminacy in the space between the inner and the outer envelopes. And it remains a test of potential not actual welfare improvement.

The foregoing analysis runs in terms of changes in consumption points associated arbitrarily with changes in the distribution of income (utility) among members of the community. Matters are made worse in one way and better in another once the production side of the general equilibrium analysis is put together with the consumption side. They are made worse because the types of change

41

that are the most interesting to consider usually involve redistributions of income from one group to another, rather than gains for some with no loss to others such as would satisfy the Pareto criterion of actual welfare gain, and so require recourse to the 'potential welfare' concept. On the other hand, they are made better by the fact that many types of change considered (such as, for example, technical progress or the opening of international trade) increase or at worst do not reduce the available quantities of each (both, in the model developed here) of the goods the community consumes, by comparison with the quantities available on the pre-change situation, and so automatically satisfy the potential welfare improvement criterion.

VI. THE THEORY OF THE FIRM AND AGGREGATION

The theory of the firm is analogous to the theory of the behaviour of the household in that both are essentially concerned with choice and maximization under constraint. But there are two significant differences between them. First, the household is assumed to seek to maximize utility, which is a non-observable magnitude, whereas the firm is assumed to maximize profits, which are objectively observable and measurable. Second, whereas the household is usually assumed to be subject to a fixed budget constraint, determined by its endowment of factors and their market prices, the firm can determine its own scale through its decision on the level of output and therefore of factor utilization at which it can most profitably operate. The analogy can be made somewhat closer by envisaging the household as having a 'reservation demand' for the factors it owns, and therefore to have to decide how much of each to rent out, but this does not make the analogy complete because the household must then be assumed to derive utility from the factor quantities held off the market for use in 'leisure' activities. A still closer but still not exact analogy arises if the household is assumed to maximize utility over a series of periods and for this purpose can lend out some of the resources provided by its budget constraint or supplement that constraint by borrowing resources from the market, in particular periods. Further, in an analysis that will for the most part preclude economic growth through the savings-investment process, the firm (or the owners of the firm) must be assumed to use its profits to consume commodities. It is therefore possible to conceive of the firm as a special type of household, that earns its income not from renting out its factor endowment (entrepreneurship) at a fixed price but by combining it with other factors that it purchases to produce goods which it then sells. The theory of the firm, in other words, can be conceived of as a special case of a more general theory of household behaviour.

Profits are defined as the excess of total revenue over total cost, and will be maximized when this excess or residual is maximized. In pursuit of this objective, the firms' behaviour is subject to two constraints, identical to those that constrain the household though the constraint imposed by each is manifested in a different way. The first is the relative factor price ratio which, from the perspective of its role as a buyer of productive factors, determines the firms' cost-minimizing combinations of productive inputs required to produce any given output level, on the assumption that the good's technology requires that some of both factors be used to produce it; the second is the relative commodity price ratio which, from the perspective of its role as a seller of commodities, determines the maximum total revenue that the firm can expect to receive from a given combination of outputs or, if the firm is identified with the production of a single commodity, from the given output of that particular good. Given factor prices, to produce any given output level, the firm can be expected to choose that combination of the two factors, capital and labour, that minimizes total expenditure on them, under the assumption that technically there exists a definite and systematic relationship between factor inputs and commodity outputs; alternatively, in closer analogy with the theory of consumer behaviour, the firm can be assumed to have an arbitrarily given budget expressed in numéraire income to spend on production, and to seek to maximize output subject to the relative factor prices facing it. Given commodity prices, output will be taken to the point where the excess of total revenue over total cost is greatest (where marginal revenue, defined as the change in total revenue per unit change of output, equals marginal cost, defined as the change in total cost per unit change in output). The assumption of the two-sector model of general equilibrium that firms are perfectly competitive with respect to their roles both as factor buyers and commodity sellers implies that commodity and factor prices will be taken as given to the firm in the analysis. Hence the process of determining the level of output of the firm becomes a process of determining the level of output of a commodity-producing *industry* composed of competitive firms, and the output is made determinate by the fall in relative commodity price and/or rise in factor costs of production consequent on the expansion of the industry in a context of fixed overall endowment of the economy with factors of production—which implies contraction of other industries and changes in factor prices as factors are transferred from the contracting to the expanding industries. One major objective of the general equilibrium model is to show precisely how industry outputs are determined consistently with profit maximization.

The above-mentioned systematic relationship between productive inputs and outputs is known in the literature as the production function. In theory, there are an infinite number of forms that the production function can take, and different forms are convenient for different purposes. In the micro-economic theory of industry equilibrium, in which factor prices are assumed to be parametric, for example, the firm is assumed to have a production function such that the cost curve is U-shaped in both the short and the long run—in the short run due to the fixity of the firm's capital equipment, in the long run because of the fixity of the firm's entrepreneurial capacity. In this case, the economic requirement that payments to factors exactly exhaust the total product while being determined by marginal productivity is satisfied because the earnings of the fixed factor are a residual (a 'rent'). In aggregative theory, where the industry and not the firm is the object of analysis, it is most convenient to assume that the production function for each firm is identical and is subject to constant returns to scale, or, as an alternative descriptive, homogeneous of degree one in the factors of production. This means that equi-proportional increase in inputs will produce the same proportional increase in outputs. Such a function has the convenient property that factor payments by marginal productivity exactly exhaust the product.

The assumption that all firms have an identical constant-returns-to-scale production function makes the output of the individual firm indeterminate, but this is not a relevant problem in the context, since industry output is determined by the condition that marginal cost (including, consistently with the initial analysis of this section, the cost of entrepreneurship) equals marginal revenue; alternatively, the condition is that average cost equals average revenue, since average and marginal revenue are equal under the assumption of a competitive industry and average cost equals marginal cost by the assumption of constant returns to scale. The same assumption implicitly removes the problem of aggregation of individual firm output into industry output.

Finally, the constant-returns-to-scale assumption has the advantage that the absolute marginal products of the factors (i.e. their marginal products in terms of the product) and therefore their relative marginal products (ratios of their absolute marginal products to one another) are independent of the scale of output, and dependent only on the ratio in which the factors are combined. This means in turn that the whole production function can be analysed in terms of a single isoquant representing an arbitrarily chosen level of output; it is frequently convenient to choose the isoquant representing a unit level of output (or, what is the same thing, to define the arbitrarily chosen output quantity as the unit quantity for output measurement), and sometimes convenient to choose the isoquant that represents the total amount of the commodity that the economy could produce if it used its total factor endowment or if it did this but were free to alter the composition (but not the value) of that endowment at a given set of factor prices. It is important to remember that an increase in the ratio of the quantity of one factor employed to all the others, the ratios of the quantities of the others among themselves remaining unchanged, must decrease both the absolute and the relative marginal product of that factor, and vice versa, because frequently in the exposition it is less cumbersome to refer only to the relevant one of these effects rather than spell both of them out in full.

The constant-returns-to-scale production function can be defined to include any number of factors of production considered useful for the analysis, including both the 'entrepreneurship' referred to in the initial analysis of this section and raw materials, components, fuel, etc. 'bought in' by the firm from other industries for use in the production process. For the purposes of this book, we wish to use the minimum number of factors consistent with representation of substitution among factors consequent on factor price changes, and hence reduce the number of factors to two, 'labour' and 'capital'. This procedure raises two questions. The first is the treatment of 'entrepreneurship', hitherto regarded as a separate and special kind of input into the productive process. Converting from the Anglo-Saxon Marshallian tradition to the Continental European tradition, we treat entrepreneurship as an activity of organization that can be performed by the owner of any factor; and we assume that it is costless and hence earns no return under competitive conditions ('profits' tend to zero in equilibrium) because in static equilibrium the organization of production is settled and unchanging and because the costs of reorganizing the economy to a new-static equilibrium are once-over costs whose amortization becomes negligible over a long enough run of the new equilibrium. The second problem, or range of problems, concerns the nature of capital as a produced factor or production, discussed previously in section II. We circumvent these problems by assuming that capital consists of physical components that are infinitely durable and malleable from one physical form into another without cost (a sort of set), thus avoiding problems of the valuation of capital, depreciation of equipment, and the adjustment of the physical form of capital to the optimum consistent with a given factor price ratio.

The production function, specified in terms of capital and labour as inputs producing a single product subject to constant returns to scale, is depicted in Figure 1.5, where the axes represent capital and labour, and the production indifference curves or production isoquants represent given quantities of output.

These isoquants slope downwards from northwest to southeast, embodying the assumption that the marginal products of both factors are positive; they are convex to the origin, reflecting the assumption of imperfect substitutability between the factors in the production process; they never intersect the axes reflecting the assumption that some of each factor is indispensable to production; and successive isoquants representing successive equal increases in output are equidistantly apart along any ray through the origin, reflecting the assumption of constant returns to scale.

The first economic problem for the firm is to choose the optimum factor combination to employ, given the factor prices. The solution can be thought of in two alternative equivalent ways. First, the firm can be considered as having a given cost budget defined in terms of the various combinations of factors it will buy, OM_2 in terms of capital as numéraire in Figure 1.5, and attempting to maximize the output and therefore the revenue it can earn with this cost budget. The maximum output obtainable with the given cost budget is X_2, where the X_2 isoquant is tangent to the cost budget line at E. Alternatively, the firm may be conceived as being required to produce output X_2, and attempting to do so at minimum cost. It could produce X_2 at the cost OM_3 by producing at either A or B, but it could lower its cost by substituting one factor for another

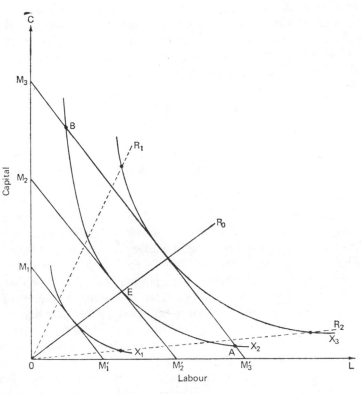

FIGURE 1.5

along the X_2 isoquant, until it reached the lowest possible cost OM_2 defined by the tangency of the X_2 isoquant with a budget line at E. The tangency solution, whether arrived at from the output-maximization or cost-minimization objective, both defines the optimum factor-utilization ratio OR_0 and implies equality of the slopes of the isoquant and the budget line. Taken with reference to the horizontal axis, the former represents the ratio of the marginal product of labour to the marginal product of capital and the latter the ratio of the price of labour to the price of capital (in symbols, along the isoquant $MP_K \cdot dK + MP_L \cdot dL = 0$ and along the budget line $P_K \cdot dK + P_L \cdot dL = 0$) so that the marginal products of the factors must be proportional to their prices. This equality is convenient for it enables us to infer changes in absolute and relative factor prices (in terms of the product) from movements along the isoquant. Further, in combination with information about the precise extent to which relative factor prices change as the factor utilization ratio changes along the isoquant (expressed technically in the 'elasticity of substitution' between the factors along the isoquant), it enables us to infer the effects of changes in the factor utilization ratio on the relative shares of the factors in the total product of the industry.

The problem just analysed involves a constraint on the firm in the form of a fixed cost budget or output level. But in contrast to the analysis of consumer behaviour, where the budget constraint is fixed by the consumer's factor endowment and the factor and commodity prices confronting him, either of these constraints is an arbitrary theoretically-imposed restriction in the firm's behaviour. The firm is in fact free to choose its output level and corresponding minimum-cost budget. In Figure 1.5, the cost budget is measured in terms of capital as numéraire; but it can easily be converted into terms of the output X by multiplication by the marginal product of capital in terms of the output. The cost of production measured in terms of X may fall short of, exceed, or just be equal to the quantity of X produced. Given that factor prices are assumed to be parametric to the firm, in the first case there would be a fixed positive profit per unit of output and the firm would have an incentive to expand production indefinitely; in the second case there would be a fixed negative profit (loss) per unit of output and the firm would cease production entirely; in the third case profits would be zero per unit and the scale of the firm's output would be indeterminate. This last case is the only one consistent with a non-zero but finite output of the *industry*. To achieve it, relative and absolute factor prices must change so as to make cost in terms of output equal to output itself. This occurs through reallocation of factors between this industry and the rest of the economy, and has the effect of changing the cost of production and therefore the relative price of the product of the other industry in terms of the output of this one.

This brings us to the extension of the analysis from the theory of the industry to the theory of the two-sector (two-industry) model.

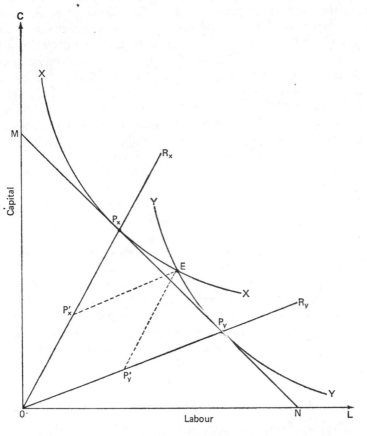

FIGURE 1.6

The initial question, the answer to which is implicit in the previous paragraph, is the basis for distinguishing between the two goods produced. To the consumer, goods can be said to differ because they possess different capacities for satisfying a given want. To the firm, goods can be distinguished by their different production function relationship. Though both goods in the two-sector model are assumed to be subject to constant returns to scale, because their production functions differ, at given factor prices the cost-minimizing ratios of capital to labour can be assumed to differ. This is illustrated in Figure 1.6 where owing to the assumption of constant returns of scale, and thus homogeneity, the production functions of each good can be represented by a single isoquant; for convenience in further analysis, these isoquants are chosen to be those corresponding to the output of each good attainable by complete specialization of the economy's endowment of productive factors (represented by the point E) on production of that good. At the particular factor price ratio given by MN, the common tangent to the two isoquants, the costs of production of the maximum outputs of the two goods are equal; and if these outputs are defined as the units of measurement of output for the two goods, the costs of production of units of the goods are equal and the price ratio between them is one-for-one. The capital-labour ratio OR_x in X is greater than the same ratio OR_y in Y, and this difference in relative factor-intensities is assumed (for simplicity) to apply at all factor-price ratios.

The Figure also permits determination of the allocation of total factor supplies among outputs of the two goods required to maintain full employment of both factors consistent with the given factor price ratio. To do this, complete the parallelogram formed by OR_x, OR_y, and the apex E to determine P_x' and P_y'. OP_x' and OP_y' are indices of the levels of output of the two goods. OP_x'/OP_y' indicates the ratio of actual to maximum potential output of X, or (given the use of the XX isoquant as the unit of measurement of X) the number of units of X produced; and similarly for Y.

V. SUMMARY OF ASSUMPTIONS AND COMMENTARY

The purpose of the two-sector model of general equilibrium is to highlight the principles of interrelatedness, of systematic response to change and of optimization that exist in the economy in order to develop a systematic approach to the understanding of economic phenomena and the organization of disciplined thinking about them. For this, recourse must be taken to a certain number of simplifying assumptions that are listed below.

These assumptions are:

1. That there exist two goods, two consumers (factor-owners) and two original factors of production in the economy. All units of a given good or factor are homogeneous in quality. This assumption excludes both a government and a foreign trade sector.

2. That the goods differ to consumers in their want-satisfying characteristics, and to producers in the relative factor-intensities that minimize production cost.

3. That both goods are normal in consumption, in the sense that as real income rises consumption of both goods increases.

4. That production of each good requires the use only of original factors of production. There are no intermediate goods (i.e. goods used in the production of other goods); and the entrepreneurial function is performed at zero cost by the owner of one or other or both factors.

5. That production functions relating factor inputs to commodity outputs exist and are determined by a given technology.

6. That these production functions are subject to constant returns to scale.

7. That both goods are consumption goods: there is no investment and saving.

8. That substitution between goods in consumption and factors in production is continuous and representable by a smoothly-shaped curve.

9. That the marginal utilities of goods and the marginal productivities of factors are always positive, so that a given level of utility or output can be maintained while one good or factor is substituted for the other.

10. That substitution of both types is imperfect, so that indifference curves in consumption and production are convex towards the origin.

11. That neither good is dispensable in consumption and neither factor dispensable in production. (These two assumptions guarantee uniqueness and stability of the equilibrium of the individual consumer and the individual industry's choice of factor intensities, subject to the next assumption of maximization; also that some of both goods will always be produced and some of both factors employed).

12. That the welfare (utility level) of the individual consumer is an increasing function of the amount of either good consumed, the amount of the other being held constant.

13. That consumers seek to maximize welfare subject to the constraints imposed on them by the amounts of factors they own, their prices and the prices of commodities facing them.

14. That consumers possess no monopsony power in product markets and no monopoly power in factor markets; they buy goods and sell factors under competitive conditions.

15. That firms behave competitively so that industries have no monopoly power in product markets and no monopsony power in factor markets; they sell goods and buy factors under competitive conditions.

16. That firms seek to maximize profits. (By assumption 4, profits are zero in equilibrium.)

17. That the amounts of each of the factors available to the economy as a whole are fixed.

18. That either money does not exist in the model, except as a unit of account, or if it exists the money price level always adjusts to keep actual equal to desired real incomes, so that the economy functions like a barter economy. In either case, it is relative prices that matter and these can be measured by selecting either commodity or factor as the numéraire.

The number and nature of the foregoing assumptions may lead the student to either one of two opposite reactions. One is that the model to be constructed and applied in the book is too complicated to be worth mastering. We hope that on the contrary we shall have made the model more easily understandable than the previous literature has done, and also communicated something of the broad range of problems understanding of which it helps to illuminate. The opposite view is that the assumptions are so hopelessly unrealistic that the model is useless for understanding the world of reality.

This later reaction raises several problems that are worth brief exploration and comment. First, it implies that full knowledge of the economic system is available, but theorists refuse to use it in favour of abstractions permitting simple answers. On the contrary, such knowledge is not and is not likely in the feasible future to be available; the purpose of abstraction is to synthesize in a coherent and usable way the knowledge available, to push out the boundaries of knowledge rather than to restrict them. Only too often the individual who prides himself on his knowledge of 'the real world' is observed employing naïve cause-effect relationships to interpret the results of complex relationships, citing specific exceptional cases to deny the existence of generally valid relationships, using logic in one practical context inconsistent with the logic applied in another practical context, and in general using detailed information to deny or prevent the possibility of broad understanding.

Be that as it may, a second problem is that the scientific issue is whether the observed deviations of the facts of experience from the content of assumptions are *empirically* significant enough to invalidate the theory. This leads to the third problem of whether the lack of correspondence between reality and the content of assumption is an acceptable test of a theory's validity or, alternatively put, the question of the circumstances under which the lack of correspondence between reality and the content of assumptions can invalidate a theory.

The question of the role of assumptions in economic theory depends on the more fundamental question of the role of economic theory in the real world. If the purpose of theory is held to be the construction of a hypothetical system that accurately describes the economy in all its real world manifestations, naturally the closer the content of assumptions to the facts of experience, the better the theory, at least in terms of this objective. But if the purpose of theory is to provide the theorist with a set of tools that helps him identify the nature of a demonstrated economic problem and its possible solutions, abstraction from the complications and the obfuscations of the real world would seem to be an essential, indeed an indispensable component of the scientific process. This procedure, in fact, represents the economist's counterpart to a controlled experiment in the physical science.

The question of the validity of a theory on the latter interpretation can only be determined in terms of whether the theory is useful in solving the given economic problem under consideration. On the basis of the hypothetical system constructed by the theorist to represent the important relations in the economy if not to describe the economy itself in full detail, the positive and normative implications of changes in its 'givens' can be determined and compared with what actually has happened in the real world when these 'givens' have in fact changed. If the empirical evidence confirms the predictions of the model, the theory, or more precisely, the use of the theory can be said to be valid, and vice versa in the circumstance when the predictions of the model are not corroborated. Theoretical validation in other words can only result from empirical investigation.

The limitations of the test of empirical verification are that it is often difficult to devise empirical tests of theories that will be generally accepted as conclusive—and this is truer the more complex the theoretical construction. Specifically, the positive implications of parametric change are more amenable to empirical testing than are its normative implications. Empirical evidence as to whether the various groups that are assumed to exist in the community have been made better or worse off by parametric change is not too difficult to assemble *ex post*, but *ex ante* predictions are often virtually impossible. Whether the community considered as an aggregate gains or loses from parametric change, whether the question is approached *ex post* or *ex ante*, is usually still more difficult if not impossible to ascertain. In this case the reality of the assumptions of the theory provides the only possible approach, albeit a shaky one, to a test of the theory. This observation must be qualified, however, in two ways. In some cases the assumptions of one theory are the validated predictions of another, or alternatively contradict those predictions, either fact being relevant to the confidence one may place in the predictions of the first theory. And there is an important distinction to be drawn between a challenging of assumptions about the nature of objectives of behaviour, and a challenging of assumptions on the grounds that the environment within which behaviour motivated by objectives is assumed to operate is not consistent with the 'observed reality' of that environment. Specifically, the assumptions of utility or profit maximization are crucial to economic theory; the assumption of perfect competition rather than monopolistic or olygopolistic competition is not.

Not all of the eighteen listed assumptions will be maintained throughout the course of the book. Indeed the method of the book like that of comparative statics itself is to relax certain of the given assumptions under *ceteris paribus* conditions and consider the effect of such relaxations on the general equilibrium outcome under the assumption of stability of equilibrium. Hence, Chapter 3 is concerned with the effect of relaxing the assumption of a fixed factor endowment and fixed demand preference functions on the general equilibrium outcome; Chapter 4 introduces taxes and other institutional factors into the analysis, and explicitly considers the economic role of government; the analysis is extended in Chapter 5 to consider the theory of government expenditure; the effects of introducing international trade are studied in Chapter 6; the analysis of tariffs in an open economy is conducted in Chapter 7; the analysis of Chapter 3 is extended to the case of an open economy in Chapter 9; and the assumption of no saving and investment is discarded in Chapter 10 to consider the theory of economic growth.

CHAPTER 2

Production, Distribution
and General Equilibrium

The theory of income distribution assumes a community composed of different groups of homogeneous individuals and seeks to establish, in a general equilibrium context, the link between parametric change and the distribution of real income between these groups. Given the assumptions of the two-sector model of general equilibrium discussed in the first chapter, certain principles of inter-relatedness can be seen to exist that allow for the study of systematic response to change. Before proceeding to a discussion of these principles in the two-sector model, however, it will be useful to summarize briefly, as a background and reference to the subsequent discussion, the one-sector model of production and distribution that was developed by J. R. Hicks in his *Theory of Wages*.

I. ONE-SECTOR MODEL

The model developed by Hicks makes use of an aggregate constant-returns-to-scale production function in which labour and capital enter as original factors of production. Its essential contributions were the introduction of the elasticity of technical substitution between the two productive factors as the parameter governing the effect of factor growth on relative income shares and influencing its effect on absolute incomes, and a classification of types of technical change according to their effect on relative income shares (to be discussed in Chapter 3). The model is illustrated in Figure 2.1, where the axes measure quantities of capital and labour and the curves are isoquants of the aggregate production function. With given stocks

C_0 of capital and L_0 of labour, maximum output is represented by the isoquant $X_0 X_0$ going through the factor endowment point E. The assumption of full employment ensures this output will be produced, in the process establishing a price ratio for labour in terms of capital represented by the slope of $M_0 M_0'$. $C_0 M_0$ represents the value of labour's contribution to output in terms of capital, i.e. the amount of labour OL_0 valued at its price in terms of capital (the slope of $M_0 M_0'$), and $C_0 M_0 / C_0 O$, the ratio of labour's income to capital's income, is the negative of the slope of $M_0 M_0'$ divided by the slope of OR_0 (the ratio of capital to labour used in production), or the reciprocal of the ratio of capital to labour multiplied by the relative price of capital.

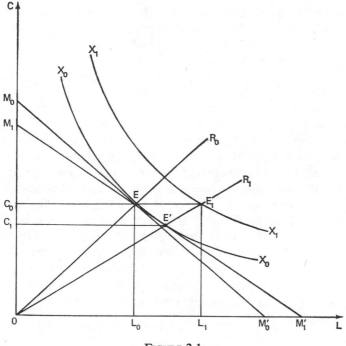

FIGURE 2.1

An increase in the stock of one factor (labour in the diagram from L_0 to L_1) must increase the absolute income of the other factor, owing to the assumptions of constant returns to scale and of

57

diminishing marginal rate of substitution between the factors in production. The latter insures that the slope of the isoquant at E' will be less than that at E with reference to the horizontal, while constant returns to scale insures that the slopes of the isoquants at E' and E_1 are the same. Consequently with the slope at E' less than that at E, the marginal product of labour falls and the marginal product of capital rises both in absolute and relative terms.

Capital's absolute income (the stock of capital times the marginal productivity of capital) must rise as the stock of labour increases given that its supply is fixed and its marginal productivity rises. The effect of the factor accumulation on labour's absolute income, however, is *a priori* indeterminate since the increase in the stock of labour tends to increase, while the fall in the marginal product of labour tends to decrease labour's absolute income. If labour's absolute income does fall, its relative share must fall as well, though a fall in the relative share of the augmented factor does not necessarily imply a fall in its absolute income. On the other hand, should labour's absolute income rise, it is possible for its relative share to rise as well. Because of constant returns to scale, which allows one isoquant to represent the entire production function, the behaviour of relative shares may be analysed in terms of the shift along the original isoquant from E to E', the ratio of labour's to capital's share changing from $C_0 M_0 / O C_0$ to $M_1 C_1 / O C_1$. These ratios, as already mentioned, are the reciprocals of the product of the relevant capital-labour ratio and relative price of capital; and labour's relative share will rise, be constant, or fall according as the fall in the capital-labour ratio between E and E' is greater, equal to, or less than the associated rise in the relative price of capital. The technically given elasticity of the capital-labour ratio with respect to the relative price of capital is defined as the elasticity of substitution; hence labour's relative share rises, is constant, or falls, according as the elasticity of substitution is numerically greater than, equal to, or less than unity.

II. TWO-SECTOR MODEL

Apart from the objection that may be raised against its treatment of the nature of capital as an original factor of production, the

Hicksian model of distribution suffers from the restrictive character-istic of one-sector models, the elimination of demand factors, which makes the functional distribution of income a mechanistic con-sequence of the available technology and factor supplies. This defect is easily remedied, however, by constructing a two-sector model in which preferences and demands for the two products influence the general equilibrium outcome that determines factor prices and distribution.

For the purpose of constructing such a model, it is assumed (as in the Hicks analysis) that endowments of the two factors, capital and labour, are given and that problems of the nature of capital can be abstracted from by identifying capital as a malleable physical stock of productive equipment. Production of each of the two goods is assumed to require the use of both factors in a constant returns-to-scale production function; commodity X is assumed to be relatively capital-intensive as compared with commodity Y, in the sense that at any factor-price ratio common to the two industries the cost-minimizing capital labour ratio is higher in X than in Y. For pur-poses of introducing demand considerations into the determination of general equilibrium, it is assumed that each of the two factors is owned exclusively by one group of the population, and that each group can be treated as having a single aggregate preference function. This assumption, while in accordance with a long tradition in economic theory going back through Marx to Ricardo, is not essential, and as seen below it is easy enough to work with the alternative assumption of two groups with unequal shares in owner-ship of the two factors. To avoid problems with corner solutions, each group is assumed always to demand some of both goods, at all relative commodity prices.

With these assumptions, construction of the model can proceed in terms of either of two geometrical techniques: the Lerner-Pearce diagram and the Edgeworth-Bowley contract box diagram. The latter is the more traditional, the former the newer and probably less familiar outside the field of international trade theory. Since both have advantages with respect to particular problems, each is developed in turn. In both cases the essential steps involve establishing a unique relationship between the production pattern, commodity prices, factor prices, and the distribution of income. This is known in the literature as the Stolper-Samuelson relation.

III. STOLPER-SAMUELSON RELATION

The Lerner-Pearce diagram, illustrated in Figure 2.2, exploits the fact that, owing to the assumption of constant-returns-to-scale, particularly the homogeneity property, the production function can be represented by a single isoquant (since relative and absolute factor marginal productivities depend only on the ratio in which factors are combined in production). In the diagram XX and YY, both going through the factor endowment point E, represent the maximum amounts of goods X and Y respectively that the economy is capable of producing with its technology and fixed factor endowment. They also can represent one-unit production of each good because of the aforementioned property. Given these isoquants, there will be a set of relative factor prices, represented by the common tangent MM' to the two isoquants, at which the two commodities will have equal per-unit costs of production in terms of the numéraire capital; at these factor prices, the cost-minimizing capital-labour ratios in the production of both goods will be OR_x and OR_y respectively. Now consider a slight rise in the price of capital relative to labour, represented by a counter-clockwise rotation of the common budget line; the optimal capital-labour ratios become OR_x' and OR_y', and the minimum cost of producing a unit X in terms of capital becomes OM_x whereas the minimum cost of producing a unit Y in terms of capital becomes OM_y. The relative cost of production of the capital-intensive good rises as the relative price of capital in terms of labour rises. There is thus a monotonic relation, given by the technology, between the relative costs (prices) of the goods and the relative factor prices, such that a rise in the relative (and absolute) marginal productivity of a factor is associated with a rise in the relative price of the good that uses it intensively. While the proof just given applies to a change in factor prices starting from an equal-cost-of-commodities situation, it is perfectly general, because units of product can always be redefined to make costs equal in the starting situation.

The monotonic relation between commodity prices and factor prices is a consequence of the assumed difference in factor intensities between commodities, and holds so long as both goods are produced. The assumed fixity of factor endowments, however, sets limits to the range of commodity and factor prices that the economy can in fact attain consistent with full employment of the given factors of

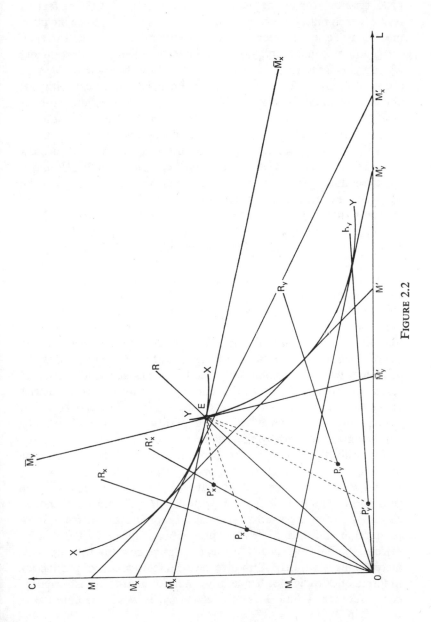

FIGURE 2.2

production. Assume that the country's endowment ratio of factors is OR (which must lie between OR_x and OR_y if MM' is to be included in the feasible set of factors and commodity prices). At one extreme, the economy could employ its total factor endowment in producing X, implying a factor-price ratio represented by the slope of $\overline{M_x M_x}'$, a cost-minimizing factor utilization ratio in X coincident with OR and a corresponding commodity-price ratio given by the ratio of $O\overline{M_x}$ to the y-intercept of a parallel tangent to the YY isoquant; at the other extreme the economy could specialize on producing Y, with a factor-price ratio given by the slope of $\overline{M_y M_y}'$, a cost-minimizing factor utilization ratio in Y coincident with OR and a correspondingly determined commodity price ratio. Thus given the factor endowment E the range of feasible factor prices for the economy ranging from complete specialization on good X to complete specialization on Y is that from the slope of $\overline{M_x M_x}'$ to $\overline{M_y M_y}'$, to which there is a corresponding range of feasible commodity prices.

The foregoing implies that, given the factor endowment, there will be a unique relation between commodity prices, factor prices, and the production pattern—the allocation of factors between the industries. This allocation can be shown diagrammatically as follows. Let E represent the actual factor endowment of the economy. Then, given the optimal factor utilization ratios in the two industries consistent with given commodity and factor prices, the allocation of resources must be such that the amounts used in the two industries add up to the overall endowment. These allocations can be determined, on the principles of vector addition, by completing the parallelogram formed by the endowment point E and the optimal factor utilization ratios in the two industries: in the specific case of the budget line MM', the factor allocations will be as shown by P_x and P_y. It is further evident that as the relative price of capital rises and of labour falls from MM' to $M_x M_x'$, P_x must shift northeast to P_x' and P_y southwest to P_y', implying an increase in X production and a decrease in Y production. Since a higher relative price of capital implies also a higher relative cost (and price) of X, increased production of X involves a rise in relative cost of production in terms of Y foregone; hence, if we were to chart a transformation curve between X and Y for the economy, it would be concave to the origin.

IV. DERIVATION OF THE TRANSFORMATION AND INCOME DISTRIBUTION CURVES

1. *Lerner-Pearce Diagram*

The Lerner-Pearce diagram thus far has been used to develop certain necessary relations among commodity prices, factor prices, and the allocation of the fixed factor endowment between industries. This gives a certain range of possible production and distribution situations that are embodied in the community's transformation curve,

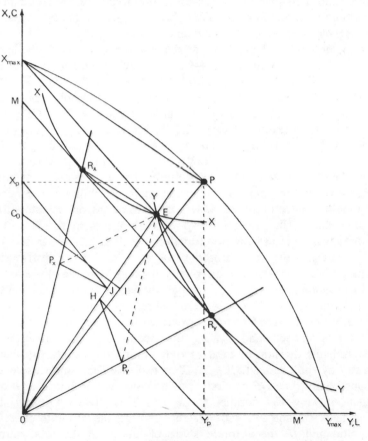

FIGURE 2.3

in the first instance, and its income distribution curve in the second. Using a technique developed by J. R. Melvin, the transformation curve can be derived directly from the Lerner-Pearce diagram in the following manner. Isoquants XX and YY in Figure 2.3 represent the production functions for both goods and pass through the factor endowment point E. These levels of output represent the maximum possible for the two commodities, which can be translated to the Cartesian axes by the line $X_{max}Y_{max}$, arbitrarily drawn except it must go through E. Measuring X and Y along the C and L axes respectively, X_{max} and Y_{max} represent the absolute maximum outputs of X and Y as linear distances from the origin. At the factor price ratio given by the slope of MM', P_x and P_y are the factor allocation points determined by the principles of vector addition. The ratio of the amount of X produced at the factor prices MM' to the maximum possible output of X is OP_x/OR_x, which can be transmitted first to OE by drawing P_xJ parallel to R_xE, and then to OX_{max} by drawing JX_p parallel to $X_{max}E$. Similarly, the ratio of Y produced at the slope of MM' to the maximum output of Y is OP_y/OR_y, which can be translated to OY_{max} in the ratio OY_p/OY_{max}. Since both OY_{max} and OX_{max} represent absolute maximum outputs, the ratios OY_p/OY_{max} and OX_p/OX_{max} determine the absolute amounts of Y and X at Y_p and X_p respectively. These points meet at point P, which is the point on the production possibility curve corresponding to factor prices MM'. By considering other factor price ratios and finding their corresponding tangents to the X and Y isoquants, the transformation function $X_{max}PY_{max}$ can be traced out.

Figure 2.3 also can be used to develop the income distribution curve. For diagrammatic simplicity, assume that the slope of the construction line $X_{max}Y_{max}$ through the factor endowment point E equals the factor price ratio MM'. OX_{max} thus represents national income measured in terms of capital; with OC_0 the income of capital in terms of itself, and C_0X_{max} the income of labour in terms of capital, the division of total income among the two factors being given by the ratio $OC_0/C_{0\,max}$. This ratio can be translated to the construction line OP by first drawing construction line $X_{max}P$ and then drawing C_0I parallel to $X_{max}P$. This divides OP into the segments OI and IP, with OI representing the absolute share of capital and IP the absolute share of labour in the total output represented by point P. Point I should be interpreted as a reference and not an actual consumption point. Capital's budget constraint is actually a line through I, with reference to the origin O, with slope equal to that of the tangent to the transformation curve at P, and similarly labour's budget constraint is the same line but of different length with reference to the origin P. Alternatively, labour's budget constraint can be determined by measuring a distance from O equal to the distance IP.

The same procedure can be used to plot income distribution curves for labour and capital passing through I and W (the reference point for labour's budget constraint with reference to the origin O—not drawn in) respectively. These curves will be reference curves, the location of the budget line being determined by the intersection of the line from the origin O to the relevant point on the transformation curve P with the reference curve. Since as the output of X expands from zero to the maximum amount possible, the marginal product of capital must rise in terms of both products and the marginal product of labour fall, the income distribution curves must have the property that as I moves southeast with P, successive budget lines for capital must lie inside their predecessors throughout their length; and conversely as W moves southeast with P, successive budget lines for labour must lie outside their predecessors throughout their length.

2. *Edgeworth-Bowley Contract Box Diagram*

An alternative approach to the Lerner-Pearce diagram for representing the two-sector general equilibrium model utilizes the contract-box diagram associated with the English economists Edgeworth and Bowley, depicted on the left-hand side of Figure 2.4. The vertical side of the box (OO_x) represents the economy's given endowment of capital, the horizontal side (OO_y) its given endowment of labour. Isoquants for X are sketched into the box with reference to the origin O_x, and for Y with reference to the origin O_y. The tangency points of the two sets of isoquants trace out the contract curve O_xQO_y, which is the locus of efficient production—that is, of factor allocations which maximize the amount of one good that can be produced given the amount of the other to be produced. Such maximization requires equality of the ratios of marginal products of the two factors in the two industries. FF, the common

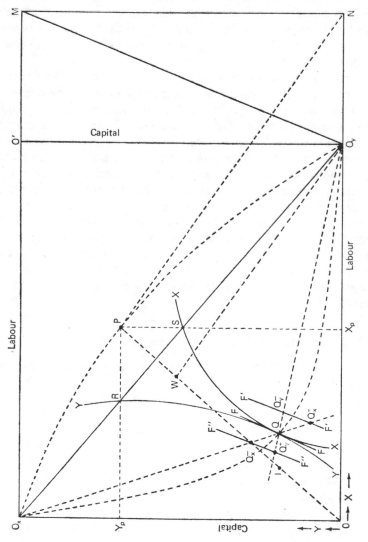

FIGURE 2.4

tangent to the isoquants for the two goods at the point Q, represents the equilibrium factor-price ratio at that point (i.e. for that combination of feasible outputs). Note that as Q moves along the contract curve in the direction of O_y, FF becomes less steep with reference to the horizontal, because such a movement involves substitution of labour for capital along the isoquants for both production functions; that is, in effect, the production point travels northeast along the X isoquant and southwest along the Y isoquant. In other words, as production of X increases and of Y decreases, the relative price of labour falls and of capital rises. This implies a rise in the marginal product of capital and a fall in the marginal product of labour in both absolute and relative terms and, as seen earlier, a rise in the relative price of X in terms of Y.

The production transformation curve between the two commodities can be constructed directly from the contract curve, utilizing a technique invented by K. M. Savosnick. This technique, of which that of Melvin is a variant, exploits the fact that owing to constant returns to scale the amount of output represented by any isoquant is proportioned to the distance of that isoquant from the origin of the isoquant map along any ray from that origin selected as a reference line. Using the diagonal of the factor box as a common reference line for the two isoquant maps, the outputs measured along this diagonal can be transferred by vertical projection to the sides of the box opposite to the origins of the isoquant maps on the southwest of the diagonal. Plotting the resultant output combinations in the interior of the box, the transformation curve can be constructed explicitly from the contract curve.

The Savosnick method is illustrated in Figure 2.4. For point Q on the contract curve, the output of X is proportional to $O_x S$ which is $O_x S/O_x O_y$ of the maximum amount of X that can be produced by the given productive factors when they are completely specialized in the production of X; similarly, the output of Y indicated at Q is proportional to the distance $O_y R$ which is $O_y R/O_y O_x$ of the maximum amount of Y that can be produced when the productive factors are completely specialized in Y. These ratios can be transferred to the sides of the factor box—$O_x S/O_x O_y$ to the horizontal and $O_y R/O_x O_y$ to the vertical—by dropping perpendiculars from points S and R on the diagonal to the X and Y axes respectively. Since by the Savosnick construction $O O_y$ is defined as the absolute maximum amount of X that can be produced and OO_x as the absolute maximum of Y, the perpendiculars mark off absolute as well as relative amounts of the two goods on the respective axes; hence, X_p and Y_p represent the absolute quantities of goods X and Y at point Q. These points determine the point P on the transformation curve corresponding to the outputs at point Q on the contract curve. Repetition of the procedure for other points on the contract curve yields the entire production transformation curve O_xPO_y with reference to the origin O.

It is evident from the construction that every P must lie to the northeast of the diagonal O_xO_y; but this does not suffice to establish the usual assumption that the transformation curve under perfect competition is everywhere concave to the origin O. To prove this, hold factor prices constant at the price ratio embodied in FF and consider equal increases and decreases in production of X from Q to Q_x^+ and from Q to Q_x^- respectively. At the given factor prices, production of Y would simultaneously decrease and increase by equal amounts, respectively from Q to Q_y^- and from Q to Q_y^+. But maintenance of initial factor price ratio is in each case inconsistent with factor market equilibrium, since it would involve an excess demand for capital and supply of labour for an increase in X production and vice versa for a decrease in X production. If factor prices are allowed to change to preserve factor market equilibrium, while X production is changed up and down by the same assumed equal amounts, the equilibrium production points must lie on the contract curve respectively somewhere right of $F'F'$ for the increase in X and somewhere right of $F''F''$ for the decrease in X. This means that production of Y decreases when X increases by more, and increases when X decreases by less, than the equal decrease and increase that would occur if factor prices were held constant. Hence, as X increases from the quantity at Q_x^- to the quantity at Q and then to the quantity at Q_x^+, a successively larger amount of Y production has to be sacrificed; and this proposition holds regardless of the magnitude of the equal successive changes in X production. Hence the transformation curve must be concave to the origin throughout.

Let us now develop the income distribution relationship. The factor-price ratio at point Q is given by the slope of FF. The value of capital in terms of labour can consequently be measured by drawing a line through O_y with the same slope as FF, to intersect O_xO' extended at M. O_xO' represents the income of labour in terms of itself and $O'M$ the income of capital in terms of labour, their ratio representing the division of total income between the two factors. Drop MN perpendicular to OO_y extended, to transfer the distribution ratio to the horizontal axis. Then draw the lines OP and NP and draw O_yW parallel to NP to intersect OP at W. This divides OP into the segments OW and WP, with OW representing the share of labour and WP the share of capital in the total output represented by point P. Similarly, the division of income could be projected on to OP, with the income of capital being measured along OP from O by drawing a line from O' parallel to MO_y to intersect O_xO_y at some point, and then a line from this point parallel to OO_y to intersect OO_x, and finally a line from this point parallel to the line O_xP to determine the point I. Alternatively, I could be found by measuring a distance from O equal to the distance WP. (Note the reversal of positions of labour's share and capital's share on OP with the contract-box diagram by comparison with the Lerner-Pearce diagram.)

As in the Lerner-Pearce diagram, the points W and I are to be interpreted as reference points, and not as actual consumption points. Labour's budget constraint is actually a line through W, with reference to the origin O, with slope equal to that of the tangent to the transformation curve at P, and similarly capital's budget constraint is the same line but of different length with reference to the origin P. Conversely, capital's income is the budget line through I parallel to the tangent at P with reference to the origin O, and labour's income is the same line with reference to the origin P.

The same procedure can be used to plot income distribution curves for labour and capital passing through W and I respectively. These curves will be reference curves, the location of the budget line being determined by the intersection of the line from the origin O to the relevant point on the transformation curve P with the reference curve. Since, as the output of X expands from zero to the maximum amount possible, the marginal product of capital must rise in terms of both products and the marginal product of labour fall in terms of both goods, the income distribution curves must have the property that as W moves southeast with P, successive budget lines for labour must lie inside their predecessors throughout their length; and conversely as I moves southeast with P, successive budget lines for capital must lie outside their predecessors throughout their length.

V. DETERMINATION OF GENERAL EQUILIBRIUM

Given the method of derivation of the transformation curve and the income distribution functions, the analysis of the general equilibrium determination of commodity and factor prices and the production pattern can now proceed without further reference to either the Lerner-Pearce or the contract-box diagram. There are two alternative ways of proceeding, technically.

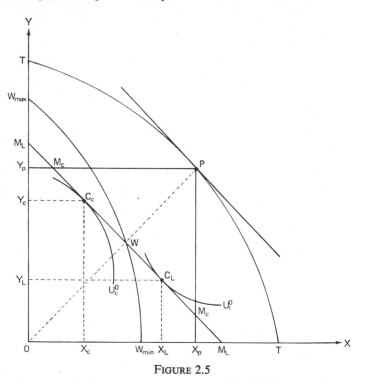

FIGURE 2.5

The first is to use a single income distribution function, with O and P as origins respectively for the indifference curve systems of the two groups of factor owners. This method is illustrated in

70

Figure 2.5 where $W_{max}W_{min}$ is the income distribution curve for labour with reference to the origin O, the income of capital being represented by reference to the origin P, the relevant point on the transformation curve. With production at P, labour's budget line with reference to O is M_LM_L, while capital's budget line with reference to the origin P is M_cM_c. Labour's indifference curves in conjunction with its budget line produce a consumption equilibrium point for labour at C_L, similarly, capital's indifference curves in conjunction with its budget line produce a consumption equilibrium point for capital at C_c. Capital's consumption demand for Y is Y_pY_c and labour's OY_L, implying an excess of supply of Y over the demand of Y_cY_L; capital's consumption demand for X is X_pX_c, and labour's OX_L, implying an excess of demand for X over the supply of X_cX_L. To achieve equilibrium, the production pattern of the economy must shift towards production of more X and less Y, implying a rise in the price of capital and a fall in the price of labour, equilibrium being restored when, for the relevant point on the transformation curve, C_L and C_c coincide.

The second possible approach is to employ two income distribution functions, one for labour and one for capital, with both sets of group indifference curves inserted in the diagram with reference to the origin O. This approach is illustrated in Figure 2.6 where $W_{max}W_{min}$ and $I_{min}I_{max}$ are the income distribution curves for labour and capital respectively. For production point P, labour's budget line is M_LM_L and capital's M_cM_c; capital's optimum consumption point is C_c, and labour's C_L. The total consumption demand of the community, derived by vector addition, is at C, implying an excess demand for X and supply of Y and requiring a rise in the relative prices of X and capital, a shift of production towards X, and a redistribution of income towards capital. Equilibrium is achieved when C_L plus C_c equals P.

To this point it has been assumed that because both groups of factor owners always demand some of both goods there must exist a point on the transformation curve consistent with the equality of C_L and C_c (Figure 2.5). But there may be more than one equilibrium as can be established by the following argument. Consider the situation in Figure 2.5 where at the price ratio given by the slope of the transformation curve at point P there exists an excess demand for X and an excess supply of Y. The impact of this excess demand

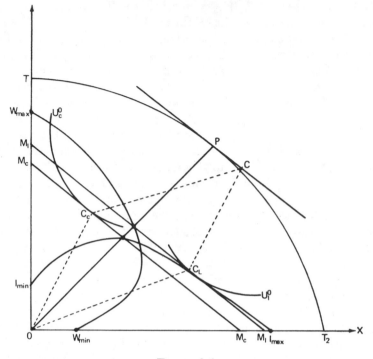

FIGURE 2.6

for X (excess supply of Y) is to increase the relative price of X which implies, on the production side, that more X and less Y will be produced and, on the consumption side, a substitution effect in favour of Y and against X on the part of both groups of factor owners (the income effect component of the price effect works against both goods). Given the normal assumption of convexity outward of the transformation curve and convexity inward (to the origin) of the preference functions, both production and consumption substitution effects are stabilizing in that both work to reduce the excess demand for X. There is, however, in addition to these production and consumption effects, an income redistribution effect attendant upon the increase in the production of the capital-intensive good which raises the price of capital and reduces that of labour. As the output of the capital-intensive good rises while that of the labour-intensive good falls, at the initial factor price ratio, labour (capital) is being absorbed by the expanding good X at a slower (faster) rate than it is being ejected from the contracting good Y, implying a rise in the price of capital and a fall in the price of labour if full employment is to be maintained. Thus as production shifts toward more of X and less of Y, the absolute (and relative) income of capitalists in terms of purchasing power over both goods increases, and the absolute income of labour falls in identical terms. If capitalists have a higher marginal propensity to consume the capital-intensive good than do workers (and there is no *a priori* reason either to believe that they should or should not), this change in the distribution of income tends to increase the demand for X as the price of X *rises*, and this effect may be strong enough to offset the stabilizing

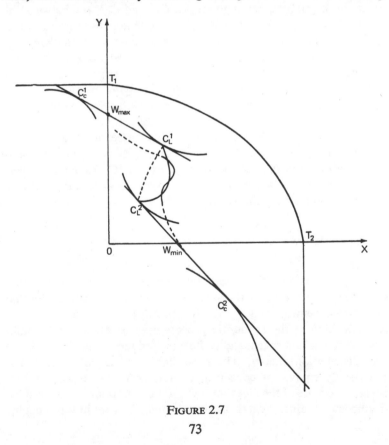

FIGURE 2.7

production and consumption substitution effects. The possibility of such behaviour in turn implies the possibility of multiple equilibrium, though multiple equilibrium must be characterized by an odd number of alternatively stable and unstable equilibria.

The possibility of multiple equilibrium is illustrated in Figure 2.7, which reproduces some aspects of Figure 2.5. When the economy is specialized on production of Y, at T_1, capitalist consumption must be at a point like C_c^1, implying (on the assumption that both groups of factor owners always demand some of both goods) an excess supply of Y. Similarly, when the economy is specialized on production of X, at T_2, capitalist consumption must be at a point like C_c^2, and labour consumption at a point like C_L^2, implying an excess supply of X. Between C_c^1 and C_c^2 must run a locus of possible consumption points for capitalists, passing between C_L^1 and C_L^2, and between the latter two points must run a locus of possible consumption points for labour. These curves must intersect at least once, implying the existence of a stable equilibrium point for the economy as a whole. But they may intersect more than once—necessarily an odd number of times—as illustrated in the diagram, implying an alternation of stable and unstable possible equilibrium points. The middle equilibrium point is unstable in the diagram but is bounded by stable equilibria both above, at a lower relative price of X, and below, at a higher relative price of X. Accordingly, it is only in the neighbourhood of the unstable equilibria, where the $C_c^1 C_c^2$ locus is positively sloped, that an increase in the price of X can lead to an increase in the excess demand for that commodity.

VI. FACTOR-OWNER PRODUCTION BLOCK APPROACH

The analysis to this point has assumed that neither factor directly produces goods but that each sells his services to entrepreneurs spending the proceeds of the sales of his services on the goods that the entrepreneurs produce with the productive factors. This conceptualization of the economic process may be called the 'circular flow of income' approach, and is the one used most often in allocative and distribution theory. There is, however, an alternative and analytically equivalent conceptualization of the economic process which makes use of the fact that under the assumptions of the model, the income obtained by a factor owner and his share in total income under different patterns of aggregate production can be determined from the hypothetical transformation curve for the factors he himself owns, because his income would be no different if his factors could be combined only with each other, and their products sold, than if the factors themselves were sold freely and combined by entrepreneurs with the factors owned by other groups in the community. This conceptualization of the economic process can be called the 'factor owner production block' approach. Its major advantage as compared with the 'circular flow of income' presentation is that it demonstrates several aspects of the distribution problem in a more geometrically explicit and thus clearer manner.

Factor owner production blocks will not be exact miniatures of the economy's total or aggregate transformation curve as might be expected, except in the special case when each factor owner possesses identical shares in the economy's total factor endowment. When ownership shares in the factors of production differ, however, each individual production block will have a different shape not only from the economy's total transformation curve but from each other as well. Furthermore, because the factors of production can be assumed to be mobile within a country, and thus between factor owners, each individual production block may lie outside the first quadrant of the Cartesian diagram, indicating negative production of one of the goods.

Negative production of a commodity serves in the analysis as a proxy for hiring factors of production, a technique for showing factor movement in terms of commodities. Just as reducing positive production in the first quadrant implies freeing or obtaining productive factors that one does in some sense own or possess, producing negative amounts of a good implies obtaining factors that one does not own—hence, borrowing factors. The concept is relevant if there are unequal factor prices (and thus unequal commodity prices as well given the one to one relation between the two) when the productive factors of both factor owners are specialized in the production of the same good, which must be the case if ownership shares of the factors of production differ. With unequal factor prices at complete production specialization points, each factor owner could hire the deficient factor from the other one at a gain for both. For example, if capital was the deficient factor at the point of complete specialization on good Y, implying in the two-factor model that labour is an abundant factor at that point, exporting labour and importing capital can be conceptualized as negative production of the capital-intensive good and increased positive production of the labour-intensive good past the point of complete specialization, since according to the Stolper-Samuelson relation this change in outputs creates an excess supply of capital and excess demand for labour at constant factor prices. The consequent fall in the absolute (and relative) price and marginal product of capital and rise in the absolute (and relative) price and marginal product of labour implies that factor movement will provide factor-price equalization.

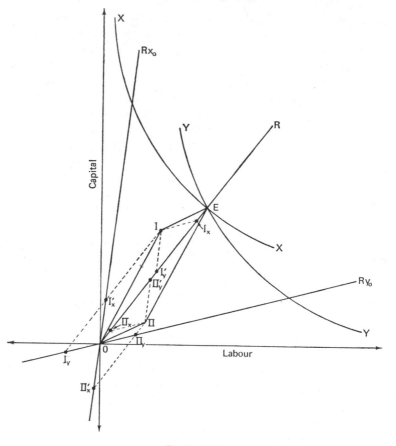

FIGURE 2.8

The factor owner production block approach to the theory of income distribution is illustrated in Figure 2.8, a further variant of the Lerner-Pearce diagram. The production function of each good again is represented by a single isoquant, and XX and YY going through the factor endowment point E represent the maximum amounts of X and Y that the economy is capable of producing with its given technology and factor endowment. Points I and II represent the endowment points of each factor owner which by the principles of vector addition must add up to E if it is assumed that all factors are fully employed. Complete specialization on X implied factor prices equal to the slope of the X-isoquant at point E and the factor utilization ratio OR in X, to which there is a corresponding point of equal slope on the Y-isoquant indicating the implicit factor utilization ratio in Y when production of Y is zero, and given in the diagram as OR_{yo}. Similarly, complete product specialization on good Y implies a factor price ratio equal to the slope of the Y-isoquant at E and the factor utilization ratio OR in Y, to which there is a corresponding point of equal slope on the X-isoquant indicating the implicit factor utilization ratio in X when production of X is zero, and represented in the diagram as OR_{xo}.

Given the optimal factor utilization ratios in the two industries when production is specialized, it is possible to determine the allocation of the resources of each factor owner between the two commodities on the dual assumptions of domestic factor mobility and that the factor quantities used in the two industries by each individual add up to his total factor endowment. These allocations are determined on the principles of vector addition by completing the parallelogram formed by the endowment point of each factor owner and the optimal factor utilization ratios in the two industries, in the separate cases of complete specialization on each commodity. When there is complete specialization on good X, OR and OR_{yo} are the relevant factor utilization ratios, in which case owner I's factor allocations are shown by I_x and I_y, indicating positive production of X and negative production of Y, while II's factor allocations are shown by II_x and II_y, indicating positive production of both goods. II's positive production of Y must, of course, offset I's negative production of this good if the economy is completely specialized on X. OR and OR_{xo} are the relevant factor utilization ratios where there is complete specialization on good Y, in which case I's factor allocations are given by I_x' and I_y' indicating positive production of both goods, while II's factor allocations are shown by II_x' and II_y' indicating positive production of Y and negative production of X, the latter being offset by an equal amount of positive production of that good by owner I. In the analysis the concept of negative production serves as a proxy for the factor movement required for factor price equalization throughout the economy.

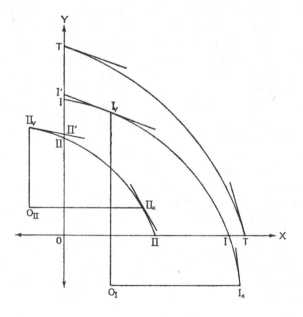

FIGURE 2.9

The production possibility curves of each factor owner are made explicit in Figure 2.9. For individuals I and II, these curves are respectively given by $I\,I$ and $II\,II$ in the first quadrant of the Cartesian diagram, but subject to the limitation imposed on the economy by its overall factor endowment and technology are capable of being extended into the second and fourth quadrants by the concept of negative production (factor hiring). The termini of each curve are defined for the range of factor prices possible for the economy as a whole, and the position of each curve is limited by the requirement that the outputs of each individual at any of the feasible commodity prices sum to the total output of the community at that price ratio.

The relationship between the economy's transformation function and that of each individual factor owner enables us to trace out the latter from the former for the range of factor prices possible for the economy as a whole. In the case where factor owners have identical factor shares, the individual transformation curves are exact miniatures of the economy's total transformation curve, and all points along the former are relevant. But where factor shares differ, some points on the production block of each factor owner will not be attainable under factor price equalization assumptions. For the factor ratio corresponding to specialization on good Y in the economy, the corresponding points on I and II's respective production blocks are I_y and II_y, the former indicating positive production of both goods and the latter positive Y but negative X production. Similarly, for the factor price corresponding to specialization on good X in the economy, we have the points I_x and II_x. The segments I_yI on I's block and II_xII on II's block therefore are not attainable since both imply factor prices outside the range possible for the economy; however, the extensions II_yII of II's block and I_xI of I's block are relevant in that through the concept of negative production they represent the factor movement required for factor price equilization when the economy is specialized in either commodity. Linking all relevant points, the 'efficient' production blocks for factor owners I and II are given respectively as I_xI_y and II_xII_y, in contrast to their actual blocks $I I$ and $II II$. In Figure 2.9 where factor ownership is non-specialized and II is assumed to possess a greater relative share of the economy's total endowment of labour and I a greater share of its capital stock, I's 'efficient' production block falls partially in the first and fourth quadrants, while II's 'efficient' block falls partially in the first and second quadrants of the Cartesian diagram under factor price equalization assumptions.

Figure 2.9 can be used to demonstrate the proposition that if factor prices are not equal at the points of complete production specialization, there are gains to each factor owner from hiring the factor of which it is deficient. In Figure 2.9, when individuals I and II are both specialized in the production of Y, the slope of II's production block is steeper than I's with reference to the horizontal, indicating a higher relative price of X (the capital-intensive good) and thus a higher relative price of capital in II than in I. Each individual gains in terms of the numéraire good Y by trading factors, in the present case, by II exporting labour and importing capital, and vice versa for I. II gains $II'II$ by producing more Y and negative quantities of X, while I gains $I'I$ by producing more X and less Y. Factor price equalization occurs, and the gains from factor mobility ceases, when the production points II_y and I_y are attained.

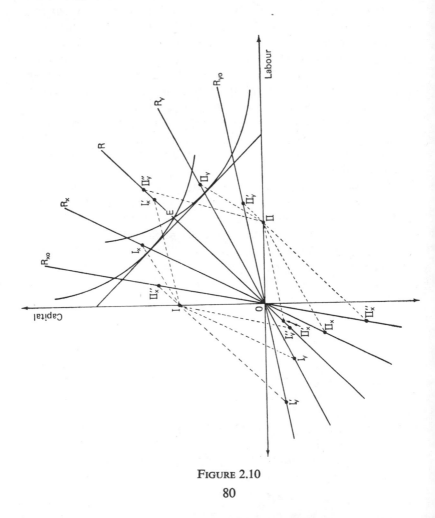

FIGURE 2.10

The factor owner production block when the two factor owners are identified with specific factors of production is illustrated in Figure 2.10. Individual I is assumed to own the economy's total supply of capital and II its total labour supply. Three representative factor price ratios are chosen for the analysis, one corresponding to complete specialization in good X, another to complete specialization in good Y and the third to non-specialized production. At these, and the entire range of possible factor prices given the economy's overall factor endowment and technology, individual I produces positive quantities of X and negative quantities of Y while II produces positive quantities of Y and negative quantities of X. In the case of specialized factor ownership, therefore, capital's 'efficient' production block falls entirely in the fourth quadrant while labour's 'efficient' block falls entirely within the second quadrant. This implies that the greater the difference of relative factor shares between individuals, the greater the divergence of the 'efficient' from the actual production block for both individuals.

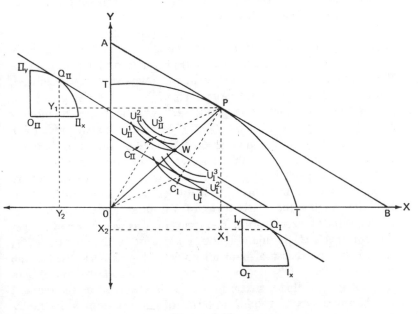

FIGURE 2.11

81

The equivalency between the 'circular flow of income' and the 'factor owner production block' approaches to the theory of general equilibrium is demonstrated in Figure 2.11 by the fact that at any feasible commodity price ratio, the corresponding outputs on the economy's transformation function are equal to the sum of the output constellations of each factor owner at that price ratio. This allows us to take as the slope of the factor owner's budget line passing through each reference point W either the slope of the corresponding point on the economy's transformation function or that of the corresponding point on the factor owner's own production block. Labour's budget line going through W can be given either by the slope of the transformation function at point P or the slope of labour's production block at point Q_{II}, and similarly for capital. One implication of this equivalency is that the income distribution curve of each factor ($W_{max}W_{min}$ and $I_{min}I_{max}$) can be derived directly from that factor's production block by tracing the locus of points given by the intersection of the factor's budget line with the ray connecting the corresponding point on the economy's transformation function with the origin of this function as production of the two goods varies.

The effect of changes in the aggregate production pattern of the economy on the distribution of income can be determined directly from each factor's (or factor owner's) production block. In the case illustrated in Figure 2.12 where factor ownership is specialized, both factor owners produce more Y (the labour-intensive good) and less X (the capital-intensive good)—II's production point moving from Q_{II} to $Q_{II'}$ and I's from Q_I to $Q_{I'}$—as the relative price of Y increases, implying a higher income for factor owner II (labour) in terms of both goods and a lower income for factor owner I (capital) in terms of both goods. If good Y is used as the numéraire good, II's income in terms of that numéraire increases from M_3 to M_3' while a fall in the relative price of X implies increased purchasing power of the numéraire good Y in terms of X as well. The new budget line for II $M_3'M_4'$ is unambiguously superior to the old one M_3M_4 since it lies northeast of it at all points. Should X be used as the numéraire good, II's income in terms of X increases from M_4 to M_4' but part of this increase in income is absorbed by the reduced purchasing power of good X in terms of good Y implicit in the increase in Y's relative price. The net effect on II's budget line when

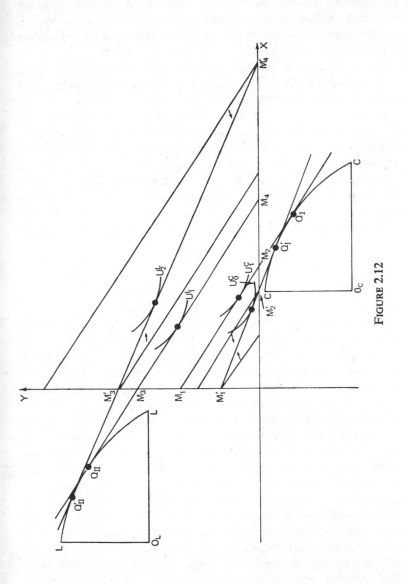

FIGURE 2.12

X is the numéraire is identical with that when Y is the numéraire. It is immaterial to the final outcome which good is used to measure the change in the absolute income position of each factor owner; in either case the change in outputs causes II's budget line to move from M_3M_4 to $M_3'M_4'$.

The same factor owner production block approach can be used to determine the effect of the change in I's production point from Q_I to Q_I' on his income. Given his initial budget constraint at M_1M_2, factor owner I (capital) is worse off in terms of both goods as a result of the change in outputs: in terms of good Y his numéraire income drops from M_1 to M_1' though part of this loss is offset by the rise in the purchasing power of good Y in terms of good X; in terms of good X he suffers both because his numéraire income falls from M_2 to M_2' and because the purchasing power of his numéraire good falls in terms of good Y. Here as before it is irrelevant which good is used as the numéraire; in either case I's new budget line $M_1'M_2'$ lies everywhere within his old one M_1M_2.

Now let us explore the effect of a change in outputs on the absolute real income position of a factor owner when it is assumed that the factor owner does not own the economy's entire stock of a particular factor of production. Consider the case illustrated in Figure 2.13 where factor owner II owns some capital as well as labour but where his relative share of the economy's labour supply is greater than that of I, so that his production block lies partially in the first and partially in the second quadrants of the Cartesian diagram. To maintain *ceteris paribus* conditions with the case of specialized factor ownership, slide II's production block down $Q_{II}M_3M_4$ with the axes of the production block kept parallel with those of the budget constraints until the production point $\bar{Q}_{II}$ is sufficiently in the first quadrant so that both the initial and subsequent production points lie in the first quadrant when prices are changed from the slope of M_3M_4 to $\overline{M}_3\overline{M}_4$ (equal to $M_3'M_4'$). We thus commence our comparison of the effect of a change in outputs on the absolute real income position of a factor owner when factor ownership is not specialized from an identical budget constraint, given an identical change in commodity prices and thus an identical change in outputs.

As in the case of specialized factor ownership, it is irrelevant which good X or Y is used to measure the change in II's real income—II's new budget constraint is given by $\overline{M}_3\overline{M}_4$. However,

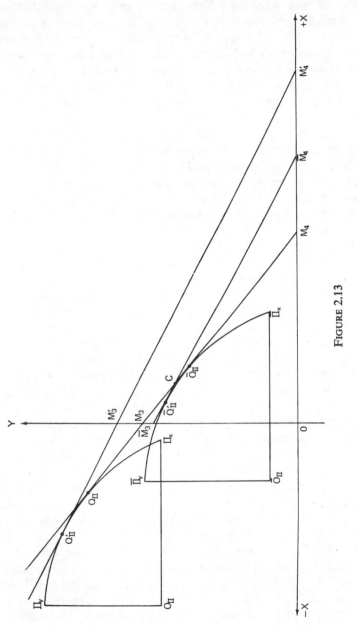

FIGURE 2.13

unlike the case where specialized factor ownership is assumed and the effect of the change of outputs on II's real income position independent of his preference function, with the new budget constraint lying everywhere outside the old one, with incomplete specialization and points $\bar{Q}_{II}$ and $\bar{Q}_{II'}$ in the first quadrant, it is not possible to determine the change in II's real income position without reference to his preference function. The new budget constraint $\overline{M_3}\overline{M_4}$ cuts the old constraint M_3M_4 at point C, so that part of $\overline{M_3}\,\overline{M_4}$ lies inside M_3M_4 and part outside it. Furthermore, it is clear from the geometry that the less specialized the factor ownership, as signified by the southeast movement of II's production block along M_3M_4 from its initial position of complete specialization of factor ownership, and thus the more southeast is the cutting point C on M_3M_4, the more likely the postulated change in outputs will reduce II's real income position rather than increase it.

The ambiguity of the distribution effect of increasing the output of Y and decreasing the output of X when both production points on II's production block lie in the first quadrant, indicating positive production of both goods, as opposed to the situation where both production points lie in the second quadrant, indicating positive production of Y and negative production of X, requires further elaboration. Let us first consider the situation where the production points $\bar{Q}_{II}$ and $\bar{Q}_{II}{}'$ lie in the first quadrant. Because $\bar{Q}_{II}$ reflects production of both commodities, for II, as a producer of X, a fall in the relative price of X in terms of Y necessarily entails a decrease in the value of X in terms of Y, even after the factor owner adjusts his outputs to the new commodity price ratio, since maintenance of his prior equilibrium income at the new commodity price ratio would imply production at a point outside the boundaries of his factor block. In quadrant II, however, the situation is not one in which the factor owner produces both goods, but one in which he produces one good Y (positive production) and trades for the other commodity X (negative production). Hence, the fall in the relative price of X in this case increases the income of the factor owner for reasons familiar from the gains from trade analysis (see Chapter 6); as the relative price of (the import) good X falls, there is a gain due to the improvement in the terms-of-trade at the initial production point, and a further gain due to the adjustment of the production point to the new commodity price ratio. The essence of the difference between the situations in the two quadrants then is that in quadrant *I* the factor owner is conceived of as a producer of *X* and thus a loser in terms of good *Y* when the price of *X* falls in terms of *Y*, while in quadrant *II* he is conceived of as a consumer of *X* and thus a gainer in terms of *Y* when the relative price of *X* falls. However, since the factor owner produces positive amounts of good *Y* in both the first and second quadrants, he gains in terms of good *X*, in each case, when the relative price of *Y* rises in terms of *X*, and there is a further gain in terms of good *X* when the factor owner adjusts his production bundle to the new commodity price ratio.

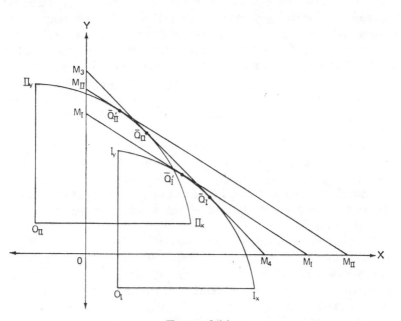

FIGURE 2.14

The analysis to this point has concentrated on the effects of changes in the aggregate pattern of production in the economy on the absolute real income position of a factor owner under conditions of specialized and non-specialized factor ownership. The question of relative income effects, of course, is a trivial one when specialized factor ownership is assumed and only becomes interesting and worth exploring when it is assumed that factor ownership is not specialized and tastes between the factor owners differ. The case where each factor owner owns both factors of production in different proportions is illustrated in Figure 2.14, where it is demonstrated that the relative income position of the factor owner possessing a greater ownership share of the factor whose marginal product has risen as a result of change must increase relative to that of the other factor owner. This is most easily accomplished by assuming an equal initial budget constraint for both factor owners I and II, so that I's production block lies tangent to M_3M_4 in the first and fourth quadrants and II's lies tangent to M_3M_4 in the first and second quadrants. The change in commodity prices must be the same under *ceteris paribus* conditions; in this case from the slope of M_3M_4 to that of $M_{II}M_{II}$ (equal to M_IM_I). II's production points shifts from $\bar{Q}_{II}$ to $\bar{Q}_{II'}$ upon this change in prices, implying a new budget constraint $M_{II}M_{II}$ which lies everywhere outside M_IM_I the new budget constraint for I when his production point shifts from $\bar{Q}_I$ to $\bar{Q}_I'$ upon the change in prices. Regardless of which good is used to measure numéraire income, it is clear that II's relative position has improved as a result of the change by M_{II}/M_I. Furthermore, it is apparent from the geometry that the greater the initial linear distance separating $\bar{Q}_I$ and $\bar{Q}_{II}$ on M_3M_4, indicating a greater difference in the relative ownership shares of the factors of production between factor owners, the greater the relative income effect of a change in prices.

Changes in commodity prices also affect factor owners differentially, though in their role as consumers rather than producers, if their tastes are assumed to differ. Groups demonstrating a relative preference (preference being defined in terms of average spending propensities) for the good whose relative price rises lose relative to groups whose preference runs in terms of the other good. This can be illustrated in Figure 2.15 where both factor owners are assumed to be subject to the same initial budget constraint M_1M_2 with I demonstrating a stronger preference for good X by comparison with II as implied by I's consumption point C_I lying southeast of C_{II}. Let us assume change serves to increase the relative price of X. The relative income effect of the change can be determined through the use of a Hicksian compensating variation in income;

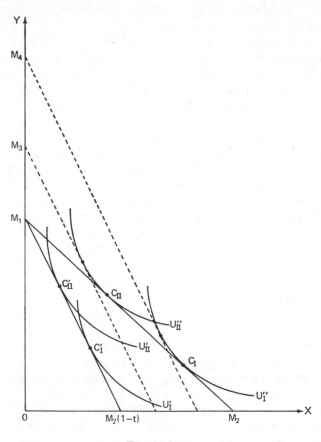

FIGURE 2.15

at the new price ratio, how much income must be given to the consumer in order to make him just as well off after the tax increase as he was before the change. M_1M_3 must be given to II in this case and M_1M_4 to I. Since M_1M_3 is less than M_1M_4, the increase in the market price of X clearly has been more adverse to I, the individual having the relative preference for X, than II; hence II's relative position improves. As the geometry of Figure 2.15 verifies, the greater the difference between II and I in the proportion of their income spent on the two goods, as implied by a greater linear distance

89

between C_{II} and C_I on M_1M_2, the greater will be the relative income effect of the change in consumer prices.

Let us now summarize the results of the foregoing analysis for the case when the relative price of X falls, the production of X falls and Y rises, so that the absolute and relative marginal product of labour rises and the price of labour rises, while the absolute and relative marginal product of capital falls and its price falls. If specialized factor ownership is assumed, regardless of the nature of the factor owner's preference functions, labour will be better off in the sense of attaining a consumption point on a higher contour of its utility map, since its absolute income in terms of both goods increases, and vice versa for capital. The larger is labour's average spending propensity for X, the good whose relative price has fallen, the greater the improvement in its absolute real income in terms of the numéraire good, while capital's absolute decline will be less the greater its average spending propensity for good X.

If non-specialized factor ownership is assumed, the less the specialization the greater the probability that the new and the old budget lines for each factor owner will cross, so that a determination as to whether the factor owner is made better or worse off in absolute terms will depend upon the precise nature of his demand preferences. Whatever the case, in relative terms, the factor owner possessing a greater share of the factor whose relative price has risen gains relative to the other factor owner, and the factor owner consuming a larger share of the good whose relative price has fallen gains relative to the other factor owner. Thus the relative positions of the two factor owners depend on the relation between their ownership shares of the factors of production and their consumption shares of the two goods.

This chapter has been devoted to the construction of a full general equilibrium two-sector model of the economy, bringing in income distribution and factor owner preferences in addition to production conditions (technology and relative factor supplies) as determinants of the full general equilibrium solution. The purpose of such an exercise, however, is not primarily to demonstrate the existence of an equilibrium on reasonable general equilibrium assumptions about tastes and technology and to explore its stability and uniqueness—though mathematical economists in particular have devoted considerable attention to these questions—but to apply the model to the investigation of economically relevant changes in the data of the system, including both exogenous changes and changes induced by policy. The next chapter will apply the apparatus to one of the purposes for which such apparatus is intended, the analysis of the effects of exogenous changes on the characteristics of the general equilibrium solution of the system. The analysis of policy induced changes is reserved for Chapter 4.

APPENDIX A

Multiple Equilibrium and the Elasticity of Technical Substitution

The condition that the factor owners have a relative marginal preference for the commodity using their factors intensively is a necessary, but clearly not a sufficient, condition for instability and multiple equilibrium. As such, it may lead to an exaggerated impression of the likelihood of these phenomena, which also require a sufficiently strong income redistribution effect for the operation of the difference in marginal propensities to outweigh the substitution and transformation affects of a rise in the price of a commodity. It can be shown that a necessary condition for this is that the elasticity of substitution between the factors in at least one of the production functions must be less than unity. While this requires more mathematical analysis than is appropriate to present here, a heuristic logical proof can be arrived at on the following lines. Assume a unitary elasticity of substitution in each industry; then each factor will have a constant share in the value of output of each industry, larger in the industry that uses it intensively than in the other. Starting from an initial equilibrium position, consider a unit increase in the value of the output of the capital-intensive industry and decrease in the value of the output of the labour-intensive industry (as a result of maximization, the value of total output is approximately constant for small variations from an initial equilibrium). Income will be transferred from labour to capital in proportion to the difference between labour's shares (or capital's shares, since the two shares add up to unity in each industry) of the value of output in the two industries. Since this must be only a fraction, and the difference between capital's and labour's marginal propensities to consume the capital-intensive good must also be a fraction, demand for the capital-intensive good can only increase by a fraction of the increase in output of it, and the initial equilibrium must be stable. For demand to increase by more than supply, the share of capital in the output of one or both industries must rise; and for this to happen with a rise in the relative price of capital requires an elasticity of substitution in production less than unity.

APPENDIX B

The Effect of Changes in the Elasticity of Technical Substitution and Differences Between Optimal Factor Utilization Ratios on the Shape and Location of the Production Possibility Curve

The purpose of this appendix is to analyse the effect of changes in (i) the elasticity of technical substitution (ETS) between labour and capital, and (ii) the difference between optimal factor utilization ratios between two commodities on the shape and location of the production possibility curve.

I. The effect of a reduction in the ETS in one of the industries of the two-sector model (assumed to be the X industry) on the shape and location of the production possibility curve depends critically on the choice of the factor utilization ratio with reference to which the reduction in the ETS is defined. Three reference capital-labour ratios in the industry where the ETS changes define the possibilities: one corresponds to complete specialization on the good in which the reduction in the ETS occurs, the second corresponds to complete specialization on the other good, and the third corresponds to some intermediate production point at which both goods are produced. The three are represented in Figure 2.B.1, where E represents the factor endowment of the economy, and XX and YY are isoquants representing the maximum levels of production of X and Y respectively obtainable with that endowment. OR_{y_o} represents the reference capital-labour ratio in X corresponding to complete specialization on good X, OR_{x_o} represents the reference capital-labour ratio in X corresponding to complete specialization on good

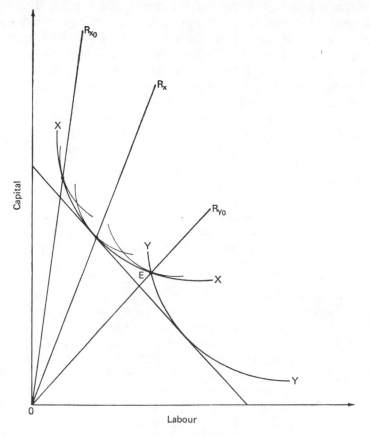

FIGURE 2.B.1

Y, and OR_x represents the reference capital-labour ratio corresponding to production of both goods at the factor price ratio represented by the slope of the common tangent to the two isoquants. The three more sharply curved isoquants tangent to XX at its intersection with the rays representing the reference capital-labour ratios depict the effects of reducing the ETS at those factor utilization ratios.

The effects of reducing the ETS on the shape of the transformation curve are at once intuitively obvious. First, the change can have no effect on the maximum possible output of the other good, since when none of the good for which the ETS has changed is produced, the change is irrelevant. Second, the change will have no effect on the levels of output of the two goods at the factor price ratio or factor utilization ratio at which the change in the ETS occurs, since at that reference point factor utilization ratios and the allocation of factors among industries, as well as the productivity of the factors, allocated to the two industries, are unchanged. But at any other factor utilization ratio, the output of one of the two goods must be less than it was before, for a given level of output of the other good, because, due to the reduction of the ETS, it will take more of both factors together to produce any given quantity of output of the commodity for which the ETS has been reduced with any given factor utilization ratio.

This point is illustrated in Figure 2.B.2, where the slopes of MN and $M'N'$ represent the initial equilibrium factor price ratio before the change in ETS occurs, and XX and YY are members of the original family of isoquants, with OP_x and OP_y representing the optimal factor utilization ratios. For equilibrium, the factor allocation points P_x and P_y must sum by vector addition to the endowment point E. Now consider any point P_x' to the right of the line MN (this means any point whatsoever, not merely the precise point P_x' shown in the diagram). It is obvious that any point P_y' found by completing the parallelogram $OP_x'EP_y'$ must lie to the left of $M'N'$. Finally, consider any reduction in the ETS occurring at some factor utilization ratio lying on the isoquant XX. If this occurs at the initial factor utilization ratio represented by the slope of OP_x (producing a new isoquant such as $X'X'$) outputs of the two goods will remain unchanged. If, however, it occurs at any other factor utilization ratio, such as OP_x' (the new isoquant being like $X''X''$), it follows that the output of the other good Y must fall for a given level of output of X. (Note that P_x' will not be a new equilibrium production point; but any such point on $X''X''$ will have to lie to the right of MN, so that the conclusion is proved by the preceding argument from completion of parallelograms.)

The effect of reducing the ETS on the slope and the curvature of the transformation curve therefore depends critically on the choice

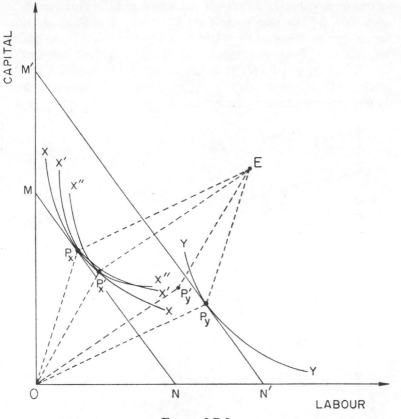

FIGURE 2.B.2

of the reference capital-labour ratio. The possibilities are illustrated in Figure 2.B.3. (*a*) If the reference ratio is that corresponding to complete specialization on production of X, the terminal points of the transformation curve are unchanged but the interior section of it shifts towards the origin: in a broad and not strictly mathematical sense, the concavity to the origin is reduced. (*b*) If the reference ratio is that corresponding to complete specialization on Y, the transformation curve shifts inwards towards the origin throughout its length to the point of complete specialization on X; whether this constitutes an increase or decrease in concavity to the origin is left to the reader's taste or the work of better mathematicians than ourselves to judge. (*c*) Finally, if the reference ratio corresponds to some positive but incompletely specialized level of *X* production, the new production possibility curve will have the same *Y*-production terminal as the old, be tangent to it at the reference-ratio level of *X*-production, and lie inside it elsewhere. Again, it is left to the reader or the mathematicians to decide whether this represents more or less concavity towards the origin.

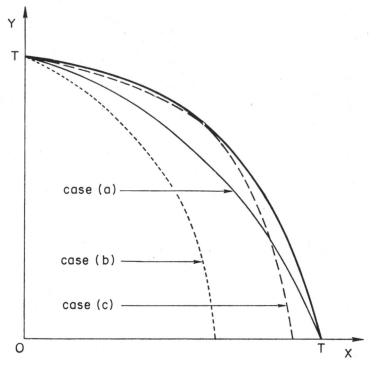

FIGURE 2.B.3

II. Investigating the production possibility effect of increasing the difference between factor utilization ratios alone is simpler than investigating a change in the ETS, for unlike the latter there is no need for a reference factor utilization ratio, independent of factor prices and optimal factor utilization ratios, at which the change is to be taken. At any of the equilibrium factor prices ranging from complete specialization on one good to complete specialization on the other, the change is simply gauged with respect to the original optimal capital-labour ratio obtaining at that price ratio. There is, in other words, only one analytical outcome not a set of possibilities for the production possibility curve when the degree of difference between factor intensities is the postulated parametric change.

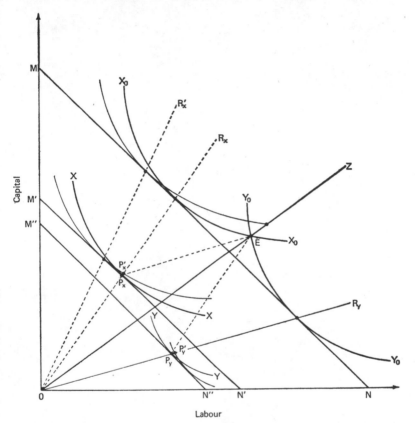

FIGURE 2.B.4

Increasing the difference in factor utilization ratios is demonstrated in Figure 2.B.4 by increasing the capital-labour ratio in X, while holding constant the factor utilization ratio in Y. Thus at factor prices MN (equal to $M'N'$ and $M''N''$), optimal factor utilization ratios OR_x and OR_y in X and Y respectively and factor allocation points P_x and P_y, increasing the difference between OR_x

and OR_y can be depicted by sliding the X-isoquant tangent to $M'N'$ at P_x northwest along $M'N'$ (and thus, because of the assumption of constant returns to scale, the isoquant X_oX_o northwest along MN) until the new optimal factor utilization ratio OR'_x is

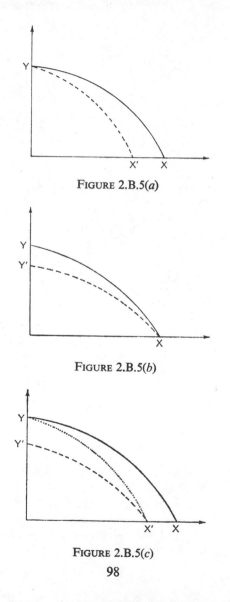

FIGURE 2.B.5(a)

FIGURE 2.B.5(b)

FIGURE 2.B.5(c)

98

obtained. It is clear from the geometry that with reference to the original optimal capital-labour ratio OR_x at factor prices $M'N'$ greater absolute amounts of both factors are required at P'_x as compared with P_x to produce the same amount of X; hence production of Y must be lower than it otherwise would be since there are less factor resources available to produce Y. The factor allocation point P''_y (not drawn in) corresponding to P_x' can be determined on the principles of vector addition by construction of the parallelogram $OP_x'EP_y''$, This analysis, of course, holds true not only with respect to the optimal factor utilization ratio corresponding to factor prices $M'N'$, but at all original optimal factor utilization ratios. Thus at OZ, the optimal factor utilization ratio corresponding to complete specialization on good X, the new isoquant passing through the factor endowment E obviously represents a smaller maximum output of X after the change than before it. The resulting transformation curve will be similar to that depicted in Figure 2.B.5(*a*) labelled YX'; it has shifted inwards towards the origin throughout its length except for the Y-production terminal. The postulated change can have no effect on the maximum possible output of Y since when none of the good for which the optimal capital-labour has changed is produced, the change is irrelevant.

Increasing the degree of difference between the optimal factor utilization ratios in the two industries has been demonstrated by increasing the capital-labour ratios in X, while holding constant the factor utilization ratio in Y. This obviously is a special case and it will now be necessary to investigate two further cases: (*i*) that in which the factor utilization ratio in X is held constant while the capital-labour ratio in Y is decreased, and (*ii*) that in which the capital-labour ratio is increased in X and decreased in Y. The method of analysis of (*i*) is identical with that illustrated in Figure 2.B.4, only in this instance increasing the difference between OR_x and OR_y is accomplished by sliding the Y-isoquant tangent to $M''N''$ at P_y southeast along $M''N''$. Once again the geometry indicates that with reference to the original optimal capital-labour ratio OR_y at factor prices $M''N''$ greater absolute amounts of both factors are required at P_y' as compared with P_y to produce the same amount of Y; hence production of X must be lower than it otherwise would be, and so on with respect to all other original optimal factor utilization ratios. The resulting transformation curve in this case will be similar to that depicted in Figure 2.B.5(*b*) labelled XY'; it has shifted inwards towards the origin throughout its length except for the X-production terminal.

Case (*ii*) where the optimal capital-labour ratio is increased in X and decreased in Y is somewhat more complex. Taken by itself the increase in the capital-labour ratio in X at the factor prices $M'N'$ means that to produce the same amount of X there are less factor resources to produce Y; hence production of Y must be lower than it otherwise would be. Also taken by itself the decrease in the capital-labour ratio in Y means that there will be less output of Y for any given factor allocation to Y—at point P_y for example, output is clearly less after the isoquant shift than before it. Thus, with reference to the original optimal capital-labour ratio OR_x at factor prices $M'N'$, to produce the same amount of X that was produced at P_x before the capital-labour ratio is increased in X and decreased in Y, the output of Y must be less than it otherwise would be for two reasons; the first, related to the increase in the capital-labour ratio in X, because the factor allocation to Y will be less than it otherwise would be, the second, related to the decrease in the capital-labour ratio in Y, because the reduced factor allocation implies a lesser output of Y than would otherwise be the case. Finally, it is clear on the basis of the above reasoning that the new X and Y isoquants passing through the factor endowment E represents smaller maximum outputs of both X and Y after the change than before it. The resulting transformation curve will be similar to that depicted in Figure 2.B.5(*c*) labelled $X'Y'$; it has shifted inwards towards the origin throughout its length including both terminal points.

It is necessary in conclusion to notice an apparent paradox. The foregoing proof shows that an increase in the difference in capital-labour ratios between the two industries pulls the transformation curve in towards the origin except at the terminus corresponding to the good whose capital-labour ratio is unchanged. But the same method of proof can also be used to show that a reduction in the difference in capital-labour ratios between the industries will have exactly the same effect. The explanation is simple: the change in the capital-labour ratio in the one industry has been defined as occurring at a given factor-price ratio and at a given total factor cost. Any change in factor-intensity so defined must reduce the total output of the industry in which it occurs attainable with the country's given factor endowment, given the level of output of the other industry (and short of zero output of this industry), as can readily be seen by mental experiment with the Edgeworth-Bowley-Samuelson contract box. Undoubtedly other definitions of an increased difference in relative factor intensities, or a reduced difference, could be found which would yield much less straightforward results.

CHAPTER 3

Exogenous Change in a Closed Economy

The characteristics of a general equilibrium solution were investigated in Chapter 2 within the context of the two-sector model of general equilibrium, given the economy's factor endowment, technology, and the demand preferences of the two groups of individuals that are assumed to comprise the economy. The purpose of this chapter is to apply this model to the investigation of the effect of changes in each of the above exogenous factors on the prices and quantities of the goods that are produced and traded, the distribution of income between the separate groups that comprise the economy and the potential welfare of the community when the latter is considered in aggregate terms. In these applications, the analytical technique employed will be to assume that prices (commodity and factor) are held constant when a change occurs, and to examine the effect of such change on excess demands and supplies at those prices, using the assumption of stability of equilibrium to predict the direction of the price change required to restore equilibrium. The focus of our analysis, accordingly, will be on qualitative rather than quantitative results.

I. CHANGE IN DEMAND PREFERENCES

Shifts of demand are the simplest to deal with and thus are dealt with first. Such shifts must involve an increase in the quantity of one good demanded by one or both groups of factor-owners, at given commodity prices and factor incomes. The result is an excess demand for one commodity and excess supply of the other at the

102

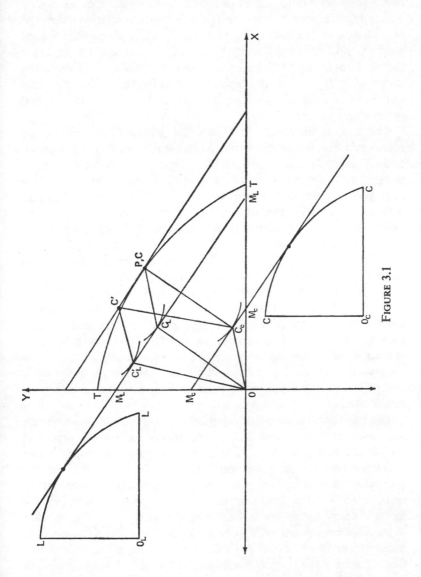

FIGURE 3.1

initial equilibrium-price ratio, requiring a change in the relative commodity-price ratio, a shift of production towards the commodity whose relative price has increased, a rise in the relative price and real income of the factor used intensively in producing that commodity, and a fall in the relative price and real income of the other factor. Thus if the preferences of a factor-owner shift towards the commodity that uses its factor intensively, both the absolute numéraire income of that factor owner and his share in national income rises as a result.

This case is illustrated in Figure 3.1 where TT represents the economy's transformation curve, LL labour's transformation curve, and CC capital's transformation curve (specialized factor ownership is assumed throughout this chapter). P,C is the initial equilibrium aggregate production-consumption point of the economy, consistent with capital's budget constraint M_cM_c and corresponding consumption point C_c, and labour's budget constraint M_LM_L and corresponding consumption point C_L; the two consumption points summing, by vector addition, to aggregate consumption at C. It is assumed that labour's preference function changes such that at M_LM_L more Y, the good that uses labour intensively in its production, and less X is demanded, as indicated by the northwest movement of C_L to $C_L{}'$ along M_LM_L. Vector addition indicates C' as the new aggregate consumption point; hence, the postulated change in preferences entails an excess demand for Y and excess supply of X at constant prices, requiring a rise in the price of Y and of labour and a fall in the price of X and of capital to restore equilibrium.

The initial and subsequent equilibrium positions of the economy are represented in Figure 3.2, where M_LM_L and M_cM_c represent the initial, and $M_L{}'M_L{}'$ and $M_c{}'M_c{}'$, the subsequent equilibrium budget constraints for labour and capital respectively. As a result of the postulated change in preferences more Y and less X is produced, as indicated by the movement from P_c to $P_c{}'$ and P_L to $P_L{}'$ on the factor owner production blocks, and capital's numéraire income, in terms of both goods falls from M_c to $M_c{}'$, and labour's numéraire income rises from M_L to $M_L{}'$. Capital's consumption point shifts from C_c on $U_c{}^1$ to $C_c{}'$ on $U_c{}^o$, and since $U_c{}^o$ and $U_c{}^1$ are comparable in that both relate to a common index of utility, the change in capital's real income in utility terms can be identified with the

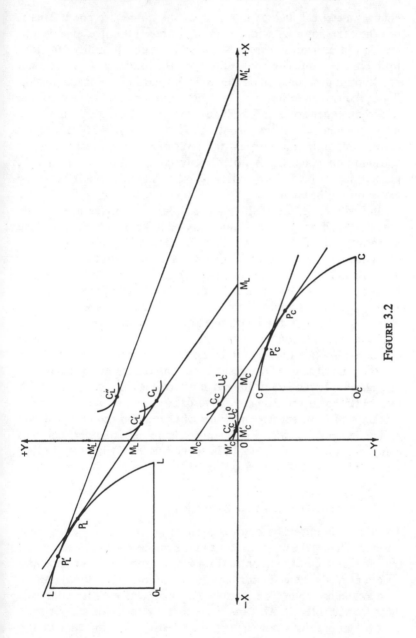

FIGURE 3.2

change in its real income in terms of the numéraire good. This is not the case, however, with the group (labour) that has experienced the shift in demand preferences, since the change in utility functions prohibits a comparison of utility in the initial and subsequent equilibrium positions, unless the different indifference maps prevailing in the two situations can be indexed in terms of some common underlying quantity of utility. Thus even though labour's numéraire income increases in terms of both goods from M_L to M_L' as a result of the shift in its preferences, the level of utility corresponding to consumption point C_L is not directly comparable to that at C_L'', hence, there is no way of telling whether labour is made better or worse off by the change.

Similarly, the effect of the change in labour's preferences on the potential welfare of the community will be indeterminate. The northwest shift of labour's utility function with reference to any given commodity price ratio induces a similar shift in the community's indifference map, indicating that more Y and less X will be produced and consumed in the new as compared with the economy's initial equilibrium. However, the levels of potential welfare indicated by the respective equilibrium consumption points are not directly comparable, since the community indifference contours on which they lie are indexed with respect to different sets of utility distributions. The result when the community is conceived in aggregate terms is and indeed must be logically consistent with that obtained in the disaggregative (distributional) analysis, for if it is impossible to specify the effect of change on the utility of one group, it similarly will not be possible to tell whether, through compensation, one group could be made better off without the other group being made worse off or not.

II. CHANGE IN FACTOR ENDOWMENT

Turning to the effects of factor accumulation, the main question that arises is whether the conclusion from the one-sector Hicksian model, that an increase in the quantity of a factor must lower its price and raise that of the other factor, continues to hold when the economy produces more than one commodity and can substitute among them (see Chapter 2). The answer is that it does. This answer rests on two propositions concerning the effects of an increase in the available quantity of a factor, if commodity prices and therefore factor prices are kept constant. The first is that, in this case, all of the additional income consequent on factor augmentation accrues to the owners of the increment of the factor, and by assumption they will wish to spend it on some of both goods, so that demand for both goods increases. The second is the so-called Rybczynski Theorem, according to which, if commodity prices and therefore

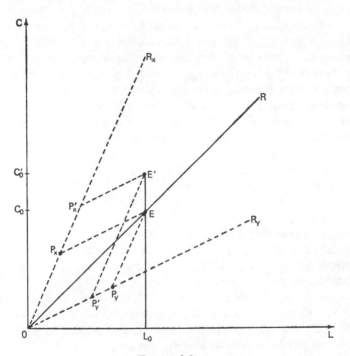

FIGURE 3.3

factor prices and optimal factor-utilization ratios in the two industries are kept constant, and the quantity of one factor is augmented, maintenance of full employment of both factors requires that the output of the industry that uses the augmented factor intensively must increase in value by more than total output, and the output of the other industry must fall absolutely. Hence, putting the demand and supply consequences of factor increase together, an increase in the quantity of one factor must produce an excess supply

107

of the commodity that uses that factor intensively, and an excess demand for the other, requiring a fall in the relative price of the commodity, and therefore in the relative price, and the marginal product in terms of both commodities, of the factor whose quantity has been increased.

The Rybczynski Theorem can be explained in literary terms as follows: in order for the increment of the augmented factor to earn the price given by the fixed factor-price ratio, it must be given the appropriate amount of the other factor to work with; and in order to release the required supply of the other factor, the industry using that factor intensively must contract and the industry using the augmented factor intensively expand, keeping employment of the augmented factor constant at the initial level but disemploying some of the unaugmented factor; the amount of the unaugmented factor thus released is then combined with the increment of the augmented factor in a further expansion of the industry that uses the augmented factor intensively.

The Theorem can be proved rigorously by use of either of the geometrical constructions employed previously to analyse the production side of the two-sector model. Figure 3.3 employs the Lerner-Pearce diagram; with the initial endowment of OL_0 of labour and OC_0 of capital represented by point E, production of X is measured by OP_x and Y by OP_y at the factor prices determining the optimal utilization ratio OR_x and OR_y. An increase of capital of $C_0'C_0'$ shifts the endowment point to E'; at constant prices production of X increases from P_x to P_x' while production of Y decreases from P_y to P_y'. Figure 3.4 employs the Edgeworth-Bowley box diagram; at Q, the initial equilibrium production point on the contract curve, the capital-labour ratio in X is the slope of O_xR_x and in Y the slope of O_yR_y. If capital increases by O_xO_x', and commodity and factor prices and therefore optimal factor-intensities are kept constant, the corresponding point on the new contract curve must lie at the intersection with O_yR_y of $O_x'R_x'$ (which is the vector O_xR_x drawn through the new origin box-corner O_x'), at the point Q'. This point necessarily involves a reduction in the production of Y and an increase in the production of X by more than the value of the total increase in national output.

The demand and supply components of the analysis of factor accumulation are combined in Figure 3.5. P,C is the initial aggregate

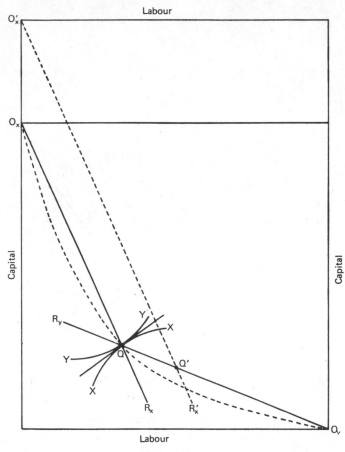

FIGURE 3.4

production-consumption equilibrium of the economy. Capital's budget constraint is $M_c M_c$ and its consumption point C_c; labour's budget constraint is $M_L M_L$ and its consumption point C_L. With an increase of capital and prices kept constant, the production point for the economy must shift southeast from P to P' along a straight-line locus RR by the Rybczynski Theorem, to which there corresponds a shift in capital's production block from CC to $C'C'$ such that the lines joining $PP'P_c P_c'$ form a parallelogram. Capital's budget line shifts from $M_c M_c$ to $M_c' M_c'$, equal to the increase in the value of output from MM to $M'M'$, capital's consumption point shifts from

109

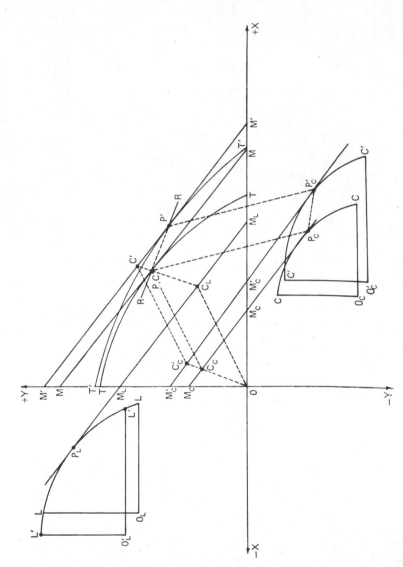

FIGURE 3.5

110

C_c to C_c', and the aggregate consumption point shifts from C to C'. (It is assumed that factor tastes are homothetic, but this is not necessary; any shift to the northeast is consistent with the assumed non-inferiority of goods and produces the same results.) The northeast shift of C to C' and the southeast shift of P to P' combine to entail an excess demand for Y and an excess supply of X at constant prices, requiring a rise in the price of Y and of labour and a fall in the price of X and of capital to restore equilibrium. Thus, as capital increases, its price must fall and that of labour rise, so that the absolute share of labour must rise. In Figure 3.5 this is represented by the northwest movement of labour's production point P_L on $L'L'$, labour's new production block, implying a rise in labour's numéraire income in terms of both goods such that labour's new budget constraint lies everywhere outside its old one. The effect of the change on relative shares (in terms of a numéraire), and whether a fall in capital's relative share will go far enough to entail a fall in its absolute share, obviously depends on a far more complex set of parameters than the aggregate elasticity of technical substitution that determines the movement of relative shares in the Hicksian one-sector model. Capital's budget constraint increases from M_cM_c to $M_c'M_c'$ as a result of the initial increase in capital at constant prices, but the movement of capital's production point northwest from P_c' along its production block $C'C'$ indicates that capital's numéraire income will be less than M_c', and should the northwest movement be sufficient, it is even possible that its new equilibrium budget constraint will cut or lie everywhere within the old one, in which case labour would not only gain the total benefits of the increase in the stock of capital but additional benefits as well. In any event, even if the accumulating factor should suffer a decrease in its absolute real income position, it is clear from Figure 3.5 that because the new transformation curve $T'T'$ lies everywhere outside the old curve TT, potential welfare in the community must increase as a result of factor accumulation; hence, it will be possible, through compensation, for gainers to compensate losers for their losses without becoming losers themselves.

III. TECHNICAL PROGRESS

Let us now turn to the question of technical progress, which for simplicity will be specified to take place only in one industry.

Technical progress can be defined in a variety of ways but it will prove convenient for our purposes to employ Hicks' definitions, by which technical progress is defined as 'neutral' if it raises the marginal products of the two factors in the same proportion so that at constant factor prices the optimal factor utilization ratio remains constant; 'labour-saving' if it raises capital's marginal product more than labour's so that the optimal factor utilization ratio rises at constant prices; and 'capital-saving' if it raises labour's marginal product more than capital's. For purposes of geometric representation of the various types of technical progress, it is useful to refer back to Figure 2.1 where technical progress can be illustrated by drawing a new isoquant with a higher product index through the original endowment point E. Neutral technical progress is the case where the new isoquant has the same slope at point E as the old one, 'labour-saving' technical progress the case where the new curve cuts the old one at point E from southeast to northwest, and 'capital-saving' where the new curve cuts the old one from northwest to southeast. It is apparent that in the one-sector model, where relative factor shares are given by the reciprocals of the product of the relevant capital-labour ratio and the relative price of capital, that relative shares are unchanged by 'neutral' progress, and that biased progress reduces the relative income share of the factor it saves.

The analytical consequences of technical progress in the two-sector model are more complex. First, with respect to the method of analysis, unlike the case of preference shifts or factor augmentation where holding commodity prices constant necessarily entails holding factor prices constant, in the case of technical progress there is a choice between holding commodity prices constant and letting factor prices adjust to the change, or holding factor prices constant and letting commodity prices adjust. The latter is the simpler assumption to make, since it entails the commodity price falling in proportion to the degree of technical progress (measured by the cost reduction at the initial factor prices), though the former is more consistent with the usual analytical approach in comparative statics of taking the effect of parametric change on excess demands and excess supplies at constant commodity prices, and predicting the direction of the price change required to restore equilibrium. In what follows both analytical methods are demonstrated.

Consider first the case of neutral technical progress in the X

industry assuming that factor prices remain constant. Its effect is to shift the X isoquant uniformly proportionately towards the origin, leaving the optimal factor-utilization ratio unchanged if factor prices remain unchanged. Hence the allocation of factors among the industries must remain unchanged, and output of Y remain constant while output of X rises proportionately to the technical progress, if factor prices are to remain unchanged. This is illustrated on Figure 3.6, where the X-isoquant shifts from XX to $X'X'$, the cost of production of X per unit falls from OM to OM_x, factor utilization ratios remain unchanged at OR_x and OR_y, and hence factor allocations to the two industries (with the given endowment E) remain unchanged at P_x and P_y respectively.

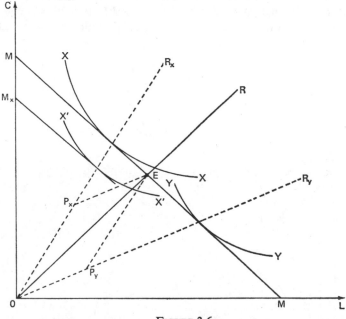

FIGURE 3.6

The situation of unchanged factor prices can be an equilibrium position after technical progress only if demand for Y is constant while demand for X expands proportionally to the increase in output. This requires a unitary elasticity of demand for X, elasticity being defined in the Hicksian sense to include both an income and a

113

substitution effect. If the elasticity of demand for X exceeds unity, there will be excess demand for X and supply of Y, the relative price of X and therefore of capital must rise, and therefore the relative and absolute share of capital must rise and that of labour fall, absolute shares being measured in terms of Y the numéraire good. Conversely, if the (Hicksian) elasticity of demand for X is less than unity, the relative price of X must fall, and with it the relative and absolute share of capital, while labour's share increases. It is necessary, however, to distinguish once again between numéraire income and welfare, because the initial reduction in the price of X relative to Y due to technical progress makes the owners of each factor better off, to the extent that they consume X. Consequently, even though a factor's absolute share falls in terms of Y, the economic welfare of its owners may still have increased (this is a case where the new budget line defined in terms of commodities cuts the old one).

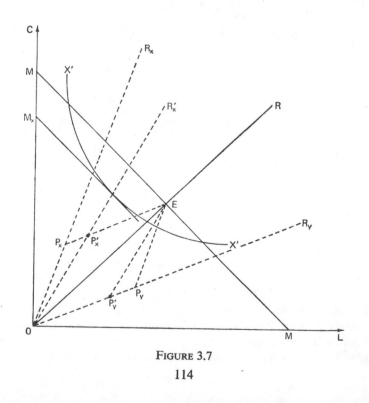

FIGURE 3.7

114

Figure 3.7 depicts the case of capital-saving technical progress, in the X (capital-intensive) industry, i.e. progress which at constant factor prices reduces the ratio of capital to labour employed while reducing the cost of production. Such a reduction, as the Figure shows, requires a redeployment of labour and capital from the Y industry into the X industry (the factor allocation points move from P_x to P_x' and from P_y to P_y'); Y production must fall, and X production increase by more than in proportion to the cost-saving brought about by the technical progress. Hence the critical value of the (Hicksian) elasticity of demand for X, which determines the movement of relative shares and of absolute shares in terms of the numéraire Y, must be something greater than unity.

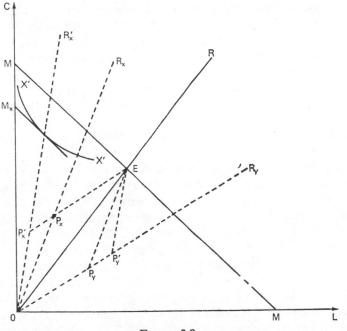

FIGURE 3.8

The opposite holds true for labour-saving innovation in the capital-intensive industry, which is depicted in Figure 3.8. Here the rise in the capital-labour ratio associated with innovation requires a redeployment out of the X industry into the Y industry (shown by the movement from P_x to $P_x{}'$ and from P_y to $P_y{}'$); the output of the Y industry must rise, while that of the X industry may fall or rise, depending on whether the resource exodus is or is not great enough to offset the improvement in productivity due to the innovation. In any case, the critical value of the Hicksian elasticity of demand for X which determines the movement of relative shares and of absolute shares in terms of the numéraire is something less than unity.

To summarize the results so far, the effect of technical progress in an industry will be to increase or decrease the relative share, and the absolute share in terms of the product of the other industry, of the factor used intensively in that industry, according as the Hicksian elasticity of demand for the product of the innovating industry is greater or less than a certain critical value. That critical value will be unity if the innovation is neutral, greater than unity if the innovation saves the factor used relatively intensively in the industry, and less than unity if the innovation saves the factor used relatively intensively in the other industry (i.e. unintensively in the innovating industry).

The results of the foregoing analysis of technical progress can be put in another, potentially illuminating, way. There is some tendency, at least in popular argument, to assume that technical progress is good or bad for labour, depending on whether it occurs in capital-intensive or labour-intensive industries, or on whether it is biased in the capital-saving or labour-saving direction. The analysis shows that there is no simple way of determining the distribution effects of innovation by its industrial location or factor-saving bias, and that reference must be made in addition to the characteristics of demands for products to answer this kind of question.

The analysis so far has taken the effect of technical progress at constant factor prices, permitting commodity prices to reflect the change in technique. Let us now employ the alternative analytical technique of assuming that the commodity price ratio rather than the factor price ratio is initially fixed, and investigate the effect of neutral technical progress in industry X. This case is illustrated in Figure 3.9 where to keep commodity prices constant, the factor price ratio must shift from MM, the slope of the common tangent to the pre-innovation isoquants, to $M'M'$ the tangent to the new X and Y isoquants. This in turn implies changes in the optimal factor utilization ratios in both industries, from OR_x and OR_y to $OR_x{}'$

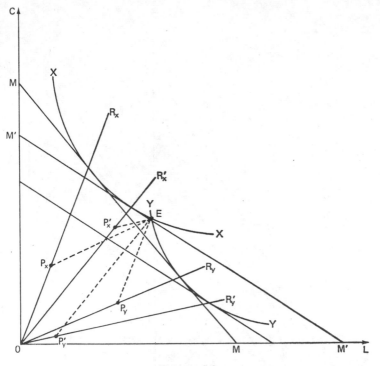

FIGURE 3.9

and OR_y' respectively, such change necessitating a re-allocation of resources from the Y industry to the X industry indicated by the movements from P_y to P_y' and P_x to P_x'. The increase in the output of X and the decrease in the output of Y is the analogue to the Rybczynski Theorem for neutral technical progress: at constant commodity prices, neutral technical progress in an industry increases the output of that industry, and reduces that of the other industry. But the analogue is not exact since in the Rybczynski case the increase in income due to factor accumulation accrues solely to the owners of the stock of the accumulating factor at constant commodity prices, while because of the change in factor prices required to keep commodity prices constant in the case of neutral technical progress, the owners of the factor used relatively intensively in the static industry lose numéraire income because of technical progress

117

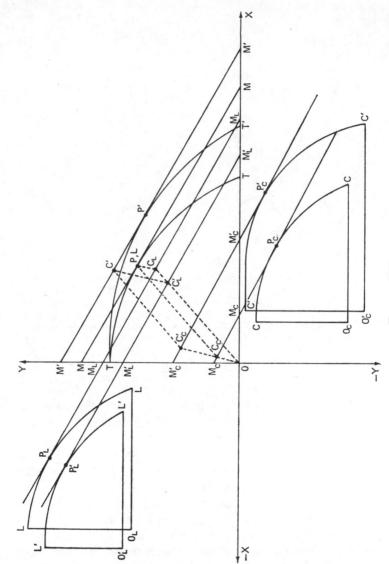

FIGURE 3.10

118

in the other industry, and more than the whole of the benefit of progress accrues to the factor used intensively in the industry in which the technical progress occurs.

The above represents the impact effect of neutral technical progress taken at constant commodity prices. Account must next be taken of the adjustment to the excess demands and supplies created at constant prices by the impact of technical progress. The full general equilibrium repercussions of neutral technical progress in X are represented in Figure 3.10. P,C is the initial production point and consumption point for the economy on TT the pre-innovation transformation curve, implying the budget line for capital M_cM_c tangent to capital's production block at P_c and labour's budget line M_LM_L tangent to labour's production block at P_L. The initial consumption points for capital and labour respectively are C_c and C_L, which by the principles of vector addition sum to C. Neutral technical progress in X must have the following effects on the *community's* transformation curve: (*a*) it can have no effect on the maximum possible output of Y when the economy is specialized in Y, since when none of the good in which technical progress occurs is produced the change is irrelevant; (*b*) it will raise the maximum possible output of X when the economy is specialized in X; (*c*) at non-specialized production points and constant commodity prices, it will raise the output of X and lower that of Y. Accordingly, at constant commodity prices, the economy's transformation curve will shift from TT to TT', and national income increases by MM'.

The distribution effects of neutral technical progress taken at constant commodity prices can be determined by reference to the factor-owner production blocks in Figure 3.10. Technical progress in industry X alone lowers the relative price of X at both endpoints of the post-progress transformation curve TT'. This plus the logical requirement that at all feasible commodity price ratios, the outputs on the economy's transformation curve equal the sum of the outputs of each factor-owner at that price ratio implies a shift in labour's and capital's block from LL and CC to $L'L'$ and $C'C'$ respectively. With CC' and LL', capital's income rises from M_c to M_c' in terms of both goods and its consumption point shifts from C_c to C_c', while labour's income falls to M_L' and its consumption point shifts to C_L'. By vector addition the new consumption points for capital and labour's sum to C', which in conjunction with the movement of the economy's production point to P' implies an excess demand for good Y and an excess supply of good X. Equilibrium in this situation requires a rise in the price of good Y, and of labour, and a fall in the price of good X, and of capital. This can be represented by a north-west movement on all three post-progress transformation curves, indicating in the new equilibrium position an increase in labour's absolute share in terms of the numéraire good Y above M_L' possibly equalling or exceeding M_L, in which case labour's post-progress budget constraint would lie everywhere outside its pre-progress constraint ensuring that labour was made better off by the change; and a decrease in capital's absolute share in terms of Y below M_c' and possibly below M_c as well. Accordingly, while the impact effect of neutral technical progress in the capital-intensive sector is to lower labour's absolute share of national income and to raise capital's absolute share by more than the increase in the value of national product at constant commodity prices, labour in fact may gain and capital lose, both in terms of the numéraire good and utility, as a result of the necessary adjustment of commodity prices and output patterns to restore competitive equilibrium in the economy.

Let us now consider the situation in the two-sector model where the nature of technical progress is biased in that at given factor prices the ratio of the marginal productivities of the two factors is altered, so that either the optimal capital-labour falls (capital-saving) or it rises (labour-saving). Biased technical progress has two initial impact effects: it decreases the cost of the commodity in which it occurs, and it frees some of the 'saved' factor for additional productive activity. Analytically, then, biased technical progress can be conceptualized as containing (*i*) a cost-saving component, and (*ii*) a factor-saving component. The analysis of the cost-saving component is identical with that of neutral technical progress, while that of the factor-saving component is identical with that of the Rybczynski Theorem.

As in the analysis of neutral technical progress, to keep commodity prices constant with biased technical progress in industry X, the relative price of capital must rise and thus the optimal factor utilization in both industries fall, indicating an increased output of X and a decreased output of Y. Given the new relationship between commodity and factor prices, the Rybczynski Theorem implies that the factor-saving effect of biased progress will be to increase the output of the commodity that uses the saved factor intensively in its production and decrease the output of the other commodity. Thus if the biased progress is capital-saving, the output of X rises and Y falls, and the changes in outputs related to both the cost-saving and factor-saving components of biased progress are in the same direction. This will always be the case when the factor saved is used intensively in the production of the commodity in which technical progress occurs. Labour-saving technical progress, on the other hand, increases the output of Y and decreases that of X, so that the combined effect on output of the cost-saving and factor-saving components is *a priori* indeterminate. If the bias of technical progress is sufficiently labour-saving unlike the case of neutral and capital-saving technical progress, the production effect of technical progress at constant commodity prices can be to increase the output of Y and decrease the output of X, which in conjunction with the assumption that both goods are normal in consumption so that increased income entails increased consumption of both good, implies an excess demand for X and an excess supply of Y, which must be corrected by a rise in the price of X and of capital and a fall in the price of Y and of labour. This case is undoubtedly prejudicial to labour and beneficial to capital, but the reader is warned that proof that such a case could exist is not equivalent to a demonstration that the case is relevant in the real world.

The present chapter has applied the two-sector model of general equilibrium to the problem of exogenous change of demand preferences, factor endowment and technology in an effort to predict the results of such change on certain key economic variables. One focus of interest has been how change can be expected to affect the distribution of income in the economy, the analysis highlighting the fact that there are no simple ways of determining the distributional effects of technical advance, factor accumulation and preference changes, in addition to demonstrating the factors relevant for such a determination. Attention continues to focus on the distributional effects of change in the next chapter, but such change is assumed to stem from deliberate acts of policy rather than from exogenous sources.

CHAPTER 4

Policy-Induced Change in a Closed Economy

The analysis of Chapter 3 was concerned with the question of exogenous change in the two-sector model of general equilibrium. We would now like to discuss the distributional effects of policy-induced change. The analysis of policy-induced changes in a closed economy raises the question of the nature of government that should be postulated in developing an economic theory relevant to the analysis of economic policy. This question already has been touched on in Chapter 1 where we sketched briefly the modern welfare economics concept of government as a neutral agency whose function on the one hand is to correct for cases of positive and negative externalities from economic activity—i.e. cases where private and social costs and benefit diverge—by either the levying of appropriate marginal taxes or subsidies on such activities or explicit regulation; and on the other hand to achieve an equitable distribution of income by making appropriate lump-sum transfers among consuming units. The first function can be called the 'resource-directing' function of government; the second the government's 'resource-transfer' function. The latter, it should be noted, relates not only to the correction of the distributional consequences of government policy, but to that of the distributional outcomes of private markets as well.

To this list of possible functions for government can be added the government's 'resource-using' function; where government is assumed to serve the private interests of the community by performing tasks that the community cannot perform, or could not perform as effiiciently, through private markets. Various reasons have been discerned for the existence of such tasks. These include the relatively crude case of 'natural monopoly' where efficient production requires a scale large enough to constitute a monopoly but monopolistic profit-maximization would lead to production and consumption below the socially optimal level, requiring government management or at least government regulation (and subsidization, where average production costs are falling); and a more sophisticated case in which government can improve social welfare by restricting the variety of differentiated goods available to consumers in order to reduce average production costs. These cases merge into the welfare economics category of externalities, but can be distinguished by the condition that performance of these tasks, regulation excluded, requires government to absorb resources from the private community. Much more recently, economic theorists have come to identify the role of government primarily with the provision of goods or services whose technical nature in consumption is such that allocation of resources to them cannot be efficiently performed through the private market. Such commodities or services are known in the literature as 'public goods', as distinguished from 'private goods', and are discussed in detail in Chapter 5.

The above-mentioned 'resource-directing', 'resource-transfer', and 'resource-using' functions of government all are related to the assumption that government serves some useful social purpose in the community; but this is not the only relevant concept of government that can be employed. An alternative, more closely allied with the Continental European tradition (particularly the Italians) than the Anglo-Saxon one, is that of an 'independent' government, assumed to have a utility function of its own which it seeks to maximize subject to unspecified constraints on its power to raise revenue by taxation, and to affect the economic welfare of the private members of the community only through the effects of its taxes on their budget constraints (i.e. the private community obtains no utility from government expenditure). The subsequent analysis of both the 'resource-using' and 'resource-transfer' functions of a welfare-oriented government also can be applied to the case of an 'independent' government, so long as it is kept in mind that the government's use or transfer of resources between private consuming units is assumed to benefit the community-at-large in the one case and not in the other; but the government's 'resource-directing' function is relevant only when the government is welfare-oriented.

Two types of budgetary policy will be discussed in this chapter: changes in budgetary scale with the pattern of government expenditure and taxation held constant; and budgetary substitution, either of one type of expenditure for another with taxes and scale held constant, or of one tax form for another with the expenditure pattern and scale held constant. Changes in budgetary scale can be related to the government's 'resource-using' function, while budgetary substitutions, either on the tax or expenditure side of budget, can be related to its 'resource-transfer' function. (Changes in budgetary scale that do not imply an increased consumption of resources by government—the combination of a tax on one factor and a subsidy to another—imply resource-transfer not resource-use.) From the perspective of the individuals or economic groups that comprise the community, the analytical question of central importance with respect to both functions is the effect that policies related to these functions are likely to have on the distribution of income among them. Changes in budgetary scale and tax substitution with scale constant both involve a transfer of resources between economic groups—the former from the tax-paying public to the government, the latter from one group of private factor-owners to another. The distributional effect of such income transfers is a standard problem in international trade theory, with the standard answer that production and the factor-price ratio will shift towards that commodity, and the factor it uses intensively, for which the transfer-receiving group has a marginal preference by comparison with the transfer-paying group. The method used to analyse both cases divides the total effect of the policy into two separate and distinct components; the impact or primary effect of the resource transfer at constant prices, and the secondary factor-price or general equilibrium adjustment of the excess demand or supply created by the impact effect. An expenditure substitution on the other hand involves the more simple economic problem of taking the general equilibrium effect of a change in government tastes at constant prices, private tastes being held constant. In this case, production and the factor-price ratio will shift towards that commodity, and the factor it uses intensively, for which the government's marginal preference increases relative to its initial preference pattern.

124

I. THE 'RESOURCE-USING' FUNCTION OF GOVERNMENT: CHANGES IN BUDGETARY SCALE

The analysis of changes in budgetary scale assumes that the patterns of both government expenditure and taxes are constant. To validate the former assumption, government's tastes must be assumed homothetic, making the income-expansion path of government a straight line. Given the government's preference function, the change in budgetary scale can be assumed to proceed from any given tax structure. Taxes can be imposed at any one of four possible points in the circular flow of income: on the household either as a supplier of the factors of production (an income tax) or as a demander of commodities (an expenditure tax); on the firm either as a demander of the factors of production (a production tax) or as a supplier of commodities (a commodity tax). All possible forms of taxation can be expressed in terms of the four varieties of factor taxes possible in the two-sector model of general equilibrium—a tax on one factor in one or both sectors and a tax on both factors in one or both sectors—and classified as general or specific according to their *impact* effect on relative factor and commodity prices. Both a tax on one factor in both sectors at an equal *ad valorem* rate (equivalent to an income tax on that factor) and a tax on both factors in both sectors at an equal *ad valorem* rate (equivalent to an income tax on both factors, a proportional commodity tax, production tax and expenditure tax) absorb resources from the private community without altering relative commodity and factor prices at impact and thus are classified as general taxes; an equally rated tax on both factors in one sector only is equivalent to a specific commodity tax on that sector that alters relative commodity prices to consumers but not producers; while a tax on one factor in one sector only is a specific factor tax that alters both relative commodity prices and the price paid for the taxed factor in the industry in which it is taxed, but not the price received by that factor in the taxed industry.

The analysis begins by assuming a general tax is used to finance the real resource transfer from the private community to government. Regardless of which form of general tax is used, the question relevant to whether there will be a secondary or general equilibrium effect is that of a difference between government and income-distribution-weighted private tastes. Consider the situation where an income tax on capital is used to finance government spending. There will be no secondary effect if the tastes of capitalists are identical with that of the government, in which case capital bears the full burden of the resource transfer. Should government have a marginal preference for the labour-intensive good as compared with capital-owners, however, the impact effect creates an excess demand for that good at constant prices, whose adjustment requires an increase in the price and output of the labour-intensive good, an increase in the price and marginal product of labour and a decrease in the price and marginal product of capital. Capital bears more than the full burden of the resource transfer in this case, and labour gains in an absolute sense. Had government had a marginal preference for the capital-intensive good, on the other hand, capital and labour would share the burden of the resource transfer, though not necessarily equally.

An identical analysis applies if it is assumed that either an income tax on labour or a general consumption tax is used to finance government spending. In the former case, labour bears the full burden of the resources transfer if the owners of labour and government have identical tastes; and each factor bears the burden of the resource transfer in proportion to its contribution to national product in the latter if the government's marginal propensity to consume either good is equal to the average of the marginal propensities of both factors to consume that good weighted by their incomes (weighting is necessary even if homothetic tastes are assumed). Should public and private tastes differ, however, there would be secondary effects to consider in both cases, which could either mitigate or augment the impact effect of the resource transfer on private factor-owners.

The analysis of a change in budgetary scale is illustrated in Figure 4.1. The government's indifference curve U_G can be interpreted in either one of two ways depending on the assumption made concerning the nature of government. The simpler, and perhaps less relevant, assumption is that government is independent of and apart from the general public, so that the latter does not benefit from the former's activities. The indifference curve here corresponds to a given level of satisfaction enjoyed by the independent government. On the alternative assumption that government does serve some social purpose, the indifference curve can be taken to represent the utility derived by the private community from the goods provided it by government's use of real resources, in which case there is an implicit assumption that the utility derived from government goods and from the private consumption bundle are additive—that is, that there are no 'feedback' effects from the scale of government services

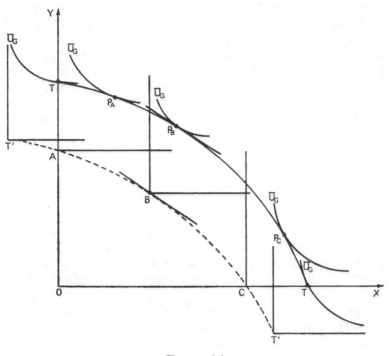

FIGURE 4.1

to private choices ('feedback' effects are discussed below). Such goods include both public goods, and private goods which for one reason or another can be provided more cheaply and/or efficiently by government than by private enterprise. Regardless of which assumption is employed, and thus the interpretation given to the government's indifference curve, it will prove convenient to the analysis of both budgetary scale and substitution effects to derive the function relating the consumption possibilities available to the

127

private community consistent with a fixed amount of government utility and the economy's fixed factor endowment and technology.

Consider the government's utility block $\bar{U}_G$ and place the vertical axes of the block coincident with that of the economy's transformation curve TT so that $\bar{U}_G$ is tangent to TT at point P_A. Now run $\bar{U}_G$ up and down TT from the point corresponding to complete specialization on Y to that corresponding to complete specialization on X, making certain that the axes of the government's block are kept parallel to those of the economy's transformation curve. The resultant constant government utility 'net' transformation curve $T'T'$ represents the set of efficient outputs available for private consumption from the economy's 'gross' set of efficient outputs consistent with the given level of government utility, whose slope at any given point such as B is equal to that of the corresponding point P_B on the economy's 'gross' transformation curve. Since negative consumption of a good is not possible, the segments $T'A$ and CT' of the 'net' curve, and the corresponding segment TP_A and P_CT of the 'gross' curve, clearly are not relevant (in a hypothetical sense, the concept of negative production can be used to geometrically represent borrowing of factors of production; see Chapter 2).

The analysis of an increase in budgetary scale can be simplified by assuming zero government in initial equilibrium and then introducing a tax-financed budget consistent with the government utility level U_G. This case is illustrated in Figure 4.2 where point P_B is assumed to be the initial equilibrium of the economy, with C_L and C_C the corresponding consumption points of labour and capital on the homothetic consumption vectors OC_L and OC_C. The relation between private and public tastes can be determined by comparing the slope of the income-distribution-weighted private consumption vector OP_B with that of government's consumption vector BP_B. When these slopes are equal, private and public tastes are identical; when BP_B is flatter than OP_B with respect to the horizontal, the government has a marginal preference for good X by comparison with the private community; and the opposite holds when BP_B is steeper than OP_B.

If the increase in budgetary scale is financed by a tax on the consumption of all goods at equal *ad valorem* rates, the impact of the tax on the consumption vectors of both factors will be to cut off a proportional distance from each, leaving $(1 - t_g)OC_C$ and

$(1 - t_g)OC_L$ as the consumption vectors of capital and labour respectively. If public and private tastes are identical, the new consumption points of capital and labour sum to B, and there are no secondary effects to consider. At the price ratio given by the slope of the 'gross' transformation curve at P_B (equal to that at B on the

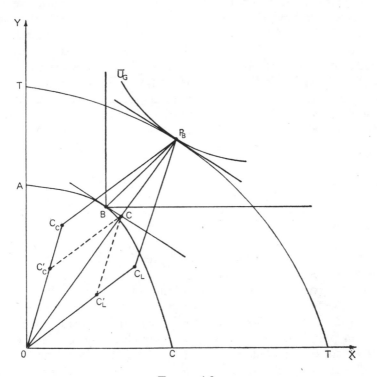

FIGURE 4.2

'net' curve) private plus public consumption equals the economy's production of the two goods, so that the initial equilibrium point remains the same. Geometrically, this case is indicated by point B lying on the vector OP_B, since the sum of the new factor-owner consumption points must lie on OP_B with a proportional commodity tax (secondary effects are excluded with an income tax on labour if point B falls on $C_C P_B$; with an income tax on capital if B falls on $C_L P_B$). If public and income-distribution-weighted private tastes differ, however, point B can lie either northwest of the vector OP_B (government marginal preference for X), in which case the impact effect of the resource transfer to government creates an excess demand for X and an excess supply of Y at the price ratio given by the slope of AC at point B; or southeast of OP_B (government marginal preference for Y), in which case the impact effect creates an excess demand for Y and an excess supply of X at that price ratio. The former (illustrated in Figure 4.2) implies an increase in the price of X and that of capital, and a decrease in the price of Y and that of labour, while the opposite occurs in the latter case.

The above assumes that a general tax of some form has been used to finance the increase in budgetary scale. It is interesting to extend this analysis to the case where such finance is provided by a specific commodity tax. As in the case of a general tax, the question of whether the impact of an increase in budgetary scale financed by a specific commodity tax creates a secondary effect depends upon the relationship between income-distribution-weighted private tastes and public tastes. Their equality, however, is no longer sufficient to preclude such effect, because the specific tax raises the price of the taxed good to the tax-paying community but not the government. A necessary condition for impact neutrality therefore is that government have a marginal preference for the taxed good as compared with private tax-payers.

The impact effect of an increase in budgetary scale financed by an excise tax on good X is illustrated in Figure 4.3 where the slope of MM represents initial commodity prices and P_B the initial equilibrium point, with C_L and C_C the respective consumption points of labour and capital corresponding to P_B. The imposition of an excise tax on good X with *factor prices and the distribution* of *income constant* shifts labour's line from $M_L M_L$ to $M_L M_L (1 - t_x)$ and capital's budget line from $M_C M_C$ to $M_C M_C (1 - t_x)$. Labour's consumption point becomes C'_L and capital's C'_C, summing by the principles of vector addition to point C, the aggregate private cum-tax consumption point at initial factor prices. For the secondary or general equilibrium effect to be zero in this case, CP_B must represent the government's consumption vector. It is clear from the geometry that because the slope of CP_B is flatter with respect to the horizontal than OP_B, the marginal preference of government for the taxed good must be greater than that of the private community to preclude

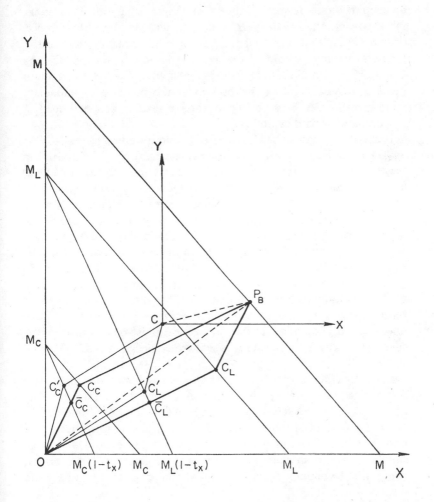

FIGURE 4.3

131

general equilibrium adjustment. When there are no secondary effects with an increase in budgetary scale financed by a specific commodity tax, each factor bears the burden of the resource transfer in proportion to its consumption of the taxed good. Taking the initial consumption vectors OC_L and OC_C as a standard of reference, should CP_B in fact represent the government's consumption vector, labour's income would drop by $C_L\bar{C}_L/OC_L$ and capital's by $C_C\bar{C}_C/OC_C$, with $C_L\bar{C}_L/OC_L$ being greater than $C_C\bar{C}_C/OC_C$. Labour bears a greater share of the burden of the increase in budgetary scale in this case, because it consumes a greater proportion of X by comparison with capital.

It should be noted that for a zero secondary effect to be possible with a partial commodity tax, the private elasticity of demand, in the Hicksian sense (including both an income and substitution effect) and appropriately weighted, must be less than unity (i.e. total expenditure on the taxed good must increase), since the private sector must wind up consuming less of both goods to be consistent with government consuming more of both. In terms of Figure 4.3, an inelastic demand for the taxed good insures that point C will be southwest of P_B, and thus that OG will have a positive slope. In terms of the formula $(cp-e)tq$ for the change in the quantity demanded of the taxed good, cp must be equal to e for the secondary effect to be zero.[1] Since cp, the government's marginal propensity to spend on the taxed good measured at factor cost, must be less than unity, so must e, the appropriately weighted Hicksian private demand elasticity.

Consider the case where government and private tastes are assumed equal ($cp < e$), illustrated in Figure 4.3 by the equality of the slopes of the vectors OG (government's marginal preference) and OP_B (the tax-paying community's marginal preference). The impact effect of the increase in budgetary scale creates an excess supply of X and an excess demand for Y at given producer prices; hence the secondary effect implies an increase in the price and

---

[1] In the formula, c is the physical quantity of the taxed good purchased by the government when its tax income increases by one unit; cp is the money value of this quantity, or the proportion of an increment of tax proceeds which is spent on the taxed good, value and expenditure being measured at factor cost; e is the Hicksian elasticity of demand; t the tax rate as a proportion of factor cost; and q the quantity initially purchased.

marginal product of labour and a decrease in the price and marginal product of capital. This case can be illustrated in Figure 4.4 by use of the factor-owner production block technique with the untaxed commodity Y serving as numéraire.

The initial equilibrium commodity price ratio is given by the slope of $M_L M_L$, which determines the production point Q_L on labour's production block, indicating the numéraire income M_L in terms of Y, and Q_c on capital's production block, indicating capital's numéraire income M_c. The cum-tax equilibrium producer price ratio is given by the slope of $M'_L M'_L$ to which both factor-owners adjust their profit maximizing production points, from Q_L to Q'_L for labour and Q_c to Q'_c for capital, with both producing more Y and less X. Labour's income increases from M_L to M'_L while capital's income falls from M_c to M'_c in terms of the numéraire good Y, indicating that labour is absolutely better off and capital absolutely worse off in terms of numéraire income as a result of the change in outputs.

Should $M'_L M'_L$ represent labour's new budget line and $M_c' M'_c$ capital's new budget line, labour would be unambiguously better off and capital unambiguously worse off in utility terms as well as in terms of numéraire income, since $M'_L M_L$ lies everywhere outside of $M_L M_L$ and $M'_c M'_c$ everywhere inside $M_c M_c$. But because the tax creates a divergence between relative commodity and relative producer prices, the cum-tax equilibrium budget lines for labour and capital emanate from points M'_L and M'_c respectively, but are steeper with respect to the horizontal than $M'_L M'_L$ and $M'_c M'_c$—the slope of the new budget lines being equal to the relative consumer price ratio, including the tax. The effect of the tax in increasing the price of X to consumers serves to decrease the real income position of both factor owners; hence, capital suffers an unambiguous decrease in its real income position. Labour, on the other hand, unambiguously gains if its cum-tax or net budget constraint lies everywhere outside its old one, as is the case with $M'_L M'_L (1 - t_x)$, but may gain or lose should its net budget constraint cut the initial one, in which case the effect of the tax on labour's real income would depend on the ratio in which it consumed the two goods. Clearly, the greater labour's average propensity to consume the taxed good X in initial equilibrium the more likely that labour will be made absolutely worse off by the tax. In the case of non-specialized factor ownership, the factor-owner possessing a relatively greater

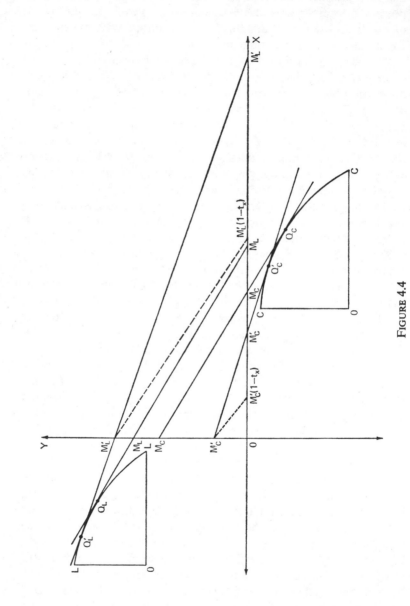

FIGURE 4.4

share of the factor whose price had risen, and consuming a greater relative amount of the untaxed commodity, gains relative to the other factor, even though in absolute terms both factor-owners can be made worse off by the budgetary change.

With one significant modification, Figure 4.3 can be used to analyse the case where the increase in budgetary scale is financed by a specific factor tax—that is a tax on one factor only in one industry. A specific factor tax raises the price of the taxed factor to producers in the industry in which the tax is imposed, and thus the price of the commodity of that industry to consumers, with net factor prices and the distribution of income held constant. The latter effect is identical to that of a specific commodity tax; hence the former constitutes the sole difference between a specific commodity and specific factor tax of equal *ad valorem* rate. The analysis of this effect is illustrated in Figure 4.5, a version of the Lerner-Pearce diagram where XX and YY going through the factor endowment point E represent the maximum output of X and Y that the economy is capable of producing with its given factor endowment and technology. If the slope of ML represents the initial factor price ratio, the optimal factor utilization ratios OR_x and OR_y are determined as are the factor allocation points P_x and P_y. Assume the specific factor tax to be on capital in industry X only. At initial net factor prices, the factor-utilization ratio falls in X to OR'_x but remains constant at OR_y in Y; hence the factor allocation points shift from P_x to P'_x and P_y to P'_y, indicating an increase in the output of X and a decrease in the output of Y. When this supply-side effect is added to the demand-side effect of the specific factor tax illustrated in Figure 4.3, it is clear that preclusion of a general equilibrium adjustment requires that the government have a greater marginal preference for the taxed good X than that indicated by the government's consumption vector OG, since the supply-side effect augments the demand-side effect in this case. The two effects would tend to offset each other, however, had the specific factor tax been imposed on labour in industry X. In either case, it is clear that when the postulated increase in budgetary scale in financed by a specific factor tax, the question of whether the impact of this budgetary change requires a general equilibrium adjustment or not depends on more than just the relationship between the income-distribution-weighted private consumption vector and the government's consumption

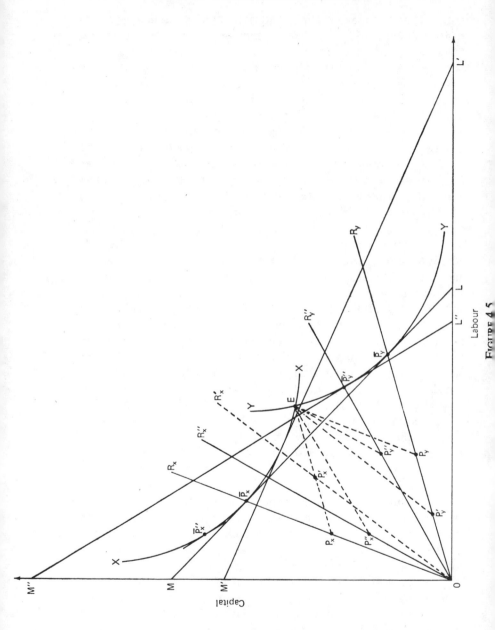

Labour

Capital

FIGURE 4.5

136

vector—the production effect of a specific factor tax is relevant as well.

On the assumption that private and government tastes are identical, the adjustment of the excess supply of X and demand for Y created by the impact effect of an increase in budgetary scale financed by a specific factor tax on capital in X implies a fall in the price and marginal product of capital in both sectors and a rise in the price and marginal product of labour. In the Figure, cum-tax equilibrium is assumed to occur at the relative factor price ratio given by the slope of $M''L''$. Producers in Y raise their capital-labour ratio to OR_y'' implying a rise in the absolute (and relative) marginal product of labour; while the general equilibrium requirement that the values of the marginal products of the non-taxed factor (labour) be the same in both industries, and thus that the slope at $\bar{P}_y''$ equals that of a point northwest of $\bar{P}_x$ given by $\bar{P}_x''$ in the Figure, implies that the marginal product of labour rises and the net of tax marginal product of capital falls in X (because of the tax there is a difference between the 'net' and 'gross' marginal products of capital in X and thus, in equilibrium, between the 'gross' values of the marginal products of capital in the two industries). The effect of a partial factor tax on capital in X on numéraire income when X is assumed to be capital-intensive is unambiguous; capital loses and labour gains, both in absolute and relative terms. But even though labour gains in terms of numéraire income, it may lose in utility terms since the increase in the price of X to consumers introduces the possibility that labour's new budget constraint may cut the old one, in which case the effect of the partial factor tax on labour's real income depends on the ratio in which labour consumes the two goods.

II. THE 'RESOURCE-TRANSFER' FUNCTION OF GOVERNMENT

1. *Budgetary Policies*

A function of modern government that does not require any changes in the government's consumption of real resources is the enforcement of a given distribution of income between private factor-owners in the community which can be expected to differ from the distribution that would result from the outcomes of private decisions in a system of markets without intervention of any kind. This can be called the government's 'resource-transfer' function in contrast to its 'resource-using' function implied by the analysis of changes in budgetary scale. Outside of the outright fixing of prices in the market-place (analysed below) government can promote what it considers to be an equitable distribution of income in the private community either through changes in its expenditure or tax patterns, or by a direct tax-subsidy policy. Substitution of one type of expenditure for another affects the private community in two ways: first, the change in the mix of public goods available to it has a direct distributional effect, since different persons in the community will benefit differentially from different classes of public expenditure; second, the change in the government's expenditure pattern will alter the budget constraints of private factor-owners through its effect on factor prices. The present analysis abstracts from the former type of distributional effect; the latter effect of government policy on the private budget constraint is the only relevant one when such policy is assumed either to consist in tax substitution or a direct tax-subsidy policy.

The assumption that the government's preference function is homothetic permits the separation of changes in budgetary scale with expenditure patterns constant from changes in the government's expenditure pattern with its budgetary scale held constant (otherwise changes in budgetary scale would imply expenditure pattern changes as well). Let us now consider the 'substitution effect' on the expenditure side of the government's budget which, because of the assumption of homothetic tastes, implies a shift in the entire indifference map of government. It is most convenient to analyse the effect of such a shift at constant commodity prices in order to isolate the private consumption vectors from the change. In doing so, however, we must take into account the effect that the change in the government's tastes has on the 'net' private transformation curve, for as the government demands more of one commodity and less of another at constant prices, there will be less of the former and more of the latter good available for private consumption at these prices. Hence, a shift in the government's utility map will cause a corresponding shift in the 'net' transformation curve.

This can be illustrated in Figure 4.3 where it is assumed that the government's expenditure pattern changes such that, at given commodity prices, it demands more of good Y and less of good X.

The change is indicated by the northwest movement of the government's consumption point along MM from P_B to P'_B, and thus the southeast movement of the private consumption point corresponding to P_B from B to B' along $M'M'$, such that the figure $BP'_B P_B B'$

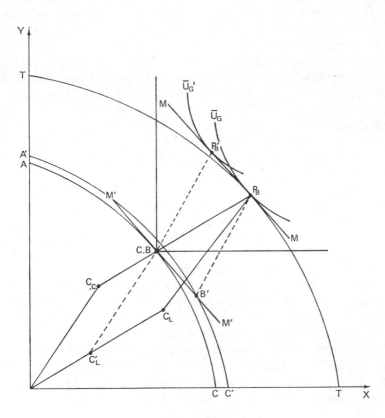

FIGURE 4.6

forms a parallelogram (alternatively, the point B' can be determined by moving the government's utility block southeast along MM until the point P'_B coincides with P_B). Point B' is but one point on the new 'net' transformation curve corresponding to the price ratio given by the slope of $MM(M'M')$; the rest of the curve can be similarly

139

determined by repeating this procedure for all price ratios ranging from complete specialization on one good to complete specialization on the other. The resultant curve, given by $A'C'$ in Figure 4.6, lies entirely outside the initial curve AC, such that its slope is less by comparison with that of AC on all rays passing through the origin.

If P_B is assumed to be the initial equilibrium point with $\bar{U}_G$ financed by income tax on labour, the initial consumption points of capital and labour are C_C and C'_L respectively. The postulated change in the government's consumption vector from BP_B to BP'_B at the price ratio given by the slope of MM creates an excess demand for good Y and excess supply of X at these prices; hence labour gains and capital loses both in absolute and relative terms. By tracing the effect of expenditure changes on private budget constraints, the analysis provides a rationale for factor-owners to lobby their government to switch its expenditure to commodities that use their factor intensively in its production.

Both the above analyses of budgetary expenditure substitution and the previous one of changes in budgetary scale assume that the utility functions of both private factor-owners are independent of changes in both the pattern of government expenditure and the budgetary scale. While undoubtedly this would be the case with a government that was independent of the private community, 'feedback' effects on private tastes from government spending can be expected when government is assumed to serve some social purpose. For example, when government provides more local security either because of increases in budgetary scale or a change in expenditure pattern, at given prices and incomes, private individuals are apt to demand less protective weapons, bodyguards, etc. Such effects can significantly alter the conclusions reached above, though explicit specification of 'feedback' effects can be built into the model.

A second method by which government can alter the distribution of income within the economy is by changing the taxes used to finance a given amount of government utility. As in the case of a change in budgetary scale, however, the direct income-distribution effect implicit in the tax substitution with budgetary scale constant can either be augmented or mitigated by a factor-price change effect, depending on whether the transfer-recipients have a marginal preference for the labour-intensive or the capital-intensive good.

The modification of the initial transfer by an adverse factor-price effect cannot, however, fully wipe out the benefit from the transfer, so long as the initial equilibrium is stable.

The case of tax-substitution with budgetary scale constant is illustrated in Figure 4.7 where the level of government utility U_G is initially financed by an income tax on labour, and the tastes of

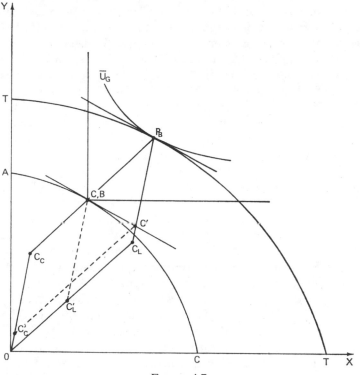

FIGURE 4.7

the government and labour identical, so that there are no secondary effects to consider. Labour's tax rate is $C_L C'_L / O C_L$ consistent with the consumption point C'_L for labour and C_C for capital, which sum to the aggregate private consumption point C coincident with the production point B on AC corresponding to point P_B on TT. Suppose that an income tax on capital is substituted for the income tax on labour so that the level of government utility remains constant at U_G. This requires an income tax imposed on capital at the rate $C_C C'_C / O C_C$. The effect of this tax substitution can be divided into an impact effect at constant prices, and a general equilibrium adjustment. The former involves an income transfer from capital to labour as labour's consumption point shifts from C'_L to C_L and capital's from C'_C to C_C; the latter, an increase in the price and marginal product of capital and a fall in the price and marginal product of labour, since the primary effect of the tax substitution creates an excess demand for X and supply of Y at constant prices due to labour's higher marginal preference for good X by comparison with capital's. Labour gains and capital loses, but the changes are less than would have been the case had there been no secondary effect or had the secondary effect worked in the other direction.

Finally, government can alter the distribution of income in the community by changing the scale of its budget without increasing its consumption of real resources by imposing a general tax whose proceeds are redistributed to the favoured factor-owners. Assume government desires to redistribute income from capitalists to labourers by this method. So long as the tax-subsidy policy applies equally to all units of each factor, it does not matter whether the tax takes the form of a proportional sales tax, with proceeds being distributed to labour, or a tax on the earnings of capital, with the proceeds being distributed to labour either directly or as a subsidy on the use of labour (the general principle is that the favoured factor should receive a greater proportion of the tax proceeds than he pays, and vice versa). In either case, the analysis is equivalent to that of budgetary tax substitution; there is a direct income transfer from capital to labour taken at constant prices, and a general equilibrium adjustment of the excess demand or supply created by the impact effect that depends on whether the labour-owning recipients have a marginal preference for the labour-intensive or capital-intensive good by comparison with capitalists. Again the mitigation of the initial transfer by an adverse secondary effect cannot fully wipe out the primary benefit, so long as the initial equilibrium is stable.

2. *Minimum-Wage Laws*

In addition to budgetary manipulations, governments can affect the distribution of income in the community by direct intervention in the marketplace by fixing either the prices or the quantities of goods and/or factors that can be exchanged. Minimum-wage laws are one example of the government pursuing its 'resource-transfer' function by legislative fiat (though by no means the only one—the analysis of price fixing and quota arrangements is left to the reader to work out), and the analysis of such laws has become traditional in economics. The standard conclusion reached by economists concerning such laws, derived from an application of partial equilibrium techniques, is that, though minimum wage laws benefit those workers who are successful in obtaining employment in the industries subject to them, they tend to create unemployment or else drive a number of workers into the equivalent of the 'subsistence sector' of the economy. Contrary to these conclusions a general equilibrium analysis of minimum-wage laws demonstrates that there are possible circumstances in which a minimum-wage law that applies to only a part of the productive activities of the economy may benefit workers in all sectors. On the other hand, if the minimum wage law applies to all sectors, the traditional conclusion can be rigorously demonstrated.

The analysis is illustrated in Figure 4.8 and 4.9, for the two alternatives of capital-intensity and labour-intensity of the minimum-wage sector. In each Figure $O_xP''PO_y$ represents the contract curve under conditions of competition. P is the point on the contract curve that would prevail under competition. It is assumed that this equilibrium is unique—the possibility that the redistribution of income between labour and capital that occurs as production shifts along the contract curve is assumed not to result in the possibility of multiple equilibrium. In other words it is assumed (for both these Figures and Figure 4.10) that an increase in the relative price of a commodity reduces the excess demand for it, through the usual income and substitution effects, regardless of the redistribution effect.

Figure 4.8 represents the case in which the minimum wage law is imposed on the X industry, the capital-intensive industry. The effect of the law is to increase the capital-labour ratio in the X industry from the slope of O_xP to the slope of $O_xP''P'$, and to make the economy's new contract curve consist of the curved section of the old contract curve between O_x and P'' and the straight line section $P''P'$ extended. The curved section of the old contract curve corresponds to those output levels for which the marginal product of labour exceeds the minimum wage; the straight-line section to the capital-labour ratio in the minimum-wage sector required to make labour's marginal product equal to the minimum wage.

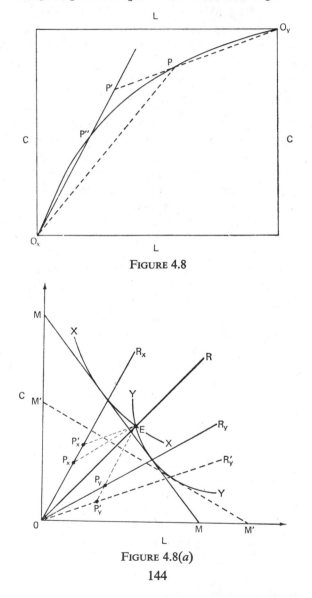

FIGURE 4.8

FIGURE 4.8(*a*)

As production moves from O_x to P'' along the old contract curve, the relative price of X in terms of Y must increase. The same holds true as production of X continues to increase along $P''P'$ extended. This is proved by reference to Figure 4.8(a). In the Figure, units of X and Y are chosen to have equal costs of production at the factor price ratio prevailing with production at P'', their common costs of production being given by the budget line MM. The overall endowment ratio of the economy is represented by OR, and the optimal factor utilization ratios in the two industries by OR_x and OR_y respectively. In order to increase the production of X, with the fixed factor utilization ratio prevailing to P'' and set by the minimum wage law, it is necessary to free the relevant capital required by reducing the capital-intensity in the Y industry, the new ratio of capital to labour in that industry being represented by OR'_y. The new factor price ratio in the Y industry will be $M'M'$. Since capital is mobile between the two industries and its price unrestricted, competition will equalize the price of its services in the two industries; hence capital can serve as the numéraire for measuring the effect of the production change on relative commodity prices. And since M' lies below M on the C-axis, the relative price of X must rise.

Return to Figure 4.8: at P'' both the production of X and the price of it in terms of Y are necessarily lower than at P; hence P'' cannot represent a possible equilibrium, which equilibrium must lie to the northeast of P'' on O_xP' extended. At P', the quantity of X produced must be lower and of Y produced higher, than at P; and the price of X in terms of Y must be higher than at P (this can be proved by considering the effect of an increase in OR_x in Figure 4.8a). With a lower quantity produced and a higher relative price of X, P' could be an equilibrium position. If it is, the marginal product of labour in the Y industry is unchanged, while its marginal product in terms of X (through exchange in the market) must be lower than at P. Hence if P' is the new equilibrium position, labour in the Y industry can at best be no worse off (if it consumes no X) and generally will be worse off than at the competitive equilibrium position P. If the demand for X is sufficiently inelastic, P' will represent an excess demand for X, and the equilibrium with the minimum wage will lie to the northeast of P'; in this case the marginal product of labour in Y will be lower than before in terms of both products, so that such labour will be unambiguously worse off. But if the demand for X is sufficiently elastic, the new equilibrium of the economy with the minimum wage law in effect will lie between P' and P''; the capital-labour ratio in the Y industry must rise as compared with competitive equilibrium, while the relative price of X in terms of Y must fall by comparison with P'. The marginal product of labour in the Y industry must rise in terms of X; and depending on the preferences of the owners of labour in consumption of the two goods, labour in the Y industry may be made better off than it would have been under competitive equilibrium in the absence of the minimum wage. This possibility constitutes the exception to the standard conclusion.

Figure 4.9 illustrates the case in which the minimum wage law seeks to raise the real wage of labour in the labour-intensive sector in terms of the produce of that sector. The new contract curve consists of the segment O_xP'' of the competitive contract curve, and the straight-line segment $P''O_y$ determined by the minimum wage law. Figure 4.9(a) shows that, as production of X increases from P'' along the straight-line segment, the relative price of X in terms of Y must fall. At P'', the point of division of the segments of the new contract curve, production of X and its relative price in terms of Y are both lower than at P; hence P'' cannot be a position of equilibrium. Nor can P', since at P' both production of Y and its relative price in terms of X are higher than at P. The new equilibrium of the economy must lie somewhere on the straight-line segment of the new contract curve between P' and O_y. The ratio of capital to labour employed in the X industry must be lower than it was under competitive equilibrium in the absence of the minimum wage law. Hence the marginal product of labour in the X industry must be lower than under competitive equilibrium; and since the price of X must also be lower in terms of Y, labour's marginal product of Y transformed into terms of X through conversion at the commodity price ratio must also be lower than under competitive equilibrium without the minimum wage law. Hence the minimum wage law must necessarily make labour in the non-included industry worse off than it would in the absence of the law.

Figure 4.10 illustrates the case in which the minimum wage law is imposed in both industrial sectors (assumed either to exhaust the economy, or to comprise the non-subsistence sectors of it), raising the capital-labour ratios in them from O_xP and O_yP to O_xP'' and

146

O_yP'' respectively. Production at P'' involves a smaller quantity and a lower price of X and hence is incapable of being an equilibrium point. There is an excess demand for X and an excess supply of Y. Reallocation of the economy's resources towards X and away from

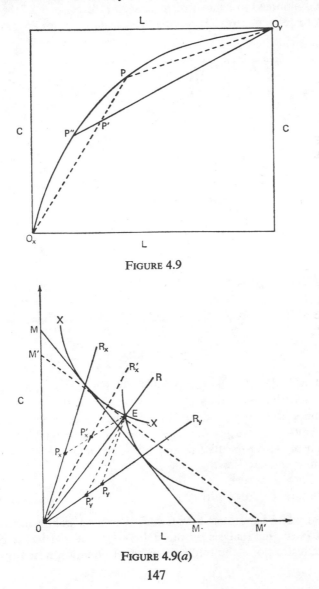

FIGURE 4.9

FIGURE 4.9(*a*)

Y, maintaining the capital-labour ratios required by the minimum wage law, releases more labour from the Y industry than can be absorbed in the X industry, given the relative capital-intensity of the X industry, and necessarily creates unemployment (or, where there is assumed to be a subsistence sector, forces part of the labour force to retreat into that sector). The resulting equilibrium of the

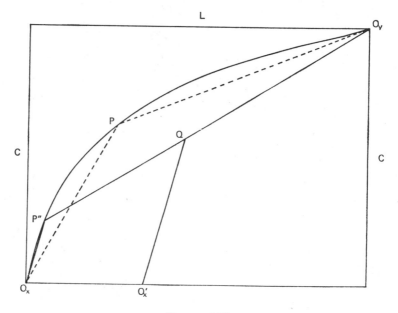

FIGURE 4.10

economy is depicted by the point Q (which may involve more or less production of X than point P, since the relative price of X as the capital-intensive good must have fallen by comparison with Y, the labour-intensive good). $O_x O'_x$, the shift or origin for the production of X, represents the amount of unemployment created by the minimum wage law.

III. TRADE-UNIONS POLICY

Policies can be initiated by private as well as public institutions, and it is to the analysis of the policies of one particular type of private institution—the trade union—that attention now turns. The monopolistic policies of trade unions and business concerns can be classified as 'resource-transfer' in that their object is to promote a redistribution of income to themselves from the rest of the community. Such policies differ from the resource transfer policies of government, however, in that the income redistribution they seek to achieve is not dictated by community consensus as to what the appropriate or equitable distribution of income consists of, but by economic self-interest. In the case of trade unions, the two may not be completely separate, since modern governments have shown themselves willing to tolerate a degree of monopoly power with respect to trade unions policies that is inconsistent with the ideals and standards of a capitalistic economy as embodied in the trust-busting function of government. Trade unions, in other words, may be one means by which the government carries out its own resource-transfer policies.

For purposes of analysis, it is assumed that the demand preferences of factor-owners—specifically, the owners of capital, of unionized labour and non-unionized labour—can be treated as an aggregate community preference system, i.e. that demand effects of income redistributions consequential on unionization can be ignored. This community preference system is further assumed to have two plausible characteristics; that a reduction of real income reduces the quantities of both goods demanded, and that a reduction in the relative price of one commodity causes substitution of that commodity for the other in consumption. Unionization itself is assumed to consist of the introduction of a fixed proportional differential excess of wages in the unionized sector over wages in the non-unionized sector, the number of unionized workers adjusting to demand given this differential. The problem is the effect of unionization so defined on the prices of capital, unionized labour, and non-unionized labour in terms of the products. As will be developed below, analysis of these effects does not constitute a full analysis of the effects of unionization on the distribution of real income.

In the absence of unionization, the production possibilities open to the economy can be depicted by the Edgeworth-Bowley production contract box technique depicted in Figures 4.11 and 4.12, in which O_xPO_y is the contract curve in the absence of unionization, and P is assumed to be the general equilibrium production point in those circumstances.

149

The effect of unionization is to make the wage rate (value of marginal product) in the unionized industry exceed that in the non-unionized industry by a certain proportion. (The analogy between trade unionization in one industry and a partial factor tax should be noted. The former can be considered the equivalent of a tax on labour in one sector only.) The values of the marginal products

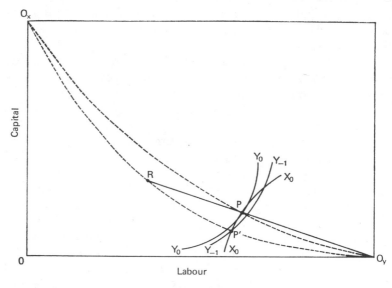

FIGURE 4.11

of capital in the two industries must, however, be equal. In diagrammatic terms, at any point of equilibrium in the allocation of factors between the industries, the slope of the tangent to the isoquant for the unionized industry must be steeper than the slope of the tangent to the isoquant for the non-unionized industry (the slopes being taken with reference to the horizontal so that they represent the price of labour in terms of capital). Figures 4.11 and 4.12 show such equilibrium points for unionization in the X and Y industries respectively, the points P' in the two figures in each case corresponding to unchanged output in the unionized industry. It is obvious that, because of the differential introduced between the marginal value products of labour in the two industries, the efficiency of production is reduced, and less output of the non-unionized industry is produced for any given output of the unionized industry. In other words, the transformation curve (as derived by the analysis presented in Chapter 2) is pulled in towards the origin except at its extreme points; it may even become convex to the origin over all or part of its length. Moreover, on the new transformation curve, because of the differential in marginal value products of labour in the two

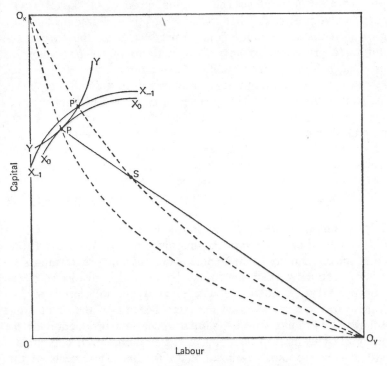

FIGURE 4.12

industries introduced by unionization, the private marginal cost of the unionized product exceeds its social marginal cost. Hence the new equilibrium will be doubly inefficient: production will be less than it could be, and consumers will choose inefficiently among points on the transformation curve (see Chapter 9).

The points P (the pre-unionization general equilibrium production point) and P' (post-unionization equilibrium with production of the

151

pre-unionization quantity of the unionized good) serve as convenient reference points for analysis of the effects of unionization. At P', the capital-labour ratio has risen in the unionized industry and fallen in the non-unionized industry, in comparison with non-unionization. Hence the marginal product of unionized labour in terms of the unionized product must have risen, and the marginal product of non-unionized labour in terms of the non-unionized product must have fallen. The marginal product of capital, correspondingly, must have fallen in terms of the unionized product and risen in terms of the non-unionized product. Since the price of the unionized product must have risen in terms of the non-unionized product, it follows that at point P' as compared with P unionized labour must be receiving wages with an increased purchasing power in terms of both goods. The earnings of capital—which must be the same in value terms in both sectors—are lower in terms of the unionized good and higher in terms of the non-unionized good. Thus, if production were to be maintained at P', unionized labour would be definitely better off, and non-unionized labour definitely worse off, while the owners of capital might be better or worse off depending on the relative quantities in which they consumed the two goods.

By assumption, however, the production point cannot remain at P' (unchanged production of the unionized product) because at that point the community's real income is less than before, owing to the loss of productive efficiency caused by the union distortion of the labour market, while the relative price of the unionized product relative to the non-unionized has risen because of the union wage differential. Production must shift towards less production of the unionized and more production of the non-unionized commodity, with a corresponding re-allocation of factors. The effects of this depend crucially on whether the unionized sector is relatively capital-intensive or relatively labour-intensive. These two alternatives are represented in Figures 4.11 and 4.12 respectively.

If the unionized sector is capital-intensive (Figure 4.11), production shifts along the new contract curve from P' towards O_x. As it does so, the ratio of capital to labour in both industries must rise, so that the marginal products of unionized and non-unionized labour in terms of their own products must rise, while the marginal product of capital in both sectors must fall. That is, by comparison with P', the gains of unionized labour must increase, and the losses of non-unionized labour fall, while capital must become worse off. It is even possible that both groups of labour gain, capital bearing the burden of this loss plus the deadweight loss in the economy's efficiency.

The point R, at which the capital-output ratio is the same as at P, is the dividing line between two sets of possibilities. In the contract curve range $P'R$, the marginal product of capital is higher and of non-union labour lower in the non-unionized product than at P, so that non-union labour is necessarily worse off and capital may be better off than at P. In the range RO_x, the converse holds—the marginal product of capital in the non-unionized product is lower, and of non-unionized labour higher, than at P, so that capital must be worse off and non-union labour may be better off than in the absence of unionization. Where the new equilibrium actually falls will depend on the demand conditions, which have not been specified here.

If the unionized sector is labour-intensive (Figure 4.12), production shifts from P' towards O_y, and the capital-labour ratio falls in both sectors, thus reducing the marginal products of both types of labour in their own sectors and raising the marginal product of capital in both sectors. As a result non-unionized labour must lose by comparison with P', and so must unionized labour; and unionized labour may even lose by comparison with non-unionization, whereas capital may gain unambiguously. The point S divides the new contract curve into two ranges, according to whether the capital-labour ratio is the unionized sector is greater or less than at P. In the range $P'S$, the marginal product of capital in terms of the unionized product is less than at P, so that capital may be worse off. In the range SO_y, the marginal product of capital is higher in both products, so that capital must be better off, while the marginal product of unionized labour may itself be made worse off. Where the equilibrium point falls depends as before on the unspecified demand conditions.

In summary, there are two possibilities, depending on whether the union sector is relatively capital-intensive or relatively labour-intensive: unionized labour necessarily better off, and non-unionized labour possibly better off; and non-unionized labour necessarily worse off, and unionized labour possibly worse off. Interestingly enough, in an empirical study of the United States based on the two-sector model, Harry Johnson and Peter Mieszkowski have found the unionized sector to be relatively labour-intensive, and the empirical values of the parameters needed in a quantitative analysis such as to make it possible that unionization has not only harmed the welfare of the non-unionized but reduced the welfare of the unionized as well.

CHAPTER 5

The Theory of Public Goods

The analysis of policy-induced change in a closed economy raised the question of the nature of government that should be postulated in developing an economic theory relevant to the analysis of economic policy. Two alternative conceptualizations were stipulated in Chapter 4: that of an 'independent' government assumed to have a utility function of its own which it seeks to maximize subject to unspecified constraints, and whose activities do not benefit the community-at-large; and a government that serves a social purpose. Such social purpose can be related to either (*i*) the correction of positive and negative externalities from economic activities by the levying of appropriate marginal taxes and subsidies on such activities, (*ii*) redistribution of income in the private community in order to achieve an equitable distribution of income, and (*iii*) the provision of goods and services for the public. The latter in fact, can be further subdivided into the provision of 'private goods' which either government can provide more cheaply and/or efficiently than private enterprise, or where private enterprise has as good or better technology as government, based on returns to scale, but private enterprise would become monopolistic and hence maximize profits by violating marginal conditions for welfare maximization (the equality between marginal production cost and marginal value to consumers); and 'public goods', whose technical nature is such that allocation of resources to them cannot be efficiently performed through the private market. The purpose of this chapter is to extend the analysis of the two-sector model to the case where one of the commodities in the model is a public good and the other a private one.

155

I. PUBLIC AND PRIVATE GOODS DEFINED

The essential characteristic that distinguishes public from private goods concerns the technical nature of the benefits conferred by the production and consumption of each. The benefit derived by a consuming unit (household or firm) from a private good—such as a piece of steak—is entirely used up in the process of consuming that good, so that consumption by one precludes any benefit to another. Since the benefit is specific to the consumer, that consumer will be willing to pay for all of it, and the producer can charge the consumer a price that captures the benefit and covers the cost of making the good available—at the margin, that is and subject to competitive conditions prevailing among both consumers and producers. By contrast, a public good in the pure sense of the term is one the enjoyment of the benefits of which by one consumer in no way prevents other consumers from enjoying a benefit (not necessarily a comparable benefit) from consumption of it, and with respect to which the producer is unable for technical reasons to charge each individual consumer a price equal to the benefit received, or consumers collectively for the benefits severally received. An example of a pure public good in this sense is a lighthouse, which enables each individual fisherman or ship's captain to navigate at night without in any way reducing the ability of others to use the light for navigation, but for which it would be impossible to charge each navigator for the individual navigational benefit received except at impossibly high transactions and enforcement costs. Consequently, lighthouses are built and maintained at the general expense of the community, acting through its government.

So defined, the terms 'private goods' and 'public goods' represent polar opposites. Between the two extreme cases where the entire benefit derivable from a good is enjoyed exclusively by one person and where all individuals in the community have equal access to the good (though, as mentioned, not necessarily deriving equal benefits from it) lies the vast majority of 'real world' goods. This can be realized by further meditation on the example cited above: the enjoyment of a good steak dinner may make a person better company for his family, friends, and colleagues; and a lighthouse conveys no benefit, direct or indirect, on a self-sufficient farmer whose acres are located far inland. Intermediate commodities, the main benefit from which accrues to an identifiable individual or

156

groups of individuals, but which also afford benefits to other members of the community difficult to identify and charge for benefits received, have both private and public characteristics, and are generally described as either 'quasi-public goods' or as 'private goods conferring externalities', depending on whether the public or the private aspect is considered to be analytically the more important. Typical examples of private goods yielding (positive) externalities are education, which benefits the person educated but also conveys benefits on the rest of the community in the form of an educated citizenry, to an extent generally assumed to vary inversely with the level of education in question (primary, secondary, college-level); and opera houses and theatres, which primarily confer a private benefit on those who attend the performances but also are held to confer a secondary benefit on those who do not attend or attend only rarely, in maintaining a cultural tradition in the community.

Three preliminary comments are relevant to an economic analysis of such 'quasi-public goods' or 'private goods yielding externalities'. First, there are 'quasi-public bads' as well as 'quasi-public goods', and negative externalities as well as positive externalities; this point is illustrated by various forms of 'pollution of the environment'. Second, consensus of informed opinion rather than vested interest should be relied on to determine the presence of a public good or externality aspect. Third, in many but not all cases laws regarding property rights and contracts provide relatively efficient ways of 'internalizing' positive or negative externalities to those generating them, for example by providing for payment of damages to those exposed to negative externalities.

The analysis of this chapter is concerned with pure public goods as a polar case. It is necessary to begin by recalling the proviso mentioned above, that equal access of all members of the community to the quantity of a public good made available does not imply that each member of the community derives an equal benefit from the availability of that quantity, and more specifically does not imply that the marginal value of an additional unit of the public good is the same to all members. On the contrary, it is obvious that, say, a pacifist will assign a much lower marginal valuation to an additional dollar of defence expenditure than a militant nationalist —possibly even a negative value.

In partial equilibrium analysis, the aggregate demand curve for private goods (price on the vertical axis, quantity on the horizontal axis) is derived by lateral (horizontal) summation of the individual demand curves; this procedure follows from the fact that a unit purchased by one individual is not available for use by other individuals. By logical extension, the demand for a public good must be obtained by vertical summation of the demand curves of the individual members of the community, since one unit caters equally to the wants of all individuals, and the marginal unit is worth the community's producing if all members who benefit at all from its presence are collectively prepared to pay the costs of producing it.

II. GENERAL EQUILIBRIUM WITH A PUBLIC GOOD: A SIMPLIFIED ANALYSIS

In order to concentrate on the analytical essence of the public goods problem, it is convenient to abstract from shifts in the personal or functional distribution of income induced by shifts in the allocation of production between the public and the private good. For this purpose it is assumed *either* that the economy possesses only one factor of production, *or* that there are two factors but that the production functions for the public good is identical, except for choice of units of measurement of quantity, with that of the private good. Either procedure yields a straight-line social (and private) transformation curve between the goods and a determinate and invariant distribution of income between factor-owners. The only difference in the analysis, as compared with that of private goods, is that the welfare of each individual factor owner depends on the amount of the private good he purchases for himself, and on the total amount of the public good provided, whether paid for by himself or by others, rather than on the amount he himself pays for.

We begin by demonstrating that, if the amount of the public good produced is not determined collectively but is left to individual decision-taking, the total amount produced will be below the socially optimal level, the reason being that each individual, in contemplating whether to produce an extra unit of the public good, has to weigh the total extra cost against the marginal benefit to himself only, since by definition he cannot charge the other individuals in the community for the benefit conferred on them by the extra output of the public good. The simplest way of showing this is to assume

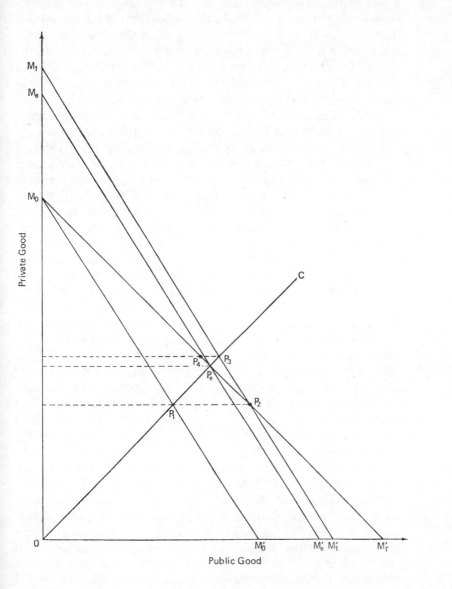

FIGURE 5.1

159

a community of two individuals, of equal incomes and with identical homothetic preference systems, each of whom acts on the assumption that what he does will have no influence on the behaviour of the others. Such a community is represented in Figure 5.1, where the slopes of the budget lines represent the relative production costs of public and private goods and OC is the income expansion path at the corresponding relative price ratio.

$M_o M'_o$ represents the budget constraint facing each consumer; and, acting independently, each will choose production point P_1. But for production point P_1 for each, the consumption combination of each will be P_2, with a new budget line for each of $M_1 M'_1$. Each will therefore attempt to shift to P_3 on the assumption that the other person's expenditure on the public good will be unchanged; but when both do, the actual consumption combination of each will be P_4, northwest of the income-expansion line OC; so each will increase expenditure on the public good in an effort to return to OC. But this will lead to overshooting of OC, causing each to cut his expenditure on the public good again, with consequent undershooting of OC, and so forth. It is obvious that the economy will converge on P_e, where the budget line $M_e M'_e$ and the straight-line locus $M_o P_4 P_e P_2 M'_r$, which represents the budget line when costs of production are equally shared, meet with the income expansion line OC. Since the indifference curve tangent to $M_e M'_e$ must cut the locus $M_o M'_r$ from right to left, both individuals could achieve higher welfare levels if they recognized the interdependence of their welfare levels through the public good and agreed to split the costs of providing it. In a community of a few individuals who knew and trusted each other, this could be done by informal agreement or by forming a 'club' to provide public goods. In a large community, however, which we shall henceforth take the two-person community to represent, the arrangements for deciding the volume of public goods to be produced and the allocation of the total costs among the citizen-taxpayers must be made formally through government. For this purpose, it is necessary to specify a process by which collective decisions (through government) on the quantity of the public good to be produced are determined. Note that it makes no difference (questions of differences in productive efficiency apart) whether the public good is produced directly by government, which hires factors of production for the purpose, or is produced and provided by private enterprise, which hires factors for the purpose, so long as the amount produced is determined by collective decision.

The simplest process of collective decision-taking to assume is one analogous to a market system of allocation. Assume that each individual is offered a share in the total costs of production of the public good, expressed as a (parametric) price per unit at which he is allowed to consume it, and asked the quantity of it which he would be prepared to buy at that price. In general, those quantities demanded will not be the same; if not, a consensus on the quantity to be produced is only possible on the basis of the smallest quantity any one would be prepared to buy. But this would imply that those who wanted more produced would be prepared to pay more than their initially-allotted cost shares for the amount of production so decided, and could induce the lowest-quantity-demanded to demand more by reducing his cost share and increasing their own. Positive income and substitution effects operating on those whose cost shares were so reduced, and negative income and substitution effects operating on those whose cost shares were increased, would move their respective quantities demanded towards a consensus involving both the cost shares and the quantity produced, such that the sum of the marginal valuations of the public good (equal to the marginal tax payments) of the various individuals in the community must sum to the total marginal cost of production of the public good. This last implies fulfilment of the conditions of Pareto optimality. Note also—a point to be taken up later—that each individual must be assumed to behave competitively, or in more emotive terminology 'be honest', in the sense that he states accurately the amounts that he would demand of the public good at the parametric price determined by his cost share, disregarding the fact that if he understates these amounts he will get less than he truly wants but more than he says he wants, because others will be willing to increase their tax shares in order to induce him to agree to a high level of production closer to what they want.

The process of collective decision on a consensus basis is illustrated in Figure 5.2, where $M_A M'_A$ and $M_B M'_B$ represent the budget lines of two individuals on the assumption that each alternatively must bear the full costs of provision of the public good. (Their total, $M_{A+B} M'_{A+B}$ represents the community's budget line.) If A paid all the costs, its consumption point would be C_A^A and B's

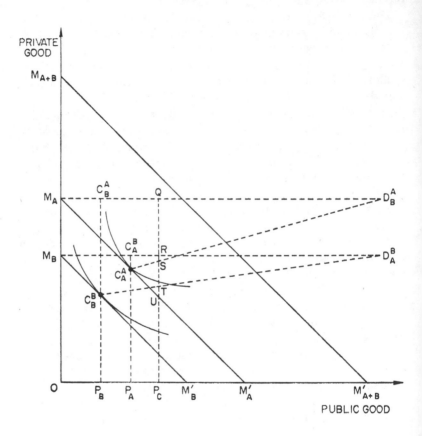

FIGURE 5.2

consumption point C_A^B; production of the public good being P_A. Conversely, if B paid all the costs, the production of the public good would be P_B and the consumption points of A and B respectively C_B^A and C_B^B. (This assumes that the public good can only be provided through government, and that if the amount so provided by taxation of one individual is less than the other individual would choose to provide himself at his own expense the latter is unable to provide the extra amount; this assumption is unrealistic, but relaxing it merely introduces problems already dealt with (since taxation of one person only is equivalent to private provision of the public good) and the following analysis shows that the result is unaffected by it. Given these alternative allocations of the total cost of producing the public good, and the assumption that the demand for neither good is satiable, however, the quantity of the public good demanded by the individual confronted by a zero price would be infinite, lying respectively along $M_B D_A^B$ and $M_A D_B^A$ respectively. Hence neither can represent a consensus on the quantity to be produced. Now experiment with reductions in the respective tax shares of the two individuals below full-cost payment. These will trace out income-cum-price-reduction expansion curves, or more briefly demand curves $C_A^A D_B^A$ and $C_B^B D_A^B$ (these curves are drawn sloping upwards from left to right, but may dip downwards over a range if the substitution effect of a tax reduction against consumption of the private good is strong enough to outweigh the income effect in favour of greater consumption of that good). The consensus equilibrium output will be P_C, where the sum of the taxes paid by A (QS) and by B (RT) is equal to the total cost of production of P_C (QU). Note that the consensus equilibrium is Pareto optimal, and that it must be unique if the demand curves slope consistently upwards from left to right (the condition for multiple and unstable equilibria is that substitution effects be sufficiently strong).

The process of collective decision-taking with respect to the provision of the public good assumed in the preceding analysis rests on two key assumptions. One is accurate indication of individual preferences as between private and public good on a tax-rate-parametric basis; the other is government decision-taking by consensus. Complications arise if either or both of these assumptions are relaxed.

To take first the question of accuracy of indication, or more specifically of incentives to individuals to 'cheat' by understating their willingness to pay for the public good, the extreme form of this can be illustrated by reference to Figure 5.2. The indifference curve for A through point S may pass to the left of C_B^A, indicating that A would be better off if he could convince B that he was unprepared to pay any of the costs of providing the public good. Similarly, the

163

indifference curve for B through point T may pass to the left of C_A^B, so that B could be better off if he could convince A that he was not prepared to pay anything towards the cost of providing the public good. Of course, if both adopted this position and maintained it adamantly, no public goods would be provided, and both would be worse off; but presumably one or both would weaken. What the outcome would be is indeterminate without further assumptions about the behaviour of the individuals concerned; but there is a virtual certainty that any resort to bluffing by either party would lead to a level of production of the public good less than P_C. It is for this reason that a number of economists have reached the conclusion that, allowing for incentives to bluff by misrepresenting preferences, the political process will lead to under-allocation of productive resources to the provision of public goods.

The opposite answer can be arrived at, however, if one abandons the assumption of consensus government in favour of that of majority government, and changes the assumptions about taxation somewhat. The problem is more complex than it seems at first sight, however. While it is tempting to assume that the use of the coercive power of majority government to redistribute income from the minority to the majority must involve over-allocation of resources to the satisfaction of the wants of the majority (in the present context, wants for public goods) to do so is implicitly to compare the presence with the absence of government, without providing any explanation of the existence of government and the acceptance of majority rule. To investigate this question fully would take the analysis too far afield into political philosophy; for present purposes, it is sufficient to translate the problem into that of the fulfilment or non-fulfilment of the Pareto conditions. To illustrate the point, assume that A is an aggregate of two persons and therefore constitutes a political majority over B. Given the assumed indispensability of both goods in the consumption of B, A could in principle tax away the whole of B's income, making its own income $M_{A+B}M'_{A+B}$ (i.e. the total social income). If A had complete freedom to spend this tax-augmented income on either public or private goods, it would choose a tangency point of one of its indifference curves with its new budget line, and the Pareto-optimality condition would approximately be fulfilled (approximately but not quite, since the marginal utility of the public good to B would be positive but negligibly small). More realistically, it might be assumed that there was a limitation on the amount of B's income that could be taken in taxation, either because B required a subsistence minimum of private goods or because if B's utility level were reduced below a certain minimum B would revolt or otherwise cease to accept the principle of majority rule. In the former case B's indifference curve would be horizontal at the subsistence level, and tax revenue subject to a maximum, in the latter the indifference curve would not be horizontal but A would obtain more tax revenue as it expanded public goods production equal to B's marginal valuation of the public good; the Pareto-optimal conditions would therefore be fulfilled in both cases. A case of over-allocation of resources to public goods production could only arise, therefore, if *either* taxation of B were conditional on the whole of the tax proceeds being spent on the provision of public goods, *and* the amount that could be provided from the proceeds of the maximum taxation of B exceeded the amount that A could choose if it could spend the tax proceeds as it wished as between private and public goods; *or* if taxation of B had to be levied as a rate per unit of public good consumed *and* A used its political majority to force B to accept a combination of tax rate and level of output of public goods that carried B beyond the level of output that would maximize its utility given that tax rate.

III. POTENTIAL WELFARE MAXIMIZATION AND SOCIAL WELFARE MAXIMIZATION

In the preceding section, it was shown that private provision of public goods must lead to the non-achievement of Pareto-optimality, and that collective decision-taking on the model of government there described must lead to a Pareto optimal situation, at least so long as citizens are 'honest' in revealing their preferences for the public good. However, the analysis there presented assumed that each individual had a given initial income fixed in terms of private goods, and was offered the opportunity to 'buy' public goods in exchange for a tax-share of cost per unit, the condition that the two individuals must have tax-shares such that they demand the same level of output of the public good determining (in general) a unique equilibrium of tax share rates, public goods output and utility levels for the two individuals. It is obvious that the two equilibrium utility levels are determined by the initial fixed incomes of the individuals in conjunction with their preference maps, and can be altered, in the specific Pareto-equilibrium-relevant sense that one can be raised and the other lowered, by a redistribution of income from one individual to another. Such a redistribution could be effected in either of two ways: by directly redistributing income measured in private goods before the collective decision-taking process determining the level of public goods production is initiated; or by taxing the individuals other than in proportion to their incomes, using the proceeds to establish a certain level of public goods production, and applying the collective decision-taking process to

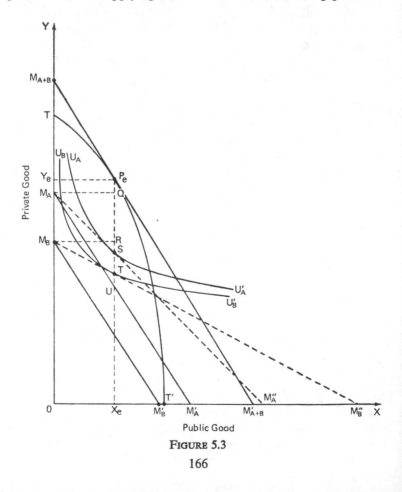

FIGURE 5.3

166

the determination of the optimal expansion of public goods production beyond the level already financed by taxation (this necessarily implies that the initial level of tax-financed public goods production must be below the optimal level for the resultant distribution of private income). Note that in either case public goods production may either increase or decrease by comparison with that corresponding to the initial distribution of income.

The resulting infinite number of combinations of utility levels for the two individuals can be charted in the form of a 'utility possibility frontier' with the utility levels of the two individuals represented on the axes. The frontier must, as a consequence of its Pareto-optimal basis of derivation, slope downwards from left to right; but because the contours of the individual preference functions are indexed only ordinally and no other restrictions on their shapes than convexity to the origin can plausibly be imposed on them, the frontier need not display a regular smoothly-varying shape. The utility possibility frontier may either be left as it is, to show the distributions of utility possible in the economy, or a social welfare function defined over the two utility levels may be brought into the diagram, tangency of one of its contours (which need not be regularly shaped or even uniformly convex to the origin) to the utility possibility frontier (or possibly a 'corner solution') indicating the maximum attainable level of social welfare and therefore, indirectly the optimal income redistribution policy in the presence of the public good.

IV. GENERAL EQUILIBRIUM WITH A PUBLIC GOOD:
THE GENERAL CASE

The simple case of general equilibrium with a public good analysed above abstracted from the effects of changes in the allocation of factors in production of the two goods on the distribution of income by assuming either a single factor, or identical production functions for the private and the public good. In the general case, the production functions will be different for the two goods, so that as production of the public good increases its marginal cost rises, the functional distribution of income shifts towards the factor that is used relatively intensively in producing the public good, and the personal distribution shifts towards the individual who owns a

167

relatively larger share of the available total of that factor as compared with the other. The general equilibrium of the system must therefore involve consistency among the outputs of private and public goods, the distribution of income between the two individuals, and the resulting aggregate demands for private and public goods (the amount of the public good demanded being the same for each individual).

The general equilibrium of the economy with a public and a private good is depicted in Figure 5.3. The central part of the Figure reproduces Figure 5.2 and the explanation of the equilibratory process is the same as in the text accompanying that Figure. TT' is the transformation curve for the economy, P_e the equilibrium point on it, and Y_e and X_e respectively the equilibrium outputs of the private and the public good respectively. The difference between the two Figures is that in Figure 5.2 the slopes of the budget lines are independent of the position of the transformation curve, whereas in Figure 5.3 they must correspond to the slope of the transformation curve at the equilibrium production point. In Figure 5.3, in contrast to Figure 5.2, the budget lines $M_A M''_A$ and $M_B M''_B$ corresponding to the tax-share prices of the public good are drawn in, as are the equilibrium utility levels of the two individuals, $U_A U'_A$ and $U_B U'_B$.

The fact that as production shifts along the transformation curve towards less or more public goods production the distribution of numéraire income shifts away from or towards the individual who owns relatively more of the factor used relatively intensively in producing the public good introduces an extra dimension to the problem of inaccurate indication of preferences as between private and public goods. The individual who stands to gain, income-distribution-wise, from increased production of public goods has an incentive to overstate his preference for them, and vice versa for the individual who stands to lose from such increased production. These incentives will be reinforced or modified, according as the individual who stands to gain from a shift towards more public goods has a relatively lower preference for such goods, so that his tax-share of their cost will be relatively small, or vice versa; and similarly, as the individual who stands to gain from a shift towards more private goods production has a relatively stronger preference for public goods, so that his tax-share of their cost will be relatively large, or vice versa.

CHAPTER 6

The Theory of International Trade

The analysis of the preceding chapters has been concerned exclusively with the economics of a single economy, which has been assumed to be somehow isolated from the effects of other economies existing in the universe. Though a convenient expositional device, the assumption of a closed economy is unnecessarily limited in that it excludes from consideration a range of potentially economically significant transactions; hence, a second economy that trades with the first must be taken into explicit account in the analysis. Theoretically such trade could consist in the services of the factors of production as well as goods, but because economies historically have been associated with nation states between which trade in goods has been empirically more significant than trade in productive factors, the theory of international trade proceeds on the assumption that while perfectly mobile within economies the factors of production do not move from one state to another. This assumption of inter-economy factor immobility, however, is not as limiting as might first appear, since it can be demonstrated that under certain assumptions commodity trade and factor mobility will be perfect substitutes for one another.

The normative analysis of the effect of free trade on a previously closed economy can be approached in either one of two ways. Aggregate criteria can be used, in which case the community's indifference map will indicate the effect of the availability of trading opportunities either on the community's *actual* welfare or economic well-being if the individuals or groups comprising the community can be assumed to be homogeneous enough both in tastes and factor

169

ownership shares to justify this assumption; or on the community's *potential* welfare should the concerned individuals or groups be sufficiently different in their tastes, shares in factor ownership, or both. In the latter more interesting case, disaggregate criteria are relevant as well, and the central problem is the effect of international trade on the distribution of income among private factor-owners. The aggregate potential welfare analysis and the disaggregate distributional analysis, of course, must be logically consistent. An increase in potential welfare, for example, is consistent either with both factors enjoying an increase in their real incomes, or with one factor gaining and the other losing but with the gainer being able to compensate the loser for his losses without becoming a loser himself; while a decrease in potential welfare in the latter case would indicate that it would not be possible through compensation for both factors to be better off or, in the limit, for one factor to be better off and the other no worse off.

I. FREE TRADE, THE DISTRIBUTION OF INCOME AND POTENTIAL WELFARE

For simplicity, the economic groups that comprise the community will be identified with specific factors of production, so that the functional and personal income distribution coincide. The analysis of the effect on the domestic economy of trade with a second economy can proceed either under the assumption that the international terms-of-trade are independent of the domestic country's demand for imports and supply of exports, in which case the terms-of-trade can be taken as given to the domestic economy, or that the domestic country is large enough to affect the terms at which it trades in international markets. For expositional purposes, the former assumption is the more convenient, but it will be relaxed in subsequent analysis.

Free trade can have no effect upon the domestic economy unless the international terms-of-trade differ from the price ratio obtaining in the home market in closed economy equilibrium. Given such a divergence, the effect of free trade is to raise the price of exportables, so promoting a re-allocation of domestic production towards exportable goods and away from importables, and in the process raising the relative price of the factor used relatively intensively in producing the country's export good and lowering that of the factor used relatively intensively in producing the country's import good. Hence the real income of the former factor increases while that of the latter factor falls as a result of free trade.

The effect of free trade in the case where international prices can be taken as given to the domestic economy is illustrated in Figure 6.1, where TT represents the economy's transformation curve and CC and LL the production blocks of capital and labour respectively. In closed economy equilibrium, the economy's aggregate production-consumption point is at P,C, with the commodity price ratio being given by the slope of the transformation curve at that point. Capital's production point is P_c, its budget constraint M_cM_c and its consumption point C_c on U_c^2; labour's production point is P_L, its budget constraint M_LM_L and its consumption point C_L on U_L^2. By vector addition the factor's consumption points C_L and C_c must sum to the aggregate consumption point C, which in equilibrium is equal to the aggregate production point P. Now if the fixed international terms-of-trade are assumed to be given by the slope of $T'T'$, indicating a higher price of Y and a lower price of X in international as opposed to domestic markets, domestic production shifts to P' on the economy's transformation curve and $P_c{}'$, $P_L{}'$ on the respective production blocks of capital and labour. Since labour is intensive in the production of the export commodity Y, whose output expands as a result of trade, and capital in the production of X, whose output falls, labour gains and capital loses as a result of free trade. Labour's budget constraint shifts to $M_L{}'M_L{}'$, indicating increased purchasing power in terms of both goods and the consumption point $C_L{}'$ on U_L^6; while capital's budget constraint falls to $M_c{}'M_c{}'$, indicating decreased purchasing power in terms of both goods and the consumption point $C_c{}'$ on U_c^1. By vector addition, the aggregate consumption point is determined as C', which is reconciled with the production P' by exporting $P'Q$ of Y for QC' of X at the international price ratio.

The effect of free international trade, as compared with self-sufficiency, is normally to raise the real income of one factor and reduce the real income of the other. The exception is the extreme case of trade which leads the country to specialize completely on the production of one of the goods, *and* establishes a price for that good sufficiently above the price at which complete specialization is

171

profitable for the factor whose income in terms of exportables is reduced to be more than compensated for the loss by the relative cheapening of imports. Excluding the exceptional case, free trade benefits one factor and damages the other. Whether free trade, as compared with self-sufficiency, benefits or harms the nation as a whole therefore is a question whose answer requires a balancing of gains against losses, and can only be decided by reference to the country's social welfare function. In the absence of a social welfare function, the question can be discussed in terms of potential welfare, that is, of whether it would be possible by transfers between factors (compensations) to make both factors better off (in the limit, no worse off) under free trade than in the absence of trade. This in turn requires a definition of what the change introduced by free trade consists in. If it is taken to consist in the change in the actual collection of goods available for the economy's consumption, it is possible that the collection of goods purchased in the free trade equilibrium could not be redistributed so as to make both factors as well off as they would be with the self-sufficiency collection. But if, as seems more sensible, it is taken to consist in the opportunity to trade at the free-trade price ratio, it can easily be shown that the country is potentially better off with free trade than under self-sufficiency, since the effect of free trade is equivalent to an outward movement of the country's transformation curve (in Figure 6.1 from TT to $T'T'$).

There are two alternative techniques of demonstrating that a country is potentially better off with free trade than under self-sufficiency, the first utilizing individual preference functions, the second the community indifference map. The former is illustrated in Figure 6.2, where C_L and C_c represent the respective initial consumption points of labour and capital at self-sufficiency prices and C the initial aggregate consumption point. The gains from free trade can be demonstrated if, in the limit, one factor can be made better off without the other factor being made worse off as a result of free trade. This easily can be demonstrated by means of vector addition since free trade shifts aggregate consumption right of MM to a point such as C'. Hold capital's consumption point constant at C_c and determine the parallelogram $OC_cC'C_L'$. It is clear from the geometry that so long as C' falls to the right of MN, C_L' also falls to the right of M_LM_L, indicating an increase in labour's real income.

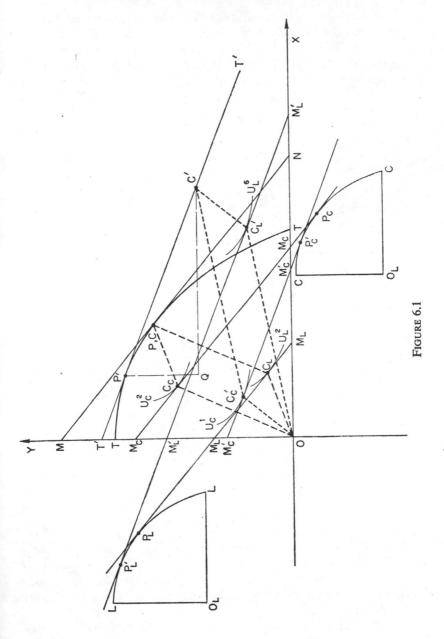

FIGURE 6.1

Thus it always will be possible for labour to fully compensate capital for any and all losses that the latter suffers as a result of free trade and still be better off with free trade than self-sufficiency. The reader should be reminded, however, that his gain is said to be potential because free trade only makes it possible for one group to gain without the other one losing—there is nothing in this

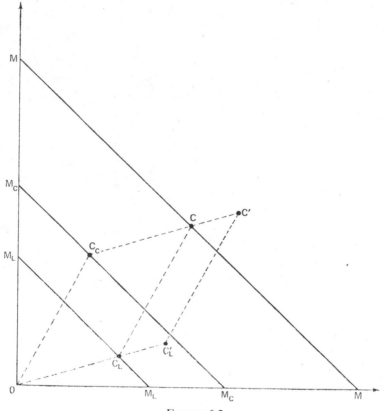

FIGURE 6.2

definition to indicate that the compensation necessary for actual welfare to increase in Paretian terms will in fact take place. Economists, in other words, cannot say that free trade actually will make the community better off, but only that it has the potentiality for doing so.

The potential welfare gains from free trade alternatively can be

174

demonstrated through the technique of the community indifference map. The community in Figure 6.3 is in closed economy equilibrium at point P,C on U_1 and is assumed to be offered an opportunity to trade at a different price ratio—the slope of $M'M'$—than that prevailing in domestic markets—the slope of MM. For purposes of analysis it will be convenient first to assess the effect of the decrease in the relative price of X to domestic consumers, assuming that the relative price of X to domestic producers remains unaffected by free trade, and then analyse the effect of the decrease in the relative price of X to domestic producers having assumed that consumers already have adjusted to the price change. In consequence, the first part of this analytical experiment is the analysis of a domestic consumption subsidy to X, the second part the analysis of a domestic production tax on X of equal *ad valorem* rate. Free trade thus can be considered as being equivalent in effect to the combination of a domestic consumption subsidy to and a domestic production tax on the imported good relative to non-trade prices; or alternatively, it can be thought of as a combination of a domestic consumption tax on and a domestic production subsidy to the export good relative to non-trade prices.

The consumption subsidy element of free trade, which is reflected by the change in prices from the slope of MM to that of $M'M'$, results in a shift in the aggregate consumption point from C to C'. This indicates a gain in potential welfare which is independent from any change in the production point, equal to the difference between U_2 and U_1 and measured by $M'M''$ in terms of either the import or export good. Given the location of the aggregate consumption point at C' the effect of the domestic production tax on the import good is to shift the production point from P to P' and consumption point from C' to C''. This entails an additional increase in potential welfare equal to the difference between U_3 and U_2 and measured by $M''M''$ in terms of either commodity. The total gain from free trade is the sum of the individual gains resulting from its consumption subsidy and production tax components: in terms of either commodity the total gain is equal to $M''M'''$, consisting of a consumption subsidy component of $M'M''$ and a production tax component of $M'M'''$. In terms of potential welfare, the total gain is equal to the potential welfare difference between the community indifference curves U_3 and U_1.

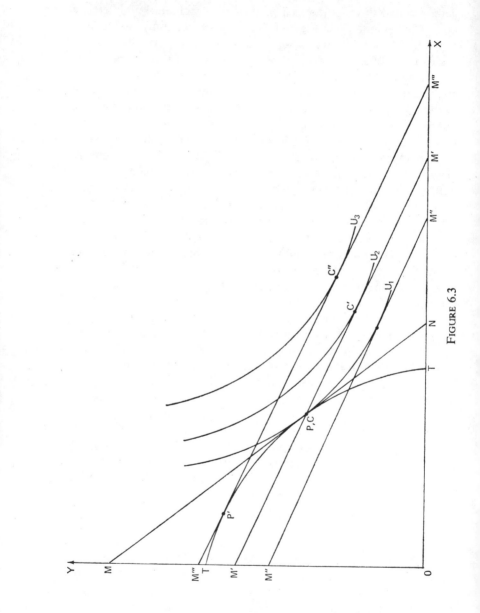

FIGURE 6.3

II. THE DETERMINATION OF INTERNATIONAL PRICES

The foregoing analysis assumes the prices of international trade goods to be given to the domestic country, and that at those given prices the country can import all of the import good it requires. While this is a convenient expositional device for investigating the effects of trade on the economy, it will now be abandoned in our examination of the determinants of international prices and quantities of traded goods. Like domestic prices in a closed economy, international prices also are a function of demand and supply, the equilibrium condition being that the excess demand for imports (excess supply of exports) be zero in international markets. The demand for imports by the domestic country at each relevant international price ratio can be expressed, in the two-sector model, in terms of the quantity of exports it would supply in exchange at those prices, and is reflected by a country's offer or reciprocal demand curve. The domestic offer curve in conjunction with the foreign offer curve, which expresses the foreign country's demand for imports in terms of its supply of exports at the various international price ratios, determines the international terms-of-trade.

There are two alternative approaches for developing a country's offer curve. The first uses the concept of the community indifference map and makes the explicit connection between the country's international offers and the level of potential welfare implied by those offers; the second makes explicit the connection between the distribution of income between factors and the country's demand for imports and supply of exports at that distribution. Each approach, the aggregate and disaggregate, is developed in turn.

1. The Aggregate Approach: Potential Welfare and the Offer Curve

As is obvious from Figure 6.3, corresponding to each relevant international price ratio there exists a unique set of profit-maximizing outputs given by the economy's transformation curve and a unique potential welfare-maximizing demand for such outputs given by the community indifference map, any imbalance thereof being reflected in international markets as that country's demand of imports in terms of its supply of exports and constituting one point on its offer curve. Utilizing this method, the necessary data for construction of the offer curve can be derived from the community's transforma-

177

tion curve and indifference map in Figure 6.3 and plotted on a separate diagram. For certain analytical purposes, however, it proves convenient to construct the offer curve from the community's transformation curve and indifference map by means of an intermediary concept known as the trade indifference map. This map consists of a set of trade indifference curves, each defined to represent a unique level of potential welfare and indicating the import and export requirements to maintain that level of potential welfare at different aggregate production and consumption points. Its derivation from the transformation curve and community indifference map is illustrated in Figure 6.4, where positive quantities of X are indicated both by movements due east and due west of the origin, while positive quantities of Y are indicated both by movements due north and due south of the origin. Hence the community's transformation curve and indifference map either can be placed in their normal position in the first quadrant of the Cartesian diagram or in the fourth quadrant of the diagram as is more convenient in Figure 6.4.

Consider the community indifference curve U_1 and transformation curve TT tangent to U_1 at point P,C, the self-sufficiency equilibrium point. Point O on the trade indifference curve I_1 then indicates that no trade is required for the community to attain the level of potential welfare indicated by U_1 with domestic production and consumption indicated as X_p and Y_p at point P,C. Holding U_1 constant, now slide the transformation curve along U_1 until, for example, some point M is reached, making sure that the axes of the transformation curve are kept parallel with those of the community indifference map. Domestic consumption at point M, indicated with reference to the origin O, is equal to Y_m of Y and X_m of X, while domestic production at point M, indicated with reference to the origin F, is MY_m' of X, or Y_mY_m' less than domestic consumption, and MX_m' of Y, or X_mX_m' more than domestic consumption. As indicated by the point F on the trade indifference curve I_1, OA (equal to Y_mY_m') units of imports of X and FA (equal to X_mX_m') units of exports of Y are necessary to attain the level of potential welfare indicated by U_1 when aggregate consumption is point M with reference to the origin O and aggregate production is point M with reference to the origin F. Comparing point M on U_1 with its corresponding point F on I_1, it is clear from the geometry that the slope of I_1 at point

178

F is equal to the common slope of TT and U_1 at point M. Thus, as the economy's transformation curve TT slides along U_1 from the point corresponding to complete production specialization on good Y to that corresponding to complete production specialization on good X the trade indifference curve I_1 is traced out, having the

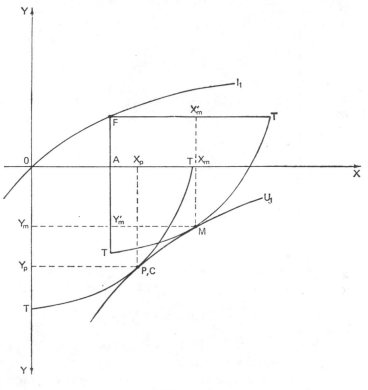

FIGURE 6.4

properties that all points along it are Pareto optimal in the sense that the domestic marginal rate of transformation between X and Y is equal to the domestic marginal rate of substitution between X and Y, and that the level of potential welfare it reflects is constant and identical to that reflected by the community indifference contour U_1.

The foregoing analysis describes the derivation of the trade

179

indifference curve I_1 corresponding to the community indifference curve U_1. It should be clear that there is a trade indifference curve corresponding to each and every curve of the community indifference map, and that these curves can be derived in an analogous manner, and have properties analogous to those of I_1. There thus exists a trade indifference map corresponding to the community's

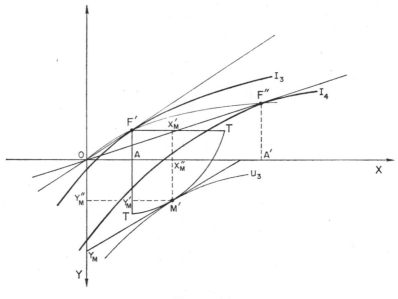

FIGURE 6.5

indifference map, each of whose contours are convex to some reference point J in the second quadrant and negatively sloped with reference to this same point such that higher levels of potential welfare are indicated by movement in the southeast direction away from that point.

We are now able to derive the domestic country's offer curve directly from its trade indifference map. Consider the arbitrarily chosen terms of trade given by the slope of OF' (equal to the slope of $Y_m M'$) in Figure 6.5. Production at these prices takes place at the point M' with reference to F', indicating outputs $M'X_m$ of good Y and $M'Y_m'$ of good X, national income OY_m in terms of good Y, and consumption $M'X_m''$ of good Y and $M'Y_m''$ of good X at point

180

M', with reference to the origin O. Excess supply of Y thus equals $X_m'X_m''$ and excess demand for $X\ Y_m'Y_m''$ at these prices so that in the first quadrant, the trade triangle can be represented as $OF'A$, F' representing the point on the offer curve corresponding to the terms of trade given by the slope of OF. Point F', of course, can be directly determined by the tangency of the terms of trade line and the trade indifference curve, and it is readily apparent from the geometry that the offer curve itself represents the loci of tangency points between various terms of trade lines and trade indifference curves as the terms of trade vary. Hence as the relative price of imports falls, the tangency point shifts to F'' and the dimensions of the trade triangle alter to $OF''A'$, implying that the offer curve has the 'normal' elastic shape—that is, as the relative price of imports fall, quantity demanded increases and total expenditure in terms of exports rises.

In a manner analogous to that described in the foregoing analysis the offer curve for the foreign country can be derived, expressing the foreign demand for imports in terms of foreign exports at the price ratios ranging from complete specialization on good Y to complete specialization on good X in that country. The two curves are superimposed in Figure 6.6, determining the slope of OE as the equilibrium terms of trade. At inferior terms of trade for the domestic country, such as that indicated by the slope of OA, there is an excess supply of the domestic import good X and an excess demand for the domestic export Y—hence an improvement in the terms of trade; while at superior terms of trade for the domestic country, such as the slope of OC, there is an excess demand for domestic imports and excess supply of domestic exports, resulting in a terms of trade deterioration. The slope of OE, in other words, is not only the equilibrium price ratio but is stabile as well.

It may be noted that since both offer curves are derived from trade indifference curves and E is a point in common, a trade indifference curve for each country will be tangent to the one for the other at the equilibrium point; in Figure 6.6 trade indifference curves I_3^f and I_5^d are tangent at point E. The normative implication of this tangency is that free trade will be Pareto optimal from the global perspective, in the sense that the residents of one country cannot be made better off in terms of potential welfare without making the residents of the other country worse off. Point E therefore represents

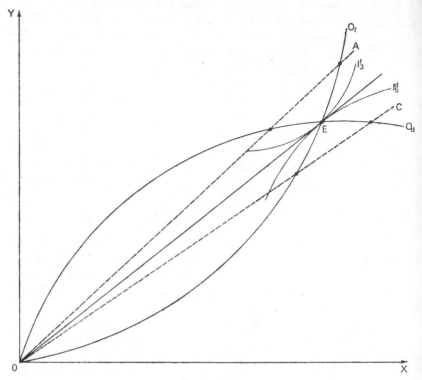

FIGURE 6.6

one point on the world's welfare frontier. There are, of course, an infinity of such points on the welfare frontier, and these correspond to the infinity of tangency points between the two systems of trade indifference curves lying on a locus through E. These other efficient points all are attainable under free trade conditions by a lump-sum income transfer from one country to another.

There are in addition to the Pareto efficient points an infinity of points that are not on the locus of indifference curve tangencies, i.e. that lie inside the world's welfare frontier, that entail a higher level of potential welfare for one country while permitting the other country to be better off with some trade than without it. Such points can be attained by use of an import or export tax, which breaks the necessary marginal equalities for full Pareto optimality in the world economy (see Chapter 7). There is accordingly no reason to regard free trade as necessarily superior to other methods of conducting trade from the national perspective when a country can affect the terms at which it trades in the international market, though free trade necessarily will be superior to no trade in this case. From a world perspective, however, free trade is the best policy for countries to follow.

2. The Disaggregative Approach: The Distribution of Income and the Offer Curve

Under free trade, the domestic price ratio is the same as the international (external); and the point on the offer curve corresponding to a particular international price ratio represents the excess of the quantity of one good that the country would produce over what it would consume, and the excess of the quantity of the other it would consume over what it would produce, at that price ratio. Given the price ratio, which determines the country's production point and the distribution of income between factors, the consumption of the two goods and therefore the point on the offer curve corresponding to the price ratio is determined by the preference systems of the factors. The derivation of the offer curve is illustrated in Figure 6.7, which reproduces Figure 2.6. The indifference curves for labour are drawn in the usual northeast direction, with the fixed origin O, and the quantities of X and Y demanded by labour are determined by the tangency of an indifference curve with labour's budget line as given by the production point on the transformation curve and the income distribution curve. The indifference curves for capital, on the other hand, are drawn in the southwest direction from the *shifting* origin of the production point on the transformation curve; and the quantities of X and Y demanded by capital are determined by the tangency of one of these indifference curves with labour's budget line, determined as above, which represents capital's budget line viewed from the point on the transformation curve as origin. The excess or deficit of the total quantity of a good demanded by both factors together, as compared with the amount of it produced, is the country's import demand or export supply of it, and is measured by the overlap or gap between the two factors' consumption points with respect to the axis for that good.

In Figure 6.7, with the price ratio equal to the slope of MN, the production point is P_1, with OB of X and OA of Y being produced, total income is given by the aggregate budget line MN, capital's budget line is M_cM_c with reference to the origin P_1, and labour's budget line is M_LM_L with reference to the origin O. Capital's consumption point is C_c, with capital demanding BX_c of X and AY_c of Y, while labour's consumption point is C_L, with labour

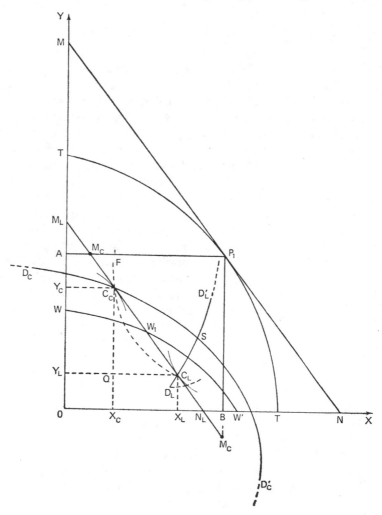

FIGURE 6.7

demanding OX_L of X and OY_L of Y. There is therefore an excess
of demand for X over domestic production (a demand for imports)
of X_cX_L at the given price ratio. More simply, at the terms of trade
given by the slope of C_cC_L, the country will supply exports of C_cQ
of Y in exchange for imports of C_LQ of $X - C_cQC_L$ is the country's
'trade triangle'.

One point on the country's offer curve has thus been defined. To
obtain other points, it is necessary to ascertain the excess demand
for X over domestic production and the excess production of Y
over domestic demand for the entire range of prices ranging from
complete specialization on Y to complete specialization on X. As
the relative price of X rises relative to the terms of trade given by
the slope of C_cC_L, the production point shifts to the right along
the transformation curve, income is redistributed towards capital
and away from labour, and the dimensions of the trade triangle
alter. The changes in exports supplied and imports demanded as
the relative price of imports rises are most conveniently analysed
in terms of the behaviour of C_L and C_c, the vertices of the trade
triangle, as the production point shifts along the transformation
curve. Movement of each factor's consumption point can be divided
into two separate conceptual components: (i) the combined income
effect resulting from (a) the change in the factor's numéraire income
as the economy's production point shifts (the production income
redistribution effect) and (b) the change in the purchasing power of
numéraire income as commodity prices change (the Hicksian
equivalent variation in income); and (ii) the Hicksian substitution
effect in consumption resulting from the change in relative commodity prices. The shift in the consumption points of labour and
capital as the relative price of the import rises is illustrated in
Figures 6.8 and 6.9 respectively, using the factor-owner production
block technique. In Figure 6.8, labour's initial income in terms of
good Y is M_L and its consumption point C_L on U_L. As the relative
price of X increases labour's production point shifts from P_L to
P_L' and its numéraire income falls from M_L to M_L'. The effect of the
production income redistribution effect on labour's consumption
point, taken at constant commodity prices given by the slope of
M_LM_L, is from C_L to C_L'. The price effect of the change in commodity prices, from the slope of $M_L'M_L'$ to that of $M_L'M_L''$ taken at
numéraire income M_L', is composed of an income effect (the Hicksian

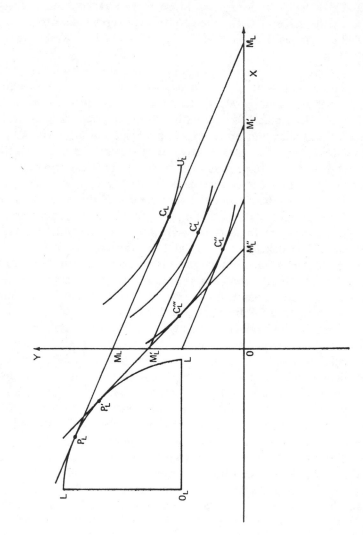

FIGURE 6.8

equivalent variation in income), indicated by the shift of labour's consumption point from C_L' to C_L'', and a substitution effect indicated by the shift from C_L'' to C_L'''. Both the income effect of the price change and the income effect of the production change work in the same direction in this case—towards the consumption of less X and less Y, so that the consumption substitution effect indicating the consumption of more Y and less X must be very strong if *net* the movement from C_L to C_L''' is to result in increased consumption of Y. Accordingly, the loci of labour's consumption points $D_L D_L'$ in Figure 6.7 is assumed to slope upwards from southwest to north-east through point C_L.

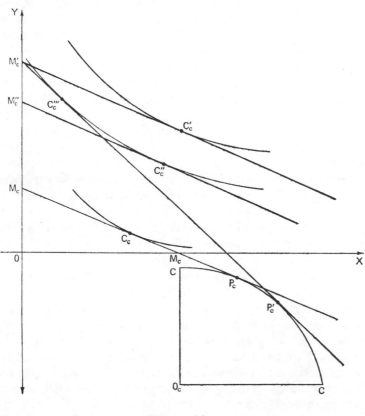

FIGURE 6.9

In Figure 6.9 where capital's initial income in terms of the export good Y is M_c and its initial consumption point C_c, capital's numéraire income rises to M'_c as its production point shifts from P_c to P'_c in response to the increase in the relative price of the import good. Measured at initial commodity prices, the production income redistribution effect results in a shift of capital's consumption point from C_c to C'_c. The price effect of the rise of the price of X comprises an income effect from C'_c to C''_c and a substitution effect from C''_c to C'''_c. The continued income effects in this case conflict, the net result being reflected in the movement from C_c to C''_c, and an increase in the demand for both goods. The consumption substitution effect works in the direction of more Y and less X being consumed, and given that the two income effect components work in opposite directions, it is more likely in this case than in the previous one that the net income effect will be outweighed by the consumption substitution effect. Accordingly, the loci of capital's consumption points is drawn in Figure 6.7 as downward sloping from northwest to southeast. Still the possibility that the net income effect might outweigh the substitution effect in this case as well implies that $D_c D'_c$ might be upward sloping but it can only slope upwards over a certain range, since, as is clear from Figure 6.7, C_c must lie to the northwest of W at one extreme (complete specialization on good Y, in which case the origin of capital's preference function assumes the point T) and to the southeast of W' at the other (complete specialization on good X, in which case the origin of capital's preference function assumes the point T').

If $D_c D'_c$ slopes downwards throughout, both sides of the trade triangle diminish as the price of X increases; and the domestic country's offer curve has the normal ('elastic demand for imports') shape, less of X being demanded and less of Y supplied as the price of X rises (Y falls). But if $D_c D'_c$ slopes upwards in the relevant range, abnormal shapes of the offer curve become possible: (a) the vertical side of the trade triangle may increase as the price of X increases, indicating an increase in the quantity of Y supplied as the price of X rises ('inelastic demand for imports'); (b) both sides of the trade triangle may increase as the price of X increases, indicating an increase in the quantity of X demanded as its price increases ('perverse elasticity of demand for imports'); (c) as the price of X decreases, the trade triangle may shrink to nothing and invert over a certain range before reverting to normal ('perverse reversal of trade direction'). This last possibility requires that $D_c D'_c$ and $D_L D'_L$ intersect three times, which means that there are three possible closed-economy equilibrium points, at successively higher prices of X and larger incomes for capital, of which the middle one is unstable.

The equilibrium volume and terms of international trade are determined by the intersection of the domestic offer curve with the

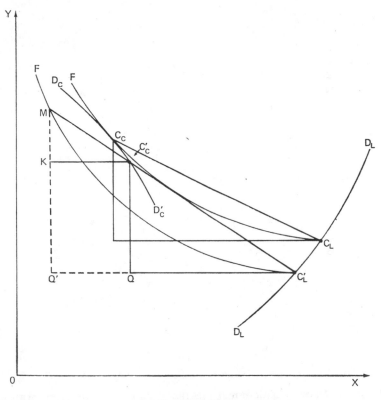

FIGURE 6.10

foreign offer curve, because the domestic country's demand for imports (supply of exports) at the price established at that inter-section is just equal to the foreign country's supply of exports (demand for imports) at that price. Geometrically, the determination of the international trade equilibrium can be depicted by sliding the origin of the foreign offer curve, assumed to have the normal elastic shape, along $D_L D_L'$ (or $D_c D_c'$) in Figure 6.7 until its intersection with $D_c D_c'$ (or $D_L D_L'$) lies on the labour budget line through its origin; for example, if the foreign offer curve were $C_L C_c F$ in Figure 6.7, $C_L Q C_c$ would represent the equilibrium volume and

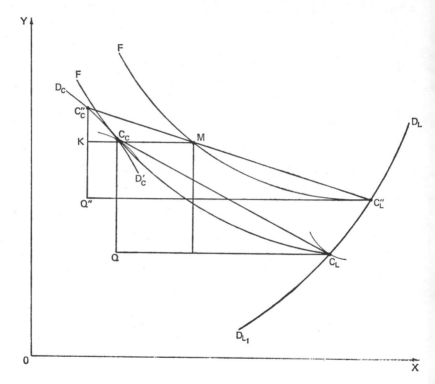

FIGURE 6.11

terms of trade. To demonstrate the stability of this equilibrium, and at the same time reinforce the conception of equilibrium itself, determine the consumption points for labour and capital at a higher relative price of $X - C_L'$ and C_c' in Figure 6.10—and place the origin of the foreign offer curve at point C_L'. At commodity prices given by the slope of $C_c' C_L'$, the domestic country demands $Q C_L'$ of imports in exchange for $C_c' Q$ of exports, but the foreign country offers

$Q'C'_L$ of exports for MQ' of imports. There is thus, in international markets, an excess demand for Y equal to MK, and an excess supply of X equal to KC'_c which will tend to lower the relative price of X and restore equilibrium. On the other hand, should the relative price of X be lower than that indicated by the slope of C_cC_L, consumption points such as C''_L and C''_c in Figure 6.11 are determined for labour and capital respectively and the domestic trade triangle is $C''_cQ''C''_L$. By sliding the origin of the foreign offer curve from C_L to C''_L, it is clear that at the intersection of the terms of trade line and the offer curve the foreign trade triangle lies inside the domestic one. There is an excess supply of Y equal to C''_cK at the terms of trade indicated by the slope of $C''_cC''_L$ and an excess demand for X equal to KM; hence, the relative price of X will rise. It is clear from the geometry that when the origin of the foreign offer curve is placed on labour's consumption point there can be no equilibrium at the terms of trade consistent with that consumption point if the foreign offer curve cuts the terms of trade line either to the left (as in Figure 6.10) or to the right (Figure 6.11) of capital's consumption point corresponding to those terms of trade.

III. THE DETERMINANTS OF INTERNATIONAL TRADE: THE HECKSCHER-OHLIN-SAMUELSON THEOREM

The analysis of the gains from trade demonstrated that so long as the international terms of trade differ from the self-sufficiency price ratio, a country is better off, in terms of potential welfare, with international trade than without it. It should be noted that this argument for international trade does not explain the divergence of the domestic and international price ratios, only the implication of such divergence; hence it is sufficiently general to be consistent with any number of alternate explanations of why comparative costs (price ratios) can differ between countries. The classical theory of international trade related differences in comparative costs to differences in the comparative productivity of labour, but did not explain the reasons for such divergence. This more fundamental task has been left to contemporary trade theorists, whose central contribution has been the Heckscher-Ohlin-Samuelson Theorem, originated by E. Heckscher, elaborated by B. Ohlin and which in its contemporary form owes much to the analytical techniques and propositions contributed by P. Samuelson. The major contention of the Heckscher-Ohlin-Samuelson Theorem is that differences in comparative costs can be related to differences in relative factor endowment between countries.

This conclusion is a direct implication of the assumptions of the Heckscher-Ohlin-Samuelson Theorem—an extension of the two-sector model of general equilibrium to a two-country world economy. Tastes are assumed to be homothetic and identical between countries in the sense that at given commodity prices the ratio in which the two commodities are consumed is the same in each country. The assumption of homotheticity makes this ratio independent of the scale of consumption—an obvious advantage since both countries could possess identical preference functions and still consume the commodities in different proportions at given prices because of differences in their income levels if homotheticity were not assumed. The analogue to homotheticity in consumption is homogeneity in production, which makes the ratio in which the two productive factors are employed in the production of a single good independent of its scale of output. These production or factor-intensity ratios can be made identical to one another in the different countries by assuming identical production functions and identical factors of production in the qualitative sense. With consumption and factor-intensity ratios the same, the only possible source of difference in comparative costs between countries in closed-economy equilibrium, given the assumptions of the two-sector model enumerated in Chapter 1 (especially constant returns to scale and perfect competition), would be differences in relative factor endowments.

It follows from the Rybczynski Theorem that the country with a relative abundance (high endowment ratio) of a particular factor would, at any given commodity price ratio, produce relatively more of the commodity that uses that factor relatively intensively; hence in closed economy equilibrium the price of that good would be relatively lower in the domestic as compared with the foreign country. Assuming the home country to be relatively abundant in labour and vice versa in the foreign country, domestics can be expected to export good Y, the commodity that used labour relatively intensively, while foreigners export good X, the commodity that used capital intensively in its production, since in closed economy equilibrium the relative price of X would be higher in the domestic as compared with the foreign market. Thus by relating these differences in domestic and international price ratios to differences in relative factor endowments between countries, the Rybczynski Theorem provides a rigorous theoretical explanation as to why comparative costs can differ between countries consistent with the notions of Heckscher and Ohlin.

The Heckscher-Ohlin-Samuelson Theorem is illustrated in Figure 6.12, where MN represents the given terms of trade ratio, deter-

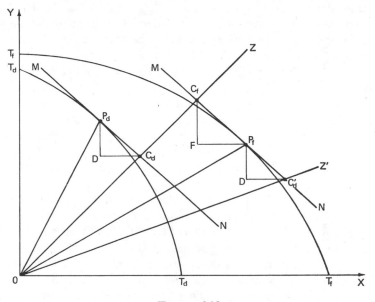

FIGURE 6.12

mining the production points P_d and P_f on the transformation curves T_dT_d and T_fT_f of the domestic and foreign country respectively. These production points indicate that the production ratio of Y to X (the slope of OP_d and OP_f in the domestic and foreign country) is higher in the domestic as compared with the foreign country, implying that the domestic country has a higher relative labour–capital factor endowment than the foreign country, since labour is assumed to be relatively intensive in the production of Y and capital in the production of X. Now consider the case where the identical tastes in the two economies are represented by the consumption vector OZ, indicating that at the price ratio given by the slope of MN there would be, in the domestic country, an excess supply of Y and an excess demand for X represented by the trade triangle P_dDC_d, and an excess supply of X and an excess demand for Y represented by the trade triangle P_fFC_f in the foreign country. If trade between the two countries was not possible, the relative price of X would rise in the domestic country and fall in the foreign one with reference to the price ratio MN (the home production-consumption vector would fall between OP_d and OZ as would the foreign one fall between OP_f and OZ). Thus in self-sufficiency equilibrium, the relative price of X would be higher in the domestic as compared with the foreign country as a consequence of the differences in relative factor endowments between the two countries. (The reader can satisfy himself that the above proof does not depend upon the position of the consumption vector OZ by choosing any other consumption vector such as OZ' where both countries demonstrate an excess demand for X but where the excess demand is greater in the home country than the foreign one. It also is clear that the proof is independent of the absolute and relative sizes of the two countries.)

The relationship between the production vectors OP_d and OP_f in Figure 6.12 and the difference in factor endowments ratios between countries is rigorously established in Figure 6.13. Consider both the factor price ratio MM corresponding to these production vectors, and thus the factor intensity ratios OR_x and OR_y; and the different factor endowment ratios OR_f and OR_d. Choose factor endowment points in the two countries E_f and E_d that represent equal national income OM at given factor prices. Determine the production points $P_x^fP_y^f$ and $P_x^dP_y^d$ in the two countries by vector addition, and compare the slopes of the lines $P_x^fP_y^f$ and $P_x^dP_y^d$. Since these slopes indicate the ratio of the production of one good to another, the difference between the slopes indicates the difference between these ratios in the two countries—with the foreign country producing a greater ratio of X to Y than the home country. That this proof is perfectly general can be determined by moving the factor endowment point in the foreign country $\bar{E}_f$ and determining the factor allocation points $\bar{P}_x^f$ and $\bar{P}_y^f$. Since $\bar{P}_x^f\bar{P}_y^f$ must be parallel to $P_x^fP_y^f$, the production vector OP_f in Figure 6.12 will be a straight line (as will OP_d for similar reasons); hence the difference between the production ratios in the two countries will be constant.

The Heckscher-Ohlin-Samuelson Theorem demonstrates that differences in relative factor endowments between countries can cause comparative costs to differ by abstracting from other possible determinants of trade—differences in tastes, technology, factor

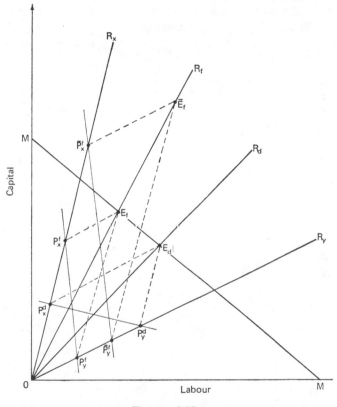

FIGURE 6.13

quality, etc. Abstraction is a perfectly legitimate scientific procedure, and such abstraction can now be used to focus on a second possible trade determinant *implicit* in the Heckscher-Ohlin-Samuelson model —differences in tastes between countries (because of the assumption of homotheticity, differences in tastes imply differences in aggregate preference functions not income levels). Figure 6.12 also can be used to illustrate this case if $T_f T_f$ is taken to represent the identical transformation curves for both countries and OZ' the home consumption vector and OZ the consumption vector in the foreign country (the proof holds regardless of the relative sizes of two countries, so long as the production vectors are the same). At the terms of trade given by the slope of MN, the home country demonstrates an excess demand for X and supply of Y, while the foreign country demonstrates the opposite; hence, in closed-economy equilibrium,

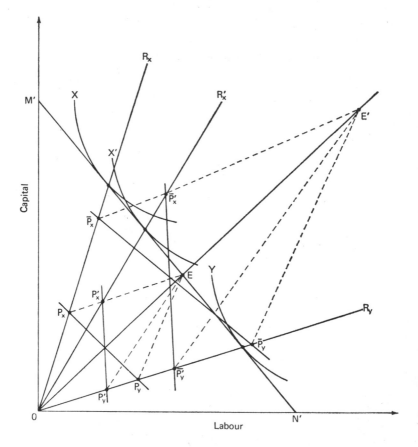

FIGURE 6.14

196

the relative price of X will be higher in the home country than in the foreign one. Trade is thus due to differences in tastes.

A third factor implicit in the Heckscher-Ohlin-Samuelson trade model that can explain differences in comparative costs between countries is differences in constant-returns-to-scale technologies (the below analysis with slight modification can be applied to the case of differences in factor quality as well). This factor can be focused upon by assuming identical factor endowment ratios, tastes and productive factors in the two countries. The analysis is similar to that of different relative factor endowment illustrated in Figure 6.12 except that in this case the difference between the production vectors OP_d and OP_f is related to different technologies in the two countries. Assume the postulated difference in technique applies only to the production of good X. This can be illustrated in Figure 6.14 for the simple case where the factor endowment point E is the same for the two countries by the home isoquant X lying northwest of the foreign isoquant X' at the factor price ratio $M'N'$ (X and X' representing the same absolute output levels), and hence OR_x being greater than OR'_x, but by the Y-isoquant, and thus OR_y, being the same in the two countries. This implies a greater absolute production of X and less absolute production of Y in the foreign as compared with the home country (this can be readily seen by comparing the production points P_x and P_y with P'_x and P'_y), and since national income is assumed to be the same, a greater relative production of X to Y in the foreign as compared with the home country. Again the proof is perfectly general, since the slopes of P_xP_y and $P'_xP'_y$, and thus the difference between these slopes will be constant regardless of the relative positions of the factor endowment point of the two countries on the common factor endowment vector OE. Comparing the factor endowment point E with E', for example, it is obvious that $\bar{P}_x\bar{P}_y$ is parallel to P_xP_y, as is $\bar{P}'_x\bar{P}'_y$ parallel to $P'_xP'_y$.

The reader at this point may be tempted to ask that if just by reversing the assumptions of the model differences in tastes, technology or factor quality (as well as decreasing costs) can logically be shown to be as capable a determinant of comparative costs as differences in relative factor endowment, is not the Heckscher-Ohlin-Samuelson Theorem's emphasis on relative factor endowment essentially an empirical proposition concerning the determinant of international trade, for which it may be added there exists a considerable amount of contradicting as well as substantiating empirical evidence. This is a matter of interpretation. If, as has become the common practice, we identify the Heckscher-Ohlin-Samuelson Theorem with the 'two by two by two' general equilibrium model (two countries, two commodities, two factors), there can be no question that the theory establishes, in a rigorous manner, a variety of possible or potential determinants of comparative cost differences, one but only one amongst which being differences in factor endowments (which many theorists happened to focus upon). Abstracting from differences in tastes and a number of other potential determinants, relative factor endowment ratios can determine the trade pattern; abstracting from differences in relative factor endowment ratios, differences in tastes, technology and factor quality also can determine the trade pattern, and so forth. On this interpretation, the Heckscher-Ohlin-Samuelson Theorem should be considered as a listing, derived by the process of theoretical abstraction of those factors present in the real world that *can* serve as determinants of international trade. There is no attempt to establish a universal law of trade determination—in any particular case any one of the above-mentioned factors may be the more important.

An alternative interpretation of the Heckscher-Ohlin-Samuelson Theorem (to some extent related to its explicit focus on relative factor endowment) is that of all possible trade determinants (the others being implicitly recognized by their inclusion in the assumptions of the theory) relative factor abundance is the only economically plausible one, in that the assumptions upon which this determinant is based (identical tastes, technology, factor quality, constant returns-to-scale, etc.) are closest to the facts of the real world. The validity of this interpretation is based both on the doubtful empirical presumption that only relative factor endowment systematically varies between countries; and the likewise doubtful methodological presumption that the purpose of economic theory is to provide universal laws that describe economic behaviour, in which case there must be a correspondence between the content of assumptions and the facts of experience. The methodological question has been discussed in Chapter 1; with respect to empirical evidence, recent findings show that advanced countries with approximately equal per-capita income trade more with each other than with less-advanced countries where per-capita income is lower. If *per capita* income can be related to capital-per-man, these findings indicate that capital-abundant countries trade more with other capital-abundant countries than with labour-abundant ones.

IV. INTERNATIONAL TRADE AND FACTOR MOBILITY: THE SUBSTITUTABILITY THEOREM

One of the major contributions to the Heckscher-Ohlin model by Samuelson was his formalization of the so-called factor-price equalization theorem; that given the unique relationship between commodity prices and factor prices (the Stolper-Samuelson relation) and the assumed identity of production functions in the different countries, the equalization of commodity prices upon trade necessarily implies the equalization of (relative and absolute) factor prices, at least so long as production remains incompletely specialized in the two countries and there are no factor-intensity reversals (see Appendix B of this chapter). Commodity trade thus serves as a perfect substitute for factor mobility, since such trade implies the equalization of factor prices even under conditions when the factors of production are immobile between countries.

Since Samuelson's extension of the Heckscher-Ohlin model, his analysis of the relationship between commodity trade and factor mobility has been similarly extended, most notably by Mundell and Nadel, to the case where either one or both of the factors of production in the 'two by two by two' general equilibrium model can move between countries. Explicit factor mobility can be assumed to take place under either one of two circumstances; where the factor-owners move with their exported factors, and where the owners of the exported factors continue to reside in the country of export. In the former circumstance, factor mobility will always be a perfect substitute for commodity trade, in the sense that the equalization of (relative and absolute) factor prices by factor mobility cuts off all commodity trade; while in the latter circumstance, four patterns of exchange are possible between economies in the 'two by two by two' consistent with factor-price equalization. Goods can be exchanged for goods (under factor immobility assumptions); the services of one factor can be exported in exchange for the import of goods; the services of the other factor can be imported in exchange for the export of goods; and the services of the exported factor can

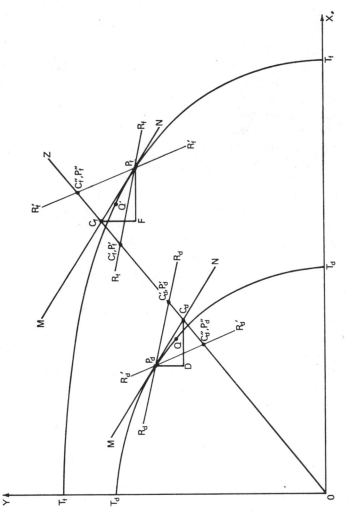

FIGURE 6.15

be exchanged for the services of the imported factor. Under the assumption that factor-owners do not move, factor mobility serves as a perfect substitute for commodity trade only in the last-mentioned exchange.

The analysis begins by considering the case where goods are exchanged for goods under conditions of factor immobility when such trade is assumed to be related to differences in relative factor endowments between countries. The domestic transformation curve is represented by $T_d T_d$ in Figure 6.15, tangent to the free-trade terms of trade line MN at point P_d, while the foreign transformation curve is represented by $T_f T_f$, tangent to MN at point P_f. Tastes are assumed to be identical and homothetic and are represented by the common income-expansion line OZ. Under free trade, the trade triangle is $P_d D C_d$ in the home country and $P_f F C_f$ in the foreign one, with $P_d D = C_f F$ and $D C_d = F P_f$.

Suppose that the home country imposes an autarkic tariff on imports of good X, so that general equilibrium with the tariff occurs at point Q on $T_d T_d$ and Q' on $T_f T_f$. The shift in the production point from P_d to Q in the home country, indicated by an increase in the output of the capital-intensive good and a decrease in the output of the labour-intensive good, implies a rise in the absolute (and relative) price and marginal product of capital and a fall in the absolute (and relative) price and marginal product of labour; while the movement from P_f to Q' on $T_f T_f$ implies the opposite in the foreign county. Points Q and Q' cannot represent equilibrium, however, if from this position of self-sufficiency all impediments to the movement of both capital and labour are removed, since in the home country the marginal product of capital will be greater, and the marginal product of labour less than the respective marginal products of these factors in the foreign country. Clearly there is a basic indeterminacy in the model; either capital can move into the home country or labour move out of the home country, or both, until marginal products and factor prices are equalized between countries. But this indeterminacy can be easily resolved by allowing for the mobility of only one factor, the procedure used by both Mundell and Nadel, and is immaterial to factor-owners in any event, since regardless of (*i*) which factor is assumed to move and (*ii*) whether the factor-owner is assumed to move with his exported factor or not, the effect of the stipulated factor mobility on the economic well-being of all factor-owners will be the same, and equal to the effect that free trade has on them.

The case where factor-owners move with their exported factors is considered in Figure 6.15. If only capital is assumed to be mobile, equilibrium in the home country will be determined where the Rybczynski line $R_d R_d$ cuts the consumption vector OZ at P'_d, C'_d; while in the foreign country equilibrium is determined where the Rybczynski line $R_f R_f$ cuts OZ at $P'_f C'_f$ (because of the assumption of identical technologies, $R_d R_d$ is parallel to $R_f R_f$). Alternatively, if only labour is assumed mobile, domestic equilibrium occurs at P''_d, C''_d where $R'_d R'_d$ cuts OZ; while foreign equilibrium occurs at P''_f, C''_f, where $R'_f R'_f$ cuts OZ. In both cases, equilibrium is characterized by (*i*) the equality of production vectors in the two countries (which because the initial difference in production vectors is assumed to be due to differences in factor endowment ratios, implies the equality of these ratios as well), and (*ii*) the equality of the common production vector with the common consumption vector, as indicated by the coincidence of OP_d and OP_f with OZ; hence the tariff could be removed and there would be no incentive for commodity trade. It should be noted that we have assumed above that *either* capital *or* labour moves in response to the factor price differentials existing between the two countries in closed-economy equilibrium; this, of course, is not necessary, and the same conclusion holds regardless of whether it is assumed that capital moves out and labour moves into the home country; or both factors move out, or both factors move in, so long as in final equilibrium the equality between the common production and consumption vectors holds. Because of the basic indeterminacy in the model, we cannot tell what the precise pattern of inter-country factor mobility will be; but this is an irrelevancy for factor prices are equalized and factor mobility will substitute perfectly for commodity trade with all possible patterns of factor movement consistent with the above-mentioned equality. (The reader can further satisfy himself of this fact by assuming an initial equilibrium with the common production vector equal to the common consumption vector. Factors can then be re-allocated between the two countries. So long as the re-allocations are proportionate in that they do not disturb the equal factor endowment ratios in the two countries, and thus the common production vectors, there will be no incentive for trade on the part of either country, and thus no commodity and factor price changes. Proportionate changes are the only relevant kind in this case, since regardless of the pattern of factor mobility, the equilibrium must fall on the vector OZ. Note that in the case where factor-owners move, the relevant criterion for establishing the equivalency of commodity trade and factor mobility must be the economic welfare of factor-owners, not a country's aggregate consumption point.)

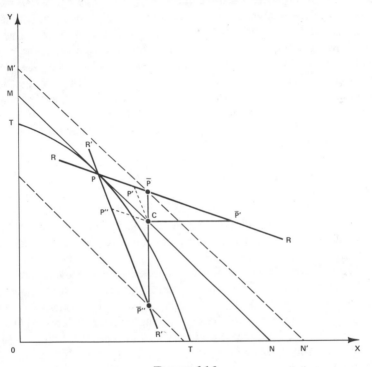

FIGURE 6.16

The case where the owners of the exported factors do not move with their exported factors is illustrated in Figure 6.16. If only capital is assumed to be mobile, factor price equalization can occur at any point southeast of $\bar{P}$ on RR, since imports of X are excluded by the assumption of an autarktic tariff. At point $\bar{P}$, interest outpayments to the foreign owners of the imported capital take the form of exports of good Y; between $\bar{P}$ and $\bar{P}'$, such payments take the form of exports of both goods X and Y; at $\bar{P}'$, the export of good X only; and southeast of $\bar{P}'$, exports of good X and imports of good Y. There is nothing in the model, however, that specifies the precise point at which factor-price equalization occurs. This is unimportant since the aggregate consumption point remains at C, regardless of which point on RR represents equilibrium, in that the increase in 'domestic' product due to the import of capital services must equal the interest out-payments to the foreign owners of capital.

It is interesting to note at this point the difference between 'national' product, a measure based on the principle of residence of factor-owner, and 'domestic' product, a principle based on the location of production; the difference between the two being their treatment of property income received from and paid abroad. Because 'national' product includes such property income under its coverage, while 'domestic' product does not, the former gives a more accurate picture of the economic well-being of the nation. At point $\bar{P}$, for example, 'domestic' product overvalues the gain from factor mobility in the country of import by MM' and undervalues it in the country of export, while 'national' product indicates that the stock of domestic factor-owners, and thus the nation, is no better off from importing capital services and exporting goods than it would be from importing the capital-intensive good and exporting the labour-intensive one.

The analysis of factor mobility can be extended to the case where only labour is mobile, and the owners of labour export their factor but continue to reside in the home country. The validity of the assumption implicit in this case, that the owners of labour can be separated from labour itself, depends upon the ownership to the property right to the service of labour. Slavery is no longer institutionally relevant, but it is a well-known phenomenon for families to send their sons abroad on condition that all earnings over and above maintenance costs be returned to the family. Thus just as the ownership of the right to the service of capital is assumed to reside with the capitalist, the ownership to the service of labour can be assumed to reside with the family of the labourer. The situation of capital and labour are not identical in this respect, however, since expropriation of factor services from its owner would appear to be more likely in the case of labour than capital, because of both the human factor and the non-symmetrical treatment given by international and national law to the two situations.

When only labour is assumed to be mobile, factor-price equalization can occur at any point southeast of $\bar{P}''$ on $R'R'$. At point $\bar{P}''$, labour remittance in-payments to the domestic owners of the exported labour take the form of imports of good $Y, \ldots$, etc. Once again the precise point on $R'R'$ at which factor-price equalization occurs cannot be pinpointed, and is irrelevant to domestic and foreign factor-owners, since the decrease in 'domestic' product due to export of labour services must equal labour remittance in-payments to the domestic owners of labour in this case. The exchange patterns between countries when only labour is mobile thus is for the home country to export labour services and import goods.

Finally, the case when the home country exports labour services and imports capital services must be examined. This case implies not only that both factors of production are mobile, and move, in response to the factor price differentials existing between the countries at self-sufficiency, but that both countries exchange equivalent values of productive factors, measured at the free trade international factor prices. Since the value of interest out-payments equals the value of labor remittance in-payments, there is no need for commodity trade. Hence, the exchange of labour services for capital services represents the 'mirror image' to the factor-price equalization theorem, since factor mobility substitutes perfectly for commodity trade. Instead of exporting the labour-intensive good and importing the capital-intensive good, the home country exports labouring services and imports capital services. This case is represented by the points P' and P'' in Figure 6.16.

APPENDIX A

Note on the Measurement of the Gains from Trade[1]

The gains in potential welfare from international trade can be measured in terms of either the import or export commodity. Consider the case in Figure 6.A.1 where trade changes the relative

---

[1] Adapted from M. B. Krauss and D. M. Winch, 'Mishan on the gains from trade', *American Economic Review* (March 1971) 61, 199–201.

prices of the two goods from the slope of Y_4X_5 to that of Y_5X_4. If we choose the import good as numéraire, we have a rise in income in terms of that good plus a rise in the relative price of the export good, the former increasing income for the economy as producers and the latter reducing it for the economy as consumers, there being a *net* gain for the economy considered together in both roles. Measuring in Y the import good, producer income increases from

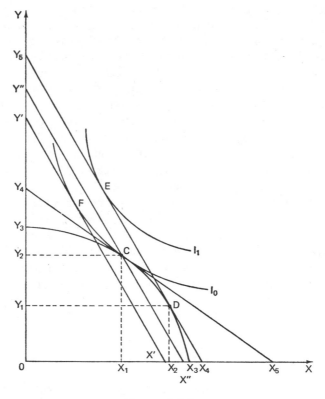

FIGURE 6.A.1

Y_4 to Y_5, but consumers need Y_4Y' more to keep potential welfare constant; hence the net gain is $Y'Y_5$. We can instead choose the export good as numéraire, in which case the value of output falls, but the purchasing power of consumers increases, there being a net gain for the community as a whole. Measuring in X the export good, consumers save $X'X_5$ for constant potential welfare, but producers lose income X_4X_5; hence the net gain is $X'X_4$, equal in value to $Y'Y_5$. With one numéraire, producer surplus gain exceeds consumer surplus loss, and vice versa with the other.

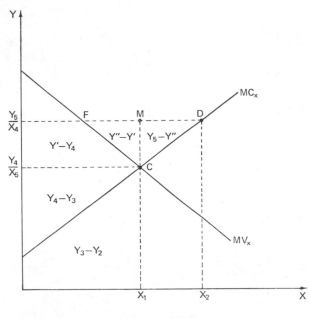

FIGURE 6.A.2

The gains from international trade alternatively can be geometrically represented in terms of marginal cost and marginal valuation curves. The transformation curve X_3Y_3 of Figure 6.A.1, derived from the familiar Edgeworth-Bowley efficiency box (not shown), is combined with a set of comparable community indifference curves I_0I_1 to yield in Figure 6.A.2, a supply (marginal opportunity cost) curve of the export commodity X and a compensated demand curve for X (marginal valuation curve), Y being the numéraire; in Figure 6.A.3, a supply curve of the import commodity Y with a compensated demand curve for Y, X being the numéraire. According to the numéraire chosen (an arbitrary choice and one that makes no real difference to the result), the movement from self-sufficiency to free trade (from point C to D) can be shown alternatively as a movement from the price ratio Y_4/X_5 to Y_5/X_4 in Figure 6.A.2, or X_5/Y_4 to X_4/Y_5 in Figure 6.A.3 (i.e. in terms of numéraire X or numéraire Y). In Figure 6.A.2 where Y is the numéraire, producers' surplus rises and consumers' surplus falls. This is because the total

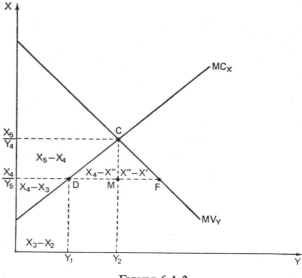

FIGURE 6.A.3

payment to factors expressed in Y rises while the purchasing power of Y in buying X falls (the price of X in terms of Y rises). Similarly, the movement from autarky to free trade can be shown in Figure 6.A.3 where X is the numéraire. Here the total payment to factors expressed in X falls while the purchasing power of X in buying Y rises (the price of Y in terms of X falls). The sum of the two changes $Y'Y_5$ or $X'X_4$ is the net welfare effect of moving from I_0 at point F to I_1 at point E in Figure 6.A.1. Whether this is represented as a net gain in producers' surplus (Figure 6.A.2) using Y as the numéraire, or a net gain in consumers' surplus (Figure 6.A.3), using X as the numéraire, is as arbitrary as the choice of the numéraire itself. To paraphrase Marshall, it is a matter of indifference which numéraire is used to express a given surplus.

208

It should be noted that the clarification of the concept of the net gain from trade—measured by $Y'Y_5$ in terms of Y, $X'X_4$ in terms of X—is independent of the partitioning of the net gain into two stages, one representing constraint of production to the initial equilibrium point, the other relaxation of this constraint. Exactly the same logic as above can be employed, for the first stage, to depict $Y'Y''$ in Figure 6.A.1, equal to the area of triangle FMC in Figure 6.A.2, as a net gain of producers surplus in terms of Y; and $X'X''$ in Figure 6.A.1, equal to the area of triangle CMF in Figure 6.A.3, as a net gain in consumers' surplus in terms of X. The second stage, corresponding to the relaxation of the production constraint, then can be depicted as $Y''Y_5$ in Figure 6.A.1, equal to the area of the triangle MCD in Figure 6.A.2 in terms of Y; while in terms of X it is depicted as the linear distance $X''X_4$, equal to the area of the triangle DCM, in Figure 6.A.3. Measuring in X, the net gain from trade can be expressed in Figure 6.A.3 as the sum of the areas of triangles DCM and CMF, the former corresponding to the domestic production tax component, the latter to the domestic consumption subsidy component of the movement from autarky to free trade; similarly, measuring in Y, the net gain from trade can be expressed in Figure 6.A.2 as the sum of the areas of triangles FMC and MCD, the former corresponding to the domestic consumption tax component, the latter to the domestic production subsidy component of the movement from autarky to free trade. For purposes of exposition and completeness, all economically relevant areas in Figures 6.A.2 and 6.A.3 are expressed as linear distances in Figure 6.A.1.

APPENDIX B

The Factor–Price Equalization Theorem and Factor Intensity Reversals

The factor price equalization theorem, that the equalization of commodity prices that would result from free trade would tend to equalize relative factor prices and, therefore, absolute factor prices as well; and would in fact exactly equalize factor prices if both countries produced both goods in free trade equilibrium, requires, in addition to the Heckscher-Ohlin assumptions required to make relative factor endowment the determinant of international trade, that either certain factual assumptions be made concerning the nature of technology—namely, that there be no factor intensity

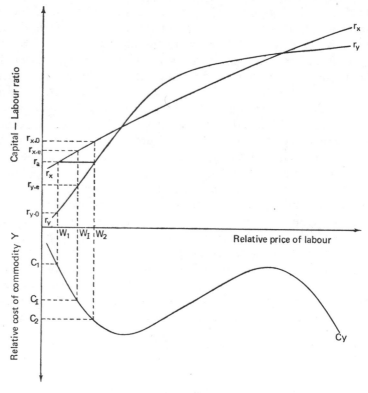

FIGURE 6.B.1

reversals regardless of factor prices—or, if factor intensity reversals are possible, that the factor endowment ratios of the two countries be not too dissimilar. The purpose of this appendix is to explain why these additional assumptions are necessary.

One implication of the Stolper-Samuelson relation is that there exists a definite relationship between optimum capital-labour ratios in the two sectors of the model, relative factor prices, and the relative costs of production of commodities, given the technical possibilities of production, summarized in the production function. This relationship is illustrated in Figure 6.B.1 where the capital-labour ratio is plotted on the north-direction of the vertical axis, the relative cost of the labour-intensive commodity Y on the south-direction of the vertical and the relative price of labour on the horizontal axis. For any given relative price of labour in terms of capital (such as w_l) there will be an optimum ratio of capital to labour in the production of each good (r_{xe} in X and r_{ye} in Y) which equates marginal productivities to factor prices, and a relative cost of X in terms of $Y(c_l)$ which embodies the ratio of their costs of production at the given factor prices with the associated capital: labour ratios.

An increase in the relative price of labour above the given level will make it profitable to substitute capital for labour in both industries, thus raising the optimum capital: labour ratio in both; it will also increase the relative cost of the labour-intensive good (Y in the neighbourhood of w), since its costs will be raised more than those of the capital-intensive good by the increase in the relative price of labour. Further increases in the relative price of labour will continue to raise the optimum capital: labour ratio in both industries; but either one of two possibilities may result with respect to the relative cost ratio, depending on the relative ease of substituting capital for labour in the two lines of production. The first, and simpler, occurs when one commodity remains labour-intensive and the other capital-intensive, whatever the relative factor price (the case we have been assuming in the text). In this case, one commodity can be definitely identified as labour-intensive and the other as capital-intensive; and the relative cost of the labour-intensive good will continue to rise as the relative price of labour rises, so that the latter can be deduced from the former. The second occurs when, owing to greater facility in substituting capital for labour in the initially labour-intensive good, the difference in capital-intensity between the two good narrows and eventually reverses itself, so that the labour-intensive good becomes capital-intensive and vice versa; such a reversal of factor-intensities may occur more than once (as illustrated in Figure 6.B.1), as variation in relative factor prices induces variation in the capital-intensity of production of both goods. In this case, a commodity can only be identified as labour-intensive or capital-intensive with reference to a range of relative factor-prices or (what is the same thing) a range of capital-intensities; and the relative cost of a commodity will alternately rise and fall as the relative price of labour rises, as that commodity varies from being labour-intensive to being capital-intensive. Consequently more than one factor price ratio may correspond to a given commodity cost ratio, and the factor price ratio cannot be deduced from the commodity cost ratio alone. The distinction between the two cases, which turns on the facts of technology, is fundamental to what follows.

The analysis so far has been concerned with the relationships implicit in the given technological possibilities of production. But only a limited range of the techniques available can actually be used efficiently by a particular economy with a given factor endowment; and the possible range of relative factor prices and relative commodity costs is correspondingly limited. The factor endowment of the economy sets an overall capital-labour ratio, to which the capital-labour ratios in the two industries, weighted by the proportions of the total labour force employed, must average out. At the extremes, the economy's resources may be used entirely in the capital-intensive industry, or entirely in the labour-intensive industry; and the relative prices of factors, and the relative costs of commodities, must lie within the limits set by these two extremes.

The restrictions imposed by the factor endowment on the techniques the economy can employ and on the possible variation of factor prices and relative costs of production are illustrated in Figure 6.B.1, where r_a represents the economy's overall capital-labour ratio. If all resources are used in the production of X, the relative price of labour will be w_1, if all are used in the production of Y the relative labour price will be w_2; the corresponding relative costs of commodity Y are c_1 and c_2. As w rises from w_1 to w_2, the capital-labour ratio in X rises from r_a to $r_{x.o}$ and the ratio in Y from $r_{y.o}$ to r_a; the increases in these ratios are reconciled with the constancy of the overall capital-labour ratio by a shifting of resources from production of X to production of Y, which frees the capital required for the increases in the ratios.

As can readily be seen from the diagram, the range of variation of relative factor prices and commodity costs possible in the economy depends broadly on two technological factors: the spread between the optimum capital-labour ratios in the two industries (reflected

212

in the vertical distance between the r_y and r_x curves), and the difficulty of substituting capital for labour (reflected in the gentleness of the slopes of the two curves). The greater the difference between optimum factor-intensities and the greater the difficulty of substituting capital for labour, the greater the range of variation of factor prices and commodity costs possible between the extremes of specialization on one or the other product. If, on the other hand, capital-labour ratios were the same in the two industries or factors were perfect substitutes, there would be no possibility of variation of relative factor prices and commodity costs.

The next stage of the argument is to introduce the possibility of international trade and examine its effects. This is done in Figure 6.B.2, which reproduces Figure 6.B.1 with the deletion of certain parts of it no longer necessary to the argument. In the diagram, the country previously analysed is represented by its factor endowment ratio r_a, and its closed-economy equilibrium factor price and comparative cost ratios w_a and c_a. The possibility of trade is introduced via a second country represented in the diagram by different closed economy factor price and comparative cost ratios, w_b and c_b. It is assumed in these examples that country A is endowed with a higher ratio of capital to labour than country B.

So long as the closed-economy equilibrium comparative cost ratios of the two countries are different, international trade will be profitable, and each country will export the good in which it has a comparative cost advantage (as measured by equilibrium commodity price ratios in the absence of trade). In the assumed absence of trade barriers, the effect of trade will be to equate the price ratios in the two economies at a level (c_e in the diagram) somewhere between the two closed-economy comparative cost ratios, this level being determined by the demand and supply conditions in the two countries taken together. Since, in closed economy equilibrium, the price of good Y is higher in country A than in B, A will export good X and B will export good Y. The increased production of X in country A implies that the relative price of labour falls in that country (capital is intensive in X), while the increased production of Y in country B implies that it rises there. As the diagram clearly indicates, when relative commodity prices are equalized at c_e, relative factor prices also will be equalized at w_e provided, of course, that production continues to be non-specialized.

The effect of trade on relative factor prices in the above case is a comparatively simple matter: owing to the one to one relationship between commodity cost ratios and relative factor prices (a technical relation), the equalization of commodity prices through trade will tend to equalize relative factor prices given that the factor endowment ratios of the two countries are similar; and if both

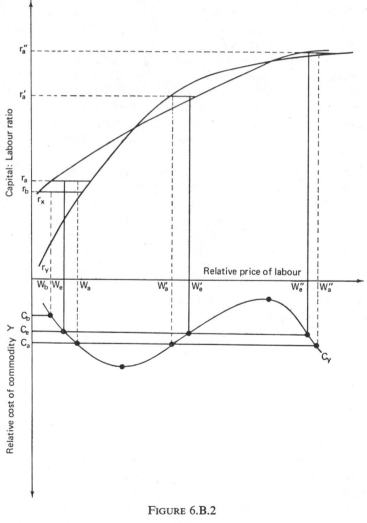

FIGURE 6.B.2

countries continue to produce both goods under international trade, equalization will necessarily be complete. But it is clear from Figure 6.B.2 that, in some cases, even when neither country is specialized under free trade conditions, the equalization of commodity prices will not only fail to equalize relative factor prices, but can result in a larger rather than smaller divergence between countries. The factor price equalization theorem, therefore, is not generally true; its validity depends on certain factual assumptions about either the nature of technology or the range of variation of factor endowments which are additional to, and much more restrictive than, the assumptions of the Heckscher-Ohlin model itself.

Consider, for example, the situation represented in Figure 6.B.2 when instead of r_a and r_b, the overall factor endowments for the two countries are r_a' and r_b; and where, in addition, the closed economy equilibrium price ratios are c_a and w_a' in country A and c_b and w_b in country B. It may be noted that despite identical production functions in both countries, the same good is capital-intensive in one country and labour-intensive in the other since the factor endowment ratios are separated by one factor reversal in this case. As before, international trade is profitable for both countries if domestic and international prices differ, and with the relative price of Y higher in country A than in B, A again will export X as will B export Y. But this time, because X is labour-intensive in country A while Y is labour-intensive in country B, increased production of the export good causes the relative price of labour to rise in both countries, i.e. factor prices move in the same direction in both countries, from w_a' to w_e' in A and from w_b to w_e in B. From the diagram, it is impossible to tell whether the initial divergence between factor prices has widened or narrowed as a result of trade in this case but, in any event, it is clear that where the factor endowment ratios of the two countries are separated by an odd number of factor intensity reversals, the equalization of commodity prices under free trade does not imply a similar equalization of factor prices.

Let us next consider the case where the number of factor intensity reversals is even; for example, when the factor endowment ratios for A and B respectively are r_a'' and r_b; and where, in addition, the closed economy equilibrium price ratios are c_a and w_a'' in A and c_b and w_b in B. In this case, the factor endowment ratios of the two countries are separated by two factor reversals, so that, as in the initial instance, X is capital-intensive and Y labour-intensive in both countries. With international trade, A exports its capital-intensive good X and B exports its labour-intensive good Y, the relative price of labour falling in A and rising in B. The effect of trade is therefore to move factor prices in the two countries in opposite directions; but the movement may be convergent or divergent. If the capital abundant country has a comparative advantage in the production of the capital-intensive commodity, factor prices in the two countries will move towards each other; if it has a comparative advantage in the production of its labour-intensive commodity, factor prices will move away from one another. The convergent pattern is illustrated in Figure 6.B.2, where country A the capital-abundant country exports X, the capital-intensive commodity. The relative price of labour falls from w''_a to w''_e in A and rises from w_b to w_e in B as a result of trade in this case. Had the comparative advantages been reversed, however, so that Y was the export commodity of country A and X that of B, initially the relative price of labour would have been higher in A than in B, and factor prices would have diverged rather than converged. In either case, factor price equalization does not hold.

In summation, the proposition that in the absence of tariffs and transport costs, and provided that no country becomes completely specialized, factor prices will equalize when commodity prices equalize requires, in addition to the Heckscher-Ohlin assumptions, that either certain factual assumptions be made concerning the nature of technology—namely that there be no factor intensity reversals regardless of factor prices—or if factor intensity reversals are possible, that the factor endowment ratios of the two countries be not too dissimilar.

APPENDIX C

The 'Transfer Problem' in International Trade

What is called the 'transfer problem' in international trade is the result of the controversy between Keynes and Ohlin concerning the question of the economic effect of German reparations after World

War I. In structure, the problem is identical with that of a resource transfer to government and budgetary tax substitution (see Chapter 4) within a closed economy—whether the direct effect of the transfer will be mitigated or augmented by a secondary effect or general equilibrium adjustment of the economic imbalances created by the transfer itself. The transfer is said to be 'overeffected' when the change in the terms of trade induced by the transfer are to the favour of the transferors, and 'undereffected' in the opposite circumstance.[1]

The transfer problem is illustrated in Figure 6.C.1 where international trade is assumed to be related to differences in homogeneous tastes (tastes must differ in the sense that the marginal propensity to spend of the transferees differs from that of the transferors if there is to be a secondary effect upon the transfer). Accordingly, the consumption vectors of the two countries OZ_d and OZ_f differ both from themselves and the common production vector $OP_{d,f}$. For diagrammatic simplicity, the countries are assumed to be of identical size so that TT represents the common transformation function. At the common equilibrium price ratio given by the slope of MN, the home country imports the capital-intensive good X and exports the labour-intensive Y—the opposite being true with respect to the foreign country—such that their respective (identical) trade triangles are given as P_dDC_d and P_fFC_f. By vector addition, the consumption points of the two countries sum to C which must lie on the (extended) production vector $OP_{d,f}$ since the initial position is one of equilibrium. The income of the world can then be measured at the equilibrium terms of trade by the line M^wN^w.

Assume that for unspecified reasons a transfer equal to MM^f (equal to MM^d) is paid from the foreign to the domestic country so that at constant terms of trade national income in the former decreases to M^fN^f and increases in the latter to M^dN^d. Accordingly, the consumption points of the two countries become C_f' and C_c', which by the principles of vector addition sum to C' on the fixed world's income line M^wN^w. Since production is not affected by

[1] The terms 'overeffected' and 'undereffected' refer to whether the surplus in the balance of payments of the transferor induced by the transfer at constant terms of trade is greater than, equal to, or less than, the transfer itself. If the induced surplus is greater than the transfer, the transferor would show net a balance of payments surplus, in which case the transfer is said to be overeffected and balance of payments equilibrium would require that the transferor's terms of trade improve, and so on.

the impact of the transfer taken at constant terms of trade, the transfer creates an excess demand for good X and excess supply of good Y on international markets, which must be adjusted by a rise in the price of good X and a fall in the price of good Y. Since the domestic country imports X and exports Y, the secondary effect of the transfer is to turn the terms of trade against the home country

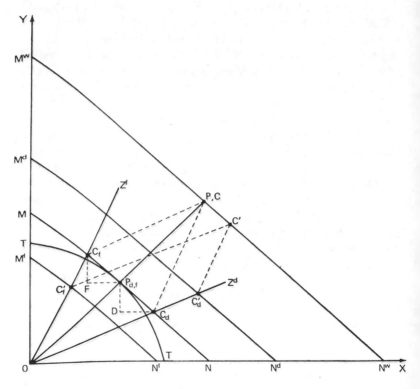

FIGURE 6.C.1

and in favour of the foreign one. Figure 6.C.1. therefore represents the case of a transfer that is overeffected.

It should be clear from the figure that whether a transfer is over- or under-effected depends upon whether the transferee has a marginal preference for its import or export good by comparison with the transferor. In the former case, the transfer creates an excess demand for the transferee's import good at constant terms of trade, which results in a deterioration of its terms of trade (an overeffected transfer), while in the latter an excess demand for the transferee's export good is created by the transfer at constant prices, resulting in a terms-of-trade improvement (an undereffected transfer). It can easily be shown through the use of the calculus (but not geometry) that when the transfer is overeffected the transferee always will gain *net* so long as the initial equilibrium is stable.

CHAPTER 7

The Theory of Tariffs

Depending upon the perspective of the theorist, the theory of tariffs is concerned with the effects of the introduction of tariffs on either the behaviour or potential welfare of the community in circumstances in which free trade would be optimal from the global point of view, or on the behaviour or individual and separate welfares of the groups that comprise the community. In character the analysis is symmetrical with that of Chapter 6. From the point of view of potential welfare, the 'costs of protection' analysis is the mirror image of that of the 'gains from trade', while the movement from free trade to autarky affects the distribution of income in a manner precisely opposite to that of the movement from autarky to free trade. To a large extent, the point from which the analysis commences is the essence of the difference between the analysis of the gains from free trade and the loss from autarktic protection.

One substantive difference, however, is that of the treatment of government. This problem was avoided in the gains from trade analysis by implicitly assuming an initial autarktic tariff and its subsequent removal, in which case the government's tariff revenue remains unaffected by the change at a zero level. The tariffs considered in this chapter will not all be autarktic; hence the question arises as to the disposition of the tariff proceeds. Two assumptions are possible. Either the tax revenue can be assumed to be returned to the community, either directly or indirectly through compensating reduction in other taxes, or the government can be assumed to consume the tariff revenues itself. The older approach to tariff theory treated government as something independent of and apart from the general public so that in imposing a tariff the government was in effect levying a tax on the general public from which no net

220

benefit to the public resulted—the real resources collected by the taxes were simply assumed to disappear without trace from the system. A more modern approach relates government's consumption of tariff revenues to its 'resource-using' function, whereby governments are assumed to provide certain goods for the community that either would not be supplied at all or would be inefficiently supplied if private markets were left to themselves (see Chapter 4). The assumption that tariff revenues are redistributed to the taxpaying community, on the other hand, could be related to the government's 'resource-transfer' function, whereby government is conceived of as enforcing a given distribution of income between private factor-owners in the community, on the assumption that there is community consensus as to what the appropriate distribution of income consists in.

I. THE DISPLACEMENT OF THE OFFER CURVE BY A TARIFF

Prices are determined by demand and supply in international markets; each country's demand for imports in terms of its supply of exports at any given price ratio being reflected by its offer curve. A crucial first step in the theory of tariffs, therefore, is to determine the effect of the tariff on the offer curve of the tariff-imposing country. For this purpose two approaches are possible, depending upon whether a disaggregative or aggregative perspective is adopted. The disaggregative approach to the question of the displacement of the domestic offer curve by a tariff focuses on the positive effect that the tariff has on the individual demands of the separate groups that comprise the community for the import and export commodities, and the analysis conducted with reference to their separate preference functions between the two goods. On the other hand, the community's trade indifference map is the vehicle for analysis when an aggregative perspective to this question is adopted, and the analysis concerned with how the tariff affects the community's desired consumption of importables and exportables. As previously noted, the two approaches must be logically consistent.

The impact of a tariff on the offer curve of the tariff-imposing country in the disaggregative case is developed first. Under conditions of free trade, the internal and world-market commodity price ratios are identical; and the quantities of imports demanded and exports supplied at a particular world-market price ratio are determined by the effects of the identical internal price ratio on the pattern of production, income distribution and demand for commodities. When a tariff is in force, this is no longer true; the internal and external price ratios differ to an extent determined by the tariff rate, and the analysis of the displacement of the offer curve by the tariff can proceed either with respect to constant internal prices, the external price of imports being lowered in proportion to the tariff rate, or with respect to constant external prices, the internal price of imports being raised in proportion to the tariff rate. The former is more convenient for our purposes; hence the effect of a tariff will be to displace the point on the offer curve corresponding to a particular internal price ratio to a new location such that the external price of imports is lower than the internal by the proportion of the tariff in the domestic price, and the quantity of imports demanded is greater, and of exports supplied is less, by the amounts demanded by the recipients of the tariff proceeds. The exact nature of the displacement is determined by the rate of the tariff and the way in which expenditure of the tariff proceeds by their recipients is divided between exportables and importables.

Since the way in which the proceeds of the tariff are spent by their recipients helps to determine the resulting displacement of the offer curve, it is necessary to specify these recipients and their behaviour. For some problems in tariff theory, it is most appropriate to consider the government as a separate consumer with its own preferences, receiving the income from the tariff and spending it according to those preferences. For the present analysis, where the emphasis is on the distribution of income between factors, it is more appropriate to assume that the tariff proceeds are redistributed to factor owners according to some principle of distribution which may range from giving all the proceeds to labour to giving them all to capital, and are spent by the recipients in the same way as would be increments of earned income. This permits the displacement of the offer curve by the tariff to be related to the marginal propensities to spend on imports of the tariff recipients.

The displacement of the offer curve by the tariff is illustrated in Figure 7.1, which reproduces the relevant parts of the central portion of Figure 6.7 with some additional detail. $C_C Q C_L$ define a point on the country's offer curve, which in the subsequent argument will be assumed to be the free-trade international equilibrium point. Now suppose that a tariff is imposed at the proportional rate $C_C R/RQ$, so that for the internal price of imports to be equal to the slope of $C_C C_L$ the external price must be equal to the slope of RC_L; and that the whole proceeds of the tariff are received by capital. With the same internal price ratio and distribution of earned income, and no share in the tariff proceeds to spend, labour's consumption

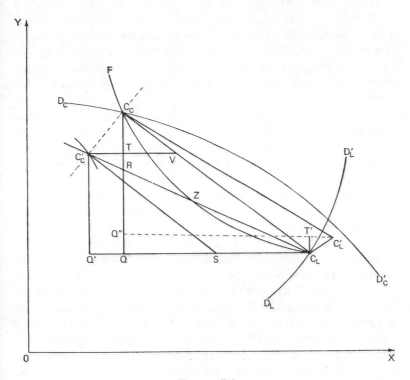

FIGURE 7.1

point must remain at C_L. Thanks to the addition of the tariff receipts to its earned income, however, capital's consumption point will move down its income-consumption line through C_C to C'_C on $C_L R$ extended. C'_C will be capital's equilibrium consumption point, because at this point total consumption of imports $Q'C_L$ from earned income plus tariff receipts is just equal to what can be paid

223

for at world market prices by the excess $C_C'Q'$ of the country's production of exportables over the demand for them from earned income plus tariff receipts. The country exports $C_C'Q'$ of Y in return for $Q'C_L$ of X, of which $SC_L = C_C'V$ accrues to capital as tariff receipts; of these receipts, $C_C'T = Q'Q$ is consumed directly by capital, and TV is used to buy C_CT of Y that would otherwise have been exported. Thus the quantity of X demanded by the country is increased by QQ', and the amount of Y supplied reduced by C_CT, these quantities being determined by the tariff rate C_CR/RQ and the ratio $C_CT/C_C'T$ in which the capital divides marginal consumption between X and Y. This latter ratio is determined by capital's marginal propensity to spend on imports and exports; since these sum to unity, the ratio can be said to depend on either propensity alone.

When all tariff proceeds go to capital, the point on the new tariff-inclusive offer curve corresponding to the same internal price ratio as the point on the free trade offer curve defined by C_CQC_L is defined by $C_C'Q'C_L$, where C_C' is determined by the intersection of the tariff-reduced external price ratio line through C_L with capital's income-consumption line through C_C. In the opposite case, when all tariff proceeds go to labour, the point on the tariff-inclusive offer curve corresponding to C_CQC_L is defined by $C_CQ''C_L'$, where C_L' is determined by the intersection of labour's income-consumption line through C_L with the line through C_C of slope equal to the tariff-reduced external price-ratio. In this case the quantity of X demanded by the country is increased by $T'C_L'$, and the quantity of Y supplied reduced by $C_LT' = QQ''$, these quantities being determined by the tariff rate and the ratio $C_LT'/T'C_L'$ in which redistributed tariff proceeds are divided between exportables and importables, or alternatively by the ratio in which labour consumes physical quantities of the two goods. On either interpretation, the location of the point C_L' on the new tariff-inclusive offer curve, corresponding to C_L on the old one, is determined by labour's marginal propensities to spend on imports and exports. In the general case in which both factors share in the tariff proceeds, the apices of the new triangle corresponding to C_CQC_L will lie on $C_C'C_C$ and C_LC_L' respectively, and the displacement of the offer curve will be determined by the tariff rate, the income-consumption lines of the two factors, and the principle of distribution of tariff proceeds; the last two of these factors can be combined conceptually in the form of a weighted-average income-consumption line, and represented diagrammatically by a line running southeast through C_C or northwest through C_L, whose slope depends on the weighted-average marginal propensities to spend on imports and exports of the tariff-recipients.

Assuming no inferior goods, regardless of how the tariff proceeds are distributed, the quantity of imports demanded is always greater, and the quantity of exports supplied always less, at any point on the tariff-inclusive offer curve than at the corresponding point with the same internal price-ratio on the free-trade offer curve. If the country's free-trade offer curve is of the normal 'elastic' shape, more exports being supplied as well as more imports demanded at a lower price of imports, the quantities of exports supplied and imports demanded at a given external price ratio must be less with a tariff in force than it would be under free trade. Hence in the disaggregative case the impact of a tariff on the tariff-imposing country's demand for imports in terms of its supply of exports is to reduce both exports and imports at any given external price ratio.

This same conclusion is reached in the aggregate case illustrated in Figures 7.2 and 7.3. When a tariff is in force the internal and the external price ratios differ to an extent determined by the tariff rate. For symmetry, the analysis is assumed to start from a given point on the country's free trade offer curve, and considers the point on the new, tariff-inclusive offer curve that corresponds to that point—in other words, the tariff is regarded as reducing the price that is offered to foreigners for trade in the world market, and changing the volumes of exports offered and imports demanded by the country in conformity with that price.

The determinants of the changes in exports offered and imports demanded depend on what role is assigned to government. The case where government consumes the tariff revenues is illustrated in Figure 7.2; that where the tariff revenues are returned to the general public (the only situation considered in the disaggregative case) in Figure 7.3. In either case, the free-trade offer curve of the home country is represented by OH, P_d is the point on it arbitrarily selected for analysis of the shift induced by the tariff, and OT is the free-trade price ratio (internal and external) corresponding to that point. The tariff (which is levied at the proportional rate $P_d R/RS$ on imports) reduces the price ratio offered to foreigners to OT'; the problem is to determine the point P_t which corresponds to the quantities of exports offered and imports demanded by the country at that price ratio in the international market.

The simplest case arises with the assumption of an independent state where the government is assumed to collect and spend taxes

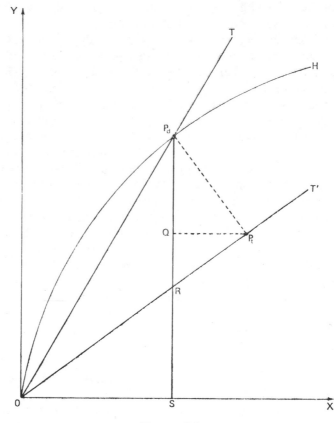

FIGURE 7.2

without its activities influencing the welfare of the community at large. This case is depicted in Figure 7.2. The government collects P_dR in tariff revenue on the volume of private trade indicated by the point P_d, leaving RS as net revenue for the government. The revenue P_dR, however, is spent partly on domestic exportable production of Y, and partly on additional imports of X on government account. In deciding on these expenditures, the government may be assumed to make its decisions on the basis of the prices of the two commodities in the world market rather than the domestic market. The location of the point P_t on the new, tariff-inclusive offer curve corresponding to the point P_d on the free-trade offer

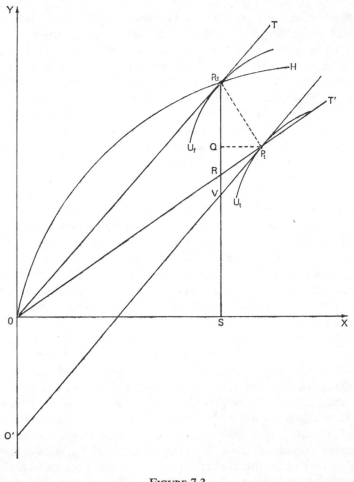

FIGURE 7.3

227

curve may be expressed in terms of the slope of the line from P_d to P_t; this slope is determined by the proportions P_dQ/P_dR and QR/P_dR in which the government divides its expenditure of tariff revenues between exportable and importable goods; alternatively, it is decided by the ratio of physical quantities of Y to physical quantities of X in governmental consumption.

The tariff revenue also can be assumed to be redistributed by the government to the community in general. In the aggregative case, where the community is treated as a single unit whose demand preferences are represented by a community indifference map, consumers are refunded the revenue received from the tariffs paid on their consumption of imports, and are free to spend it as they wish, choosing between the two commodities on the basis of the domestic (not the international) price ratio. This case is depicted in Figure 7.3. In equilibrium the tariff revenue collected on imports must be just sufficient, when added to income earned from production, to induce consumers to choose to consume (at the domestic price ratio) the volume of imports that yields that tariff revenue. In the diagram, OO' (equals P_dV) is the tariff revenue redistributed to consumers; the location of the point P_t on the new tariff-inclusive offer curve corresponding to P_d on the free-trade offer curve (the slope of P_dP_t) is determined by the proportions P_dQ/P_dV and QV/P_dV in which redistributed tariff revenue is divided between exportable goods and importable goods, or alternatively by the ratio in which consumers consume physical quantities of the two goods. On either interpretation, the location of the point P_t on the new offer curve corresponding to P_d on the old one is determined by the community's marginal propensity to spend incremental income on imports. In the disaggregated case, tariff proceeds are assumed to be distributed between owners of labour and owners of capital according to some distribution formula, and the slope of P_dP_t represents a weighted average marginal propensity to spend on imports of the community as a whole, the weights being determined by the distribution formula. Regardless of whether the community is aggregated or disaggregated for normative analysis and how the government is treated, it is obvious that, on the assumption that inferior goods are absent, P_t must lie to the southeast of P_d, which implies that so long as the home offer curve is of greater than unit elasticity at any given external price ratio such as OT', both exports supplied and imports demanded will be less with a tariff than under free trade.

The impact of a tariff on the tariff-imposing country's offer curve has now been specified: in the 'normal' case of an offer curve of greater than unit elasticity the tariff will cause a clockwise rotation of the offer curve through the origin. The effect of this change on both the *equilibrium* internal and external price ratio depends on the shape of the foreign offer curve. If the tariff-imposing country is assumed to be a small one, changes in its demand for imports in terms of its supply of exports *by assumption* will have no effect on the terms of trade; hence the tariff in these circumstances will reduce the volume of the home country's international trade and raise the internal price ratio in proportion to the tariff rate with respect to its free trade level. The small country assumption implies that the shape of the foreign offer curve will be a straight line with positive slope going through the origin.

On the other hand should the foreign offer curve have a less than perfectly elastic shape, the excess supply of imports (excess demand for exports) at the free trade external price ratio would tend to reduce the price of imports and thus improve the tariff-imposing country's terms of trade. Internal prices in comparison with their free trade level rise less than in proportion to the tariff rate in this case, but so long as the foreign offer curve has greater than unit elasticity internal prices can never fall below the free trade level as a result of the tariff—that is, the improvement in the external price ratio due to the tariff can never be such that the relative internal price of imports (the external price plus the tariff) falls in the domestic country. For the internal price ratio, including the tariff, to be equal to free trade internal (and external) prices in post-tariff equilibrium, the foreign country must be willing to offer more exports for less imports at what is for them inferior terms of trade as compared to free trade to precisely balance the tariff-imposing country's offer of less exports for more imports at what for them is superior terms of trade induced by the tariff. This, of course, is inconsistent with the assumption that the foreign offer curve has greater than unit elasticity under which *less* not more exports will be offered for less imports at inferior terms of trade. One theoretically important implication of this analysis, however, is that internal prices, inclusive of the tariff, may fall below their free trade level if the foreign country's offer curve is inelastic. For this, there must be an excess supply of the export good of the foreign country at the external price ratio corresponding to constant internal prices in the home country.

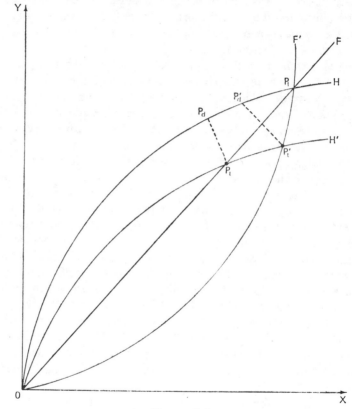

FIGURE 7.4

A comparison of the free trade and post-tariff equilibrium positions of the economy is illustrated in Figure 7.4. OH represents the home country's free trade offer curve and P_f the free trade equilibrium point at the terms of trade given by the slope of OF. The offer curve shifts to OH' as a result of tariff imposition with points P_t and P'_t corresponding to P_d and P'_d respectively; the slopes of the lines P_dP_t decrease from left to right, because as the price of imports falls a higher ratio of imports to exports is consumed. If the small country assumption is made, OF can be taken as the foreign offer curve, in which case the equilibrium point shifts from P_f to P_t. The terms of trade remain the same and the volume of international trade falls. OF' represents the situation of a less than perfectly elastic foreign offer curve with greater than unit elasticity at all points, in which case the equilibrium point shifts from P_f to P_t'. The terms of trade of the home country improve from the slope of OP_f to that of OP_t' and the volume of international trade declines.

The case of a foreign offer curve of less than unit elasticity is

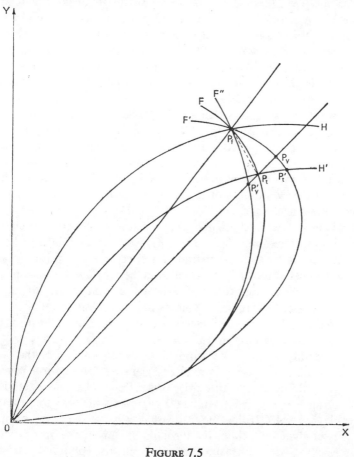

FIGURE 7.5

231

illustrated in Figure 7.5 where once again OH represents the free trade domestic offer curve of greater than unit elasticity throughout and P_f the free trade equilibrium point. The tariff shifts the domestic offer curve to OH' with P_t the point on the tariff-inclusive offer curve corresponding to P_f. Should the foreign offer curve emanating from the origin go through both points P_t and P_f, implying less than unit elasticity in this region, the terms of trade improvement for the home country is such that the tariff-inclusive internal price ratio is the same as that prevailing under free trade, the slope of OP_f. However, should the foreign offer curve pass through P_j rather than P_t, as does OF', there would be an excess supply of good X (excess demand for good Y) at the external price ratio corresponding to the constant internal price ratio in the home country, in which case the terms of trade would fall to OP'_t indicating that the domestic internal price ratio falls in comparison with its free trade level (this is known in the literature as the 'Metzler case'). On the other hand, should the foreign offer curve pass through P'_j rather than P_j, there would be an excess demand for good X at the external price ratio given by the slope of OP_t, and the domestic internal price ratio would be less favourable to the home country than the slope of OP_f, even though the foreign offer curve was of less than unit elasticity in the relevant region. Inelasticity of the foreign offer curve in other words is not a sufficient condition for the 'Metzler case', only a necessary one.

So long as the foreign offer curve is less than perfectly elastic, and the tariff reduces the trade volume demanded by the home country, the latter's terms of trade improve upon tariff imposition. For analytical completeness it will now be worthwhile to consider the case where the imposition of tariff worsens the terms of trade of the tariff-imposing country. A necessary condition for this is that the domestic offer curve be inelastic in the relevant region. This is the famous 'Lerner case'. For the terms of trade to turn against the tariff-imposing country, the imposition and disposition of the tariff proceeds must increase the country's demand for imports beyond what it would be at the same price under free trade. This possibility is illustrated in Figure 7.6 where OT represents the free trade terms of trade line and OH the free trade offer curve of the home country of greater than unit elasticity throughout. Given the specification that P_t must lie southeast of P_d, it is clearly impossible for the

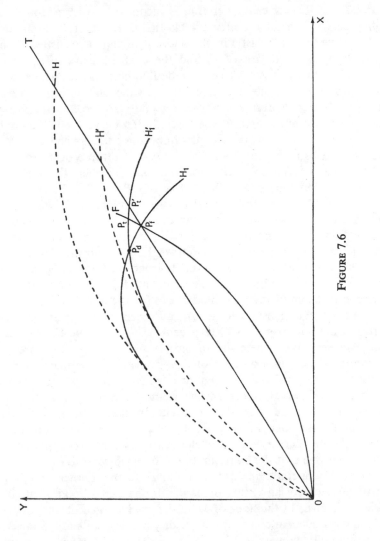

FIGURE 7.6

tariff-inclusive offer curve to cut the free trade terms of trade line anywhere but southwest of the cutting point of the free trade offer curve, indicating an excess supply of the import good at free trade prices. The 'Lerner case' therefore is inconsistent with a domestic offer curve of greater than unit elasticity. However, a domestic offer curve that is inelastic in the relevant region is consistent both with P_d lying northwest of P_t and the tariff-inclusive offer curve cutting the free trade of terms of trade line northeast of where it is cut by the free trade offer curve, as shown by the relationship between OH_1 the free trade domestic offer curve and OH_1' the corresponding tariff-inclusive offer curve. If the foreign offer curve OF is then put through the point P_f, it is clear that imposing a tariff when the offer curve is inelastic in the relevant region can result in a deterioration of the terms of trade, as is the case in Figure 7.6 where the terms of trade shift from the slope of OP_f to that of OP_t.

Both the 'Lerner' and 'Metzler' cases are identical with that where an excess demand for the taxed good is created by an excise tax in a closed economy (illustrated in Figure 4.3); hence both involve an income redistribution effect outweighing a substitution effect, and thus an inelastic demand. In the 'Lerner case' where the income transfer is from the public to the government of the domestic country, there must be an increase in the demand for the import good in the home country at constant terms of trade even though the (internal) price of the import good (X) rises as a result of the tariff; while in the 'Metzler case', where the income transfer is from the foreign public to either the domestic one or domestic government, there must be an increase in the foreign demand for their import good (Y) at constant internal prices in the domestic country and thus a higher relative price of good Y in foreign markets. That an inelastic demand for the good whose price increases is a necessary condition for both the 'Lerner' and 'Metzler' cases is illustrated in Figure 7.6(a). Assume that the community indifference curve U_1 is tangent to the terms of trade line MN at point E. In the 'Lerner' case, the tariff must create an excess demand for the taxed good X at the price ratio given by the slope of MN. The production cost component of the tariff taken at constant commodity prices results in a decrease in community numéraire income from OM to OM' as the community's budget constraint shifts from MN to $M'N'$; the consumption cost component shifts the budget constraint from $M'N'$ to $M'N'$

$(1 - t_x)$. Point E'' represents the consumption point on $M'N'(1 - t_x)$ consistent with the initial consumption of X X_1 in the case where the government spends all the tariff revenue on X (most favourable to X assumption). On the assumption that the taxed good is not inferior in consumption, point E'' can be referred to some point E on $M'N'$ to ascertain the demand elasticity. Given that E'' lies southwest of E, this must be less than unity. Accordingly, for the demand for X to increase as a result of a tariff on X at constant terms of trade, the demand elasticity for the taxed good must be less than unity. This, however, is only a necessary condition for the 'Lerner' case, since the government's marginal preference for the taxed good must be sufficiently strong as well. Figure 7.6(a) also can be used to represent the 'Metzler' case, but now U_1 refers to potential welfare in the foreign country and the import good Y is placed on the horizontal axis with the export good X on the vertical. In the 'Metzler' case, the tariff on X in the home country creates

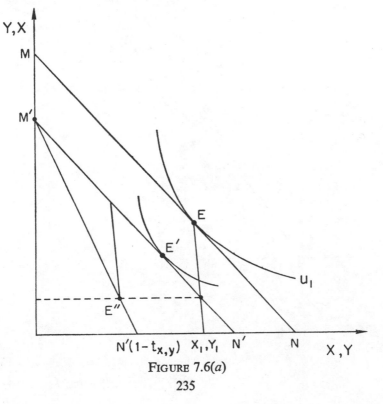

FIGURE 7.6(a)

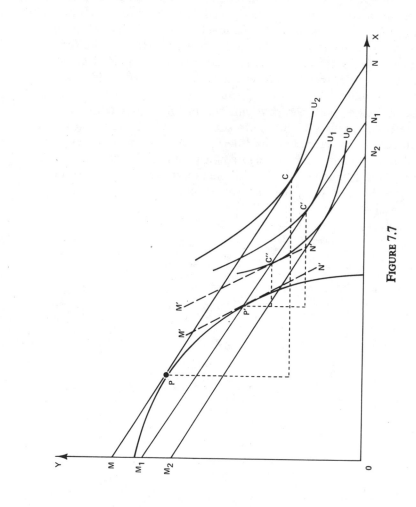

FIGURE 7.7

an excess demand for good Y in the foreign country at constant terms of trade, but a higher internal price of Y in the foreign country. The analysis proceeds in an identical manner to that of the 'Lerner' case, and the conclusion is identical as well. A less than unit elasticity of demand for the import good also is a necessary condition for the 'Metzler' case.

Both the 'Lerner' and 'Metzler' cases are special cases; hence attention must properly concentrate on the normal result that tariffs improve the terms of trade of the tariff-imposing country, raise the internal price of imports above their free trade level and reduce the volume of international trade below that obtaining under free trade. The normative implications of these changes for the potential welfare of the community when the latter is conceived in aggregate terms, and for the individual and separate welfares of the individual groups that comprise the community when a disaggregative perspective is adopted, must now be determined.

II. THE COSTS OF PROTECTION: TARIFFS AND POTENTIAL WELFARE

To focus attention on the potential welfare effects of the rise in the internal relative price of imports due to tariff imposition, the analysis abstracts from terms of trade effects for the time being by employing the small country assumption. Under these conditions, the analysis of the costs of protection is the mirror image of that of the gains from trade with the exception of the treatment of government. For just as the potential welfare gains in moving from autarky to free trade can be partioned into two exhaustive components—the gain from substituting lower for higher cost goods in consumption, and the gain from diverting resources from direct higher cost to indirect lower cost goods that can be imported from abroad—the potential welfare costs of protection, regardless of whether protection is autarktic or not, symmetrically can be partitioned into consumption and production cost components.

The costs of protection analysis is illustrated in Figure 7.7 where under free trade conditions producers and consumers face the given terms of trade line MN under free trade, indicating the aggregate production point P on the community's transformation curve TT and the consumption point C on U_2. The trade triangle is PQC

with exports PQ of good Y being exchanged for QC imports of good X at the international terms of trade given by the slope of MN. A tariff imposed in this circumstance raises the internal price of imports to both consumers and producers in proportion to the tariff rate, thereby creating a cleavage between the domestic commodity price ratio and the fixed external commodity price ratio. For purposes of analysis, it will be convenient first to assess the effect of the increase in the relative price of X to domestic *producers*, assuming that the relative price of X to consumers remains unaffected by the tariff, and then analyse the effect of the increase in the relative price of X to *consumers* having assumed that producers already have adjusted to the price change. In effect, the first part of this analytical experiment is the analysis of a domestic production subsidy to X at an *ad valorem* rate equal to that of the tariff; the second part the analysis of a domestic consumption tax on X of equal *ad valorem* rate. The tariff, in other words, can be considered as being equivalent in effect to the combination of a domestic production subsidy and a domestic consumption tax on importables relative to free trade prices.

The production subsidy element of the tariff, which is reflected by the change in relative producer prices from the slope of MN to that of $M'N'$, results in a shift in the production point from P to P'. Given that in our analytical experiment consumers are assumed to continue to consume at the external price ratio, the consumption point moves from C on U_2 to C' on U_1. The potential welfare effect of the production subsidy (cost) component of the tariff therefore is an inward shift of the consumption possibility curve from MN to M_1N_1, implying a potential welfare loss indicated by the difference between U_2 and U_1.

Given the location of the new production point at P', the effect of the consumption tax element of the tariff is to increase the relative price of imports to consumers at the given external price ratio. This creates an excess supply of imports which can only be adjusted by a fall in the volume of imports since the terms of trade are fixed. The consumption point moves from C' to C'' along M_1N_1, indicating that imports (and thus exports) are decreased as the trade triangle shrinks from $P'Q'C'$ to $P'Q''C''$. Since C' is the Pareto optimal point on M_1N_1, the new consumption point C'' necessarily implies a lower level of potential welfare than at C'. The effect of the consumption

238

tax (cost) component of the tariff therefore is to constrain the community to a Pareto non-optimal position on the restricted consumption possibility curve, which implies a loss of potential welfare equal to the difference between U_1 and U_0. The total loss from the tariff is the sum of the individual losses resulting from its production subsidy and consumption tax components: in terms of good Y the total loss is equal to MM_2, consisting of a production cost component of MM_1 and a consumption cost component of M_1M_2. In terms of potential welfare, the total loss is equal to the difference between the community indifference curves U_2 and U_0.

The trade triangle can serve as a convenient reference point of summarizing the costs of protection analysis. Under free trade the trade triangle is PQC, the slope of the hypotenuse being equal to the external terms of trade and the sides to the volume of exports offered in exchange for the volume of imports at that price ratio. The production cost component of the tariff diminishes the area of the triangle to $P'Q'C'$, since the increased domestic production of importables and decreased production of exportables as the production point shifts in response to the change in internal prices implies a reduced demand for imports in terms of its supply of exports at the fixed terms of trade. The consumption cost component of the tariff further diminishes the area of the trade triangle from $P'Q'C'$ to $P'Q''C''$ because of the decreased demand for imports implied by the higher price of imports to consumers. Thus, as the tariff increases from zero to autarky, the volume of international trade and hence the gains from more efficient consumption and production are reduced. Given that the terms of trade are fixed by assumption these losses in potential welfare due to the reduced volume of trade cannot be offset, either partially or fully, by the effect the tariff might have in improving the terms of trade for the tariff-imposing country. The greater the reduction in the volume of trade from that obtaining under free trade, the greater the loss of potential welfare.

III. THE OPTIMUM TARIFF ARGUMENT

The conclusion that the potential welfare of the tariff-imposing country falls as the tariff is increased by marginal amounts from zero upwards must be amended when changes in the terms of trade from tariff imposition are taken into explicit account. Since the terms of trade depend on the volume of trade, the less the trade volume the greater the terms of trade improvement; losses due to the decreased trade volume being offset, either partially or fully, by gains from the improvement of the terms of trade. Hence the possibility that tariffs can increase the potential welfare of the tariff-imposing country, at least over certain ranges of tariff imposition, must now be considered. Specifically, if an infinitesimally small tariff is introduced and its rate gradually raised, the country's potential welfare will first increase and then decrease as the tariff

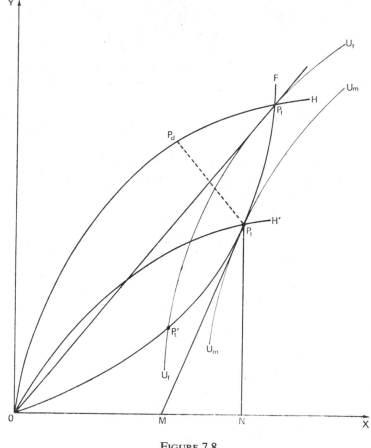

FIGURE 7.8

240

rate increases, eventually falling below the level of potential welfare achieved under free trade. The tariff rate that maximizes potential welfare is known as the optimum tariff, defined by the tangency of a trade indifference curve with the foreign offer curve.

The optimal tariff argument is illustrated in Figure 7.8 where under free trade the home country is in equilibrium at point P_f on the trade indifference curve U_f, indicating a certain level of potential welfare defined by the U curve. So long as the effect of the tariff is to shift the home offer curve as to cut the foreign offer curve between the points P_f and P'_t, the two points at which U_fU_f cuts the foreign offer curve, the tariff must make the community better off in comparison with the level of potential welfare it enjoys under free trade. In effect, the foreign offer curve represents the consumption possibilities open to the home country through trade, any point of which being obtainable through the proper use of the tariff. Presumably the point on the foreign offer curve representing the maximum amount of potential welfare for the home country will be chosen. The tariff required for this purpose shifts the home offer curve through P_t, the point of tangency between the foreign offer curve and the trade indifference curve U_mU_m. The home country gains relative to its free trade position but this gain is at the expense of the foreign country. The theory of the optimum tariff thus represents a specific example of the general principle that the use of monopoly power, though good for the monopolist, is bad for everybody else.

In Figure 7.8, at point P_t the internal price of imports is $p = P_tN/MN$ and the world market prices is $W = P_tN/ON$. The optimum tariff rate is defined by $p = (1 + t)W$, whence $t = (P/W) - 1 = (ON/MN) - 1 = (OM/MN)$; this last ratio is a geometrical measure of the reciprocal of the elasticity of the foreign supply of imports with respect to their price, one of the standard formulas for the optimum tariff.

The theory of the optimum tariff leads into the theory of tariff retaliation, a subject too complex to be pursued further in this analysis. The key points of that theory, however, are worth summarizing briefly. First, even if the foreign country retaliates to the imposition of a tariff by the home country by imposing a tariff of its own, provided that it imposes an optimum tariff, it is not necessarily the case that the home country will be worse off than if neither country imposed a tariff. Second, and consequently, while it can be shown that starting from an optimum tariff in each country both could gain by negotiating reciprocal reductions up to the point at which one country at least practices free trade, it is not necessarily true that both would gain from the restoration of world free trade— to establish free trade to mutual benefit, it may be necessary for one country to offer an income transfer to another.

Finally, the validity of the theory of optimum tariff depends upon the assumption made with respect to the nature of government (see Chapter 4). The traditional argument, illustrated in Figure 7.8, assumes the government redistributes the tariff revenue to the general public, and a variant of this argument, consistent with its underlying assumption about government, is that the tax proceeds are used by government to provide the community with public goods, assuming that the demand for such goods exists (see Chapter 5). The argument would appear to be invalid, however, if an independent government is assumed.

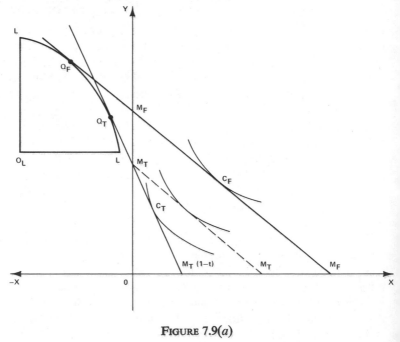

FIGURE 7.9(a)

The consumption point for the community when an 'independent' government is assumed must lie on the home offer curve, and it is clear from the geometry that all attainable points with a tariff are inferior to P_f the free trade point in this respect, since all lie southwest of P_f on the domestic offer curve OH. But, though the private community must be made worse off in terms of potential welfare in this case, it is not clear whether the entire community, including the government, is worse off since the welfare of the 'independent' government undoubtedly increases with its increased consumption. Unless the government's welfare function is specified and, moreover, made comparable to that of the private community, the overall potential welfare effect of the tariff will be *a priori* indeterminate.

IV. TARIFFS AND THE DISTRIBUTION OF INCOME

Except in the 'Metzler case', the effect of the imposition of a tariff is to raise the internal price of imported goods, so promoting a

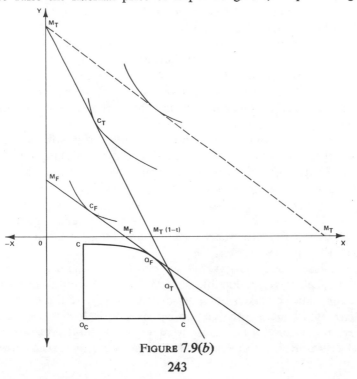

FIGURE 7.9(*b*)

re-allocation of domestic production towards importable goods and away from exports, and in the process raising the relative price of the factor used relatively intensively in producing the country's import good and lowering that of the factor used relatively intensively in producing the country's export good. The effect of a tariff in the normal case, therefore, is to increase the real earnings of the factor used relatively intensively in the 'protected' industry, and to reduce the real earnings of the factor used relatively intensively in the export industry.

The income-distribution effects of a tariff when the government is assumed to consume the tariff revenues, are illustrated in Figure 7.9, where the situation of labour is shown in Figure 7.9(a) and that of capital in Figure 7.9(b). Under free trade the terms of trade are given by the slope of the line $M_F M_F$; M_F is the income of labour in terms of Y the numéraire good, Q_F the production point generating this level of income, and C_F labour's free trade consumption point. The tariff increases the internal price of imports to the slope of labour's production block at point Q_T; the production subsidy component of the tariff shifts labour's production point from Q_F to Q_T and its income drops by $M_F M_T$ as a result. However, $M_T M_T$ is not labour's new budget line since account must be taken of the tariff's consumption tax component. The latter tends to shift labour's budget line to $M_T M_T (1 - t)$ on which labour is in equilibrium at point C_T. Thus, labour unambiguously loses as a result of the tariff.

On the other hand, capital's free trade production point is Q_F, its level of income M_F in terms of good Y and its consumption point C_F. The production subsidy component of the tariff shifts the production point to Q_T and income rises to M_T as a result. The consumption cost component shifts capital's post-tariff budget line to $M_T M_T (1 - t)$; hence capital unambiguously gains from tariff imposition in this case where the government is assumed to consume the tariff revenues.

The case where the government redistributes the tariff proceeds to the factors of production, however, is more complicated since account must be taken not only of the earnings of the productive factor but its share in the tariff proceeds as well. It should be recognized that receipt of any share whatever in the tariff proceeds must increase a factor's real disposable income above its earned income;

hence, making allowance for the distribution of the tariff proceeds does not alter the conclusion that the factor used relatively intensively in the production of imports must enjoy an unambiguous increase in real income as a result of the imposition of the tariff. It does, however, modify the conclusion that the tariff will damage the factor used relatively intensively in the export industry, since that factor may gain more from its share in the tariff proceeds than it loses by the reduction in its real earnings. It is even conceivable that the gain may be so great that the relative share of this factor in the country's income increases, and the relative share of the 'protected' factor decreases.

Such a result is impossible if the foreign offer curve is perfectly elastic, so that the country's terms of trade are fixed and independent

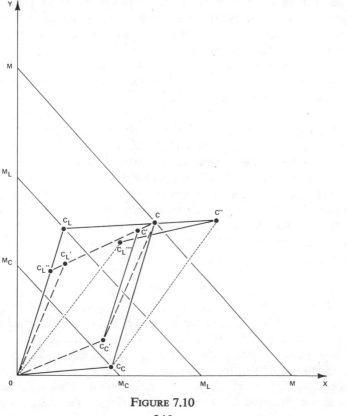

FIGURE 7.10

of its volume of trade; for in this case the country as a whole must lose by the distortion of consumption and production away from the optimum conforming with the equalizing of the internal marginal rates of substitution in production and consumption with the marginal rate of transformation of exports into imports through foreign trade, while the protected factor must enjoy a higher real income. This point is easily illustrated by reference to Figure 7.10 where MM is the free trade fixed terms of trade and $M_L M_L$ and $M_C M_C$ the budget lines for labour and capital respectively. Capital's initial consumption point is given by C_C and labour's by C_L, which by the principles of vector addition must sum to C, the aggregate consumption point on the terms of trade line. Capital is assumed to be made better off by the tariff which in the diagram can be expressed by the movement of capital's consumption point from C_C to C_C'. If the aggregate consumption point remains at point C, labour's consumption point shifts to C_L' as a result, implying a lower real income for labour. The tariff, however, will move the aggregate consumption point southwest, in the diagram from C to C'. Assuming C_C' to be given, this requires a southwest shift in labour's consumption point from C_L' to C_L'', implying a further deterioration in labour's real income position. It is quite clear from the diagram that so long as (*i*) the aggregate consumption point moves due west, due south or southwest, and (*ii*) capital is made better off, that labour's real income must decline even if it receives the entire proceeds of the tariff. It will be possible for the real income position of both factors to improve only when the consumption point assumes a position such as C'', which clearly is impossible if the terms-of-trade are fixed. A necessary condition for both factors to be made better off when the tariff revenues are redistributed to the community therefore is that the foreign offer curve be of less than perfect elasticity.

In conclusion, it should be mentioned that the analysis presented in this section has been concerned (aside from the welfare implications for the foreign country of changes in the terms of trade) only with the effects of the imposition of a tariff on the economy of the tariff-imposing country. In so far as it changes the international price ratio, however, the imposition of a tariff by one country will necessarily alter factor prices, the distribution of income, and the allocation of resources between industries in the other country.

246

The nature of these consequential changes can, however, be readily inferred from the analysis presented of the effects in the tariff-imposing country.

V. THE SYMMETRY BETWEEN IMPORT AND EXPORT TAXES

The theory of tariffs demonstrates that, under 'normal' circumstances, the imposition of a tariff will have the effect of improving the terms of trade of the country imposing it, while raising the internal or domestic price of its imports relative to its exports. It will now be demonstrated that the country imposing the tariff could obtain an identical cleavage between domestic and international prices, improving its own terms of trade while increasing the relative price of the import good to domestic producers and domestic consumers the same amount, by imposing an export tax of equal *ad valorem* rate. This proposition, first stated by Marshall but developed by Lerner, is known as the 'symmetry theorem'.

Assume two countries whose offer curves OH and OF meet at the free trade equilibrium point P_f in Figure 7.11. A tariff of *ad valorem*

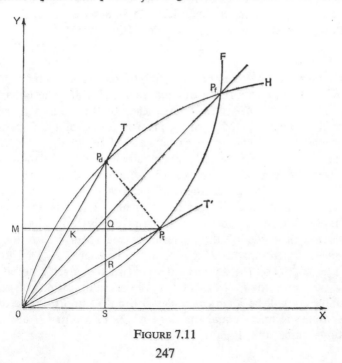

FIGURE 7.11

rate P_dR/RS is imposed by country H, yielding H's government P_dR amount of tariff proceeds in terms of good Y. From the free trade position, the effect of the tariff is to improve $H's$ terms of trade from OP_f to OP_t, while the relative price of imports rises from OP_f to OP_d domestically. In the interests of diagrammatic simplicity H's tariff-inclusive offer curve is omitted from Figure 7.11; further, the home government is assumed to consume the tax revenues, and the public conceived of in aggregative terms.

At the new domestic and international prices, importers in country H demand MQ (equal to OS) amount of good X, while exporters in F offer MP_t, an excess supply on international markets equal to QP_t; and importers in country F demand QS (equal to OM) amount of good Y, while exporters in H offer P_dS, an excess supply of P_dQ. If OT and OT' are to be the equilibrium price ratios, H's government must divide its expenditure of the tariff proceeds (equal to P_dR) between exportable and importable goods in the proportion P_dQ/P_dR, since general equilibrium requires that all excess supply functions equal zero. Let us therefore assume that H's government consumes P_dQ of its exportables, and trades the residual QR for QP_t of good X at international prices (since a given amount of Y is worth more in the international as opposed to the domestic market).

Country H now can be assumed to replace its import tax of P_dR/RS with an export tax of equal rate, P_tK/KM. The equality of P_dR/RS and P_tK/KM is a consequence of the similarity between triangles OSP_d and OMP_t. At the price ratios OT and OT', residents of country F are willing to exchange P_tM of good X for OM of good Y, but country H's residents require only KM of X in exchange for OM, the residual P_tK representing the proceeds from the export tax that accrues to government of country H in terms of good X. Since the price ratios and import demand functions are identical to those above, the symmetry theorem requires only that, in each case, the proceeds of the government be spent in an identical manner. Accordingly, if H's government consumes P_tQ of good X and trades KQ on the domestic market (where a given amount of X is worth more) for P_dQ of good Y, the overall positions of general equilibrium will be identical under either the import or the export tax; domestic prices equal the slope of OT in country H and international prices the slope of OT'.

The equivalence between an import and an export tax of equal *ad valorem* rate, given the same preferences of the government, from the point of view of resource allocation does not imply an equivalence from the monetary viewpoint however. Suppose domestic wages and exchange rates are fixed. An import duty raises the price of imports and, assuming the import elasticity is greater than unity, reduces foreign exchange spending on them. An export duty, assuming greater than unit elasticity, reduces revenue from exports; hence the imports duty improves the balance of payments at current prices, so that balance of payments adjustment requires either exchange rate appreciation or a rise in domestic wages, whereas an export duty can be expected to work the other way round. For a complete answer, however, income effects as well as elasticities must be considered.

The 'symmetry theorem' has several important and interesting policy implications. It explains, for example, why the combined introduction of general import taxes and export subsidies of equal *ad valorem* rate does not distort efficient resource allocation, while introduction of either the tariff or the export subsidy by itself does. The potential welfare effect of either the tariff or the export subsidy is to create a divergence between both the marginal rate of transformation between commodities in domestic production and the marginal rate of substitution between commodities in domestic consumption, and their marginal rate of transformation through foreign trade. But when the tariff and export subsidy are jointly imposed at equal *ad valorem* rate, their combined impact on resource allocation and the balance of payments is identical with that of substituting an import tax for an export tax of equal *ad valorem* rate. This can be easily demonstrated by assuming the initial existence of a general export tax in the economy. Given this tax, the combined imposition of an import tax and an export subsidy at an *ad valorem* rate equal to that of the export tax in effect converts the export tax into an import tax. In equation (1):

$$ET + (IT + ES) = IT \qquad (1)$$

Since the import tax and export tax are identical with respect to their effect on resource allocation by the 'symmetry theorem', the imposition of equal general import taxes and export subsidies does not distort efficient resource allocation. Such imposition will, however, move the domestic country's balance of payments towards surplus provided the trade elasticities have the required values which, on the further assumption that the international adjustment mechanism is functioning, results either in currency application or increase in domestic wages and prices, or converse movements in the foreign country. This is just another way of stating the well-known proposition of international monetary theory that currency depreciation (the analytical equivalent of the combined imposition of equal import taxes and export subsidies), though neutral with respect to resource allocation, causes domestic inflation of money wages and prices in the country of depreciation proportional to the depreciation, provided once again that the trade elasticities have the required values and the monetary authority does not offset the monetary consequences of the balance of payments surplus by compensatory policies. The effect of currency appreciation on the other hand (the combined imposition of equal general import subsidies and export taxes) is equivalent to that of substituting an import tax for an export tax, and thus while neutral with respect to resource allocation, can be expected to move the appreciating country's balance of payments towards deficit, with analogous consequences for internal money prices and wages.

An alternative demonstration of the neutrality of the combined imposition of equal general import taxes and export subsidies, with respect to potential welfare, uses the equivalency of the tariff with a domestic consumption tax and a domestic production subsidy to the import good on the one hand; and the equivalency of an export subsidy with a domestic consumption tax and a domestic production subsidy to the export good on the other. In the 'two by two by two' trade model we have:

$$IT_x = CT_x + PS_x \tag{2}$$
$$ES_y = CT_y + PS_y \tag{3}$$

Starting from an initial position of free trade, if the import tax and export subsidy are of equal *ad valorem* rate, the domestic consumption taxes on the import and export good cancel themselves out, as do the domestic production subsidies to the import and export good. Hence, the overall effect of imposing both the import tax and export subsidy is to leave the initial free trade position undisturbed.

CHAPTER 8

The Theory of Distortions

The theory of tariffs serves as a convenient point of departure for the theory of distortions. The 'cost of protection' analysis of a tariff concludes that under conditions in which free trade is optimal from the vantage point of a single country, including given terms-of-trade, the tariff serves to reduce potential welfare below the maximum possible given the economy's factors of production, technology and the international terms-of-trade; while the 'optimal tariff' argument calls for the imposition of a tariff on imported goods, at the proper rate, for purposes of potential welfare maximization when the economy has some monopoly-monopsony power in international markets and thus can affect the terms at which it trades. These results can be interpreted in either one of two ways. The first is that given the imposition of a tariff, its evaluation, in the one case as a 'distortion' that serves to reduce potential welfare below the maximum possible level, and in the other as a necessary and sufficient condition for potential welfare maximization, obviously depends, in a critical manner, upon the nature of the economic conditions of the community upon which the tariff is imposed. The major policy implication of this interpretation is that, from the perspective of potential welfare, there can be no *a priori* judgements as to the beneficiality or otherwise of a tariff and, by analogous reasoning, of any other tax or subsidy arrangement. The second interpretation is that given the nature of the economic conditions of the community, the potential welfare effect of a tariff will depend upon the *ad valorem* rate at which it is imposed. The major policy implication of this interpretation is that, given these same economic conditions, there must exist some tariff arrangement, free trade included as a special

251

case, that can maximize potential welfare in the community subject to the technical constraints which limit the community's production possibilities.

I. DISTORTIONS DEFINED

Highlighting the conditions or characteristics of the economy as the prime determinant of the potential welfare effect of any given tax or subsidy arrangement, whether levied on international trade or domestic production and consumption, raises the important question as to what these conditions or characteristics precisely consist in. A reconsideration of the well-known first-order marginal conditions of Pareto optimality is helpful for this purpose. These conditions specify that for welfare maximization the marginal social rate of substitution between goods in consumption must be equal to the marginal social rate of transformation between goods in production, and in an open economy include transformation through international exchange as well as transformation through domestic production. If in a market economy the commodity price ratio can be identified both with the marginal social rate of substitution in consumption and the marginal social rate of transformation in production, the first-order marginal conditions for Pareto optimality would be satisfied if both producers and consumers adjust their behaviour to the same commodity price ratio. Accordingly, as defined by economists, a welfare distortion is anything that prevents (*i*) the identification of the commodity price ratio with the marginal social rate of substitution between goods in consumption; (ii) the identification of the commodity price ratio with relative factor costs; and (iii) the identification of relative factor costs with the marginal social rate of transformation between goods in production, which in an open economy includes transformation through international exchange as well.

The assumption that private factor-owners maximize utility insures that the marginal private rate of substitution between goods in private consumption is equal to the commodity price ratio faced by consumers; hence any divergence between the marginal social rate of substitution between goods and commodity prices must be related to a divergence between the marginal *social* and marginal *private* rates of substitution between goods in consumption. Since

252

the source of such divergence can be either external economies or diseconomies in consumption, the presence of such consumption externalities is one of the characteristics or conditions of the economy relevant to a determination of the potential welfare effect of any particular intervention mechanism. Similarly, a divergence between the marginal *social* and marginal *private* rate of transformation between goods in production, due to the presence of externalities in production, which makes marginal cost as it appears to private producers differ from marginal social cost, constitutes a relevant characteristic of the economy to consider since it prevents the identification of the commodity price ratio with the marginal social rate of transformation between goods.

Divergencies between marginal social value and marginal social cost can be related to such institutional factors as the nature of competition and tax and social policy. The presence of monopoly or oligopoly conditions in the production of a good, for example, raises the price of that good to consumers above its marginal private cost of production, just as would the imposition of an excise tax on that good. Taxes on particular factors of production in particular industries, and specific applications of minimum-wage laws for whatever motive, also raise commodity price above the marginal private cost of production and, in addition, serve to reduce the production possibilities of the economy below their maximum level, because of the inefficiency they induce in factor allocation. For an accurate assessment of the potential welfare effect of any particular intervention mechanism, full acount must be taken of all existing obstacles to the achievement of Pareto optimality, 'distortions' as they are called by economists, including those exclusively related to the foreign trade sector of the economy.

Given the existence of a distortion in the economy, potential welfare maximization requires policies that are designed to 'equal' the distortion in the sense of completely offsetting it. Such interventions are known in the literature as 'first-best' policies. There can be circumstances, however, where 'first-best' policies are ruled out, because the policy-maker, for one reason or another, is denied the use of the policy-instrument necessary for its effectuation. The best the policy-maker can do in this situation is partially offset the distortion. Policies geared to maximize potential welfare subject to both the constraint imposed upon the economy by technology and its fixed factor endowment, and the political constraint that prevents use of the policy-instrument required for a 'first-best' solution, are know in the literature as 'second-best' policies. The analysis in the first part of this chapter deals with 'first-best' policies; that in the second with 'second-best' policies.

II. PRINCIPLE FOR 'FIRST-BEST' POLICIES

The specification of the factors relevant to the determination of the potential welfare effect of a tariff or a domestic tax of subsidy, specifically the nature and number of pre-existing distortion, raises the question of the existence of any general 'rule of intervention' for determining the 'first-best' policy in any given situation. The answer is that there does exist such a rule, this being that the intervention must be imposed at the precise point at which the distortion occurs, and be equal to the degree of distortion, for it is only in this case that the inequality related to the distortion will be removed without a new inequality being created in the process. Hence, if the inequality is related to a distortion in domestic commodity markets, the 'first-best' policy must be in domestic commodity markets; if related to a distortion in domestic factor markets, the 'first-best' policy must be in domestic factor markets; and if in the foreign trade sector the 'first-best' intervention must be in the foreign trade sector of the economy.

To demonstrate, consider the optimal tariff argument where under conditions of free trade $DRS = DRT \neq FRT$, because of the existence of monopoly-monopsony power in international markets.[1] The optimal tariff removes the inequalities existing between both DRS and FRT, and DRT and FRT, without creating an inequality between DRS and DRT. On the other hand, had DRS been equated with FRT at the expense of the equality between DRS and DRT—as would be the case with a domestic consumption tax on importables— or DRT equated with FRT at the expense of the equality between DRS and DRT—the case of a domestic production subsidy to

[1] DRS refers to the marginal rate of substitution between commodities in domestic consumption; DRT to the marginal rate of transformation between commodities in domestic production; and FRT to the marginal rate of transformation between commodities in foreign trade. All of these are defined in terms of the amount of good Y given up in exchange for a unit increment of good X.

importables, it would be impossible to predict on *a priori* grounds—that is, without comprehensive empirical information on the tastes and technology of the economy—whether the economy had been made better off or not by the change, since in these cases the intervention would imply the substitution of one violation of the Paretian optimality conditions for another. Switching Paretian inequalities rather than removing them results in these cases, because the distortion exists in the foreign trade sector and the intervention mechanism is in the domestic commodity market, and thus does not achieve the required discrimination between foreign and domestic consumption or production.

III. RELEVANCE AND APPLICABILITY OF OPTIMAL INTERVENTION ANALYSIS

The fact that a 'first-best' policy exists in any given situation does not mean that such a policy will be adopted by government. The relevance of optimal intervention analysis vitally depends on the assumption that legislators do not normally know what makes for improvement of potential welfare, are interested in maximizing potential welfare, and thus would be prepared to act on better information if it could be provided. If this assumption was not accepted by economists, their research on economic policy would have to be oriented differently, depending on the theory of government adopted. For example, if governments were assumed to be all-wise and all-knowing, research on tax policy might be concerned with inferring from actual tax structures either the divergences between social and private costs, and benefits, discovered by the collective wisdom of the legislators to exist in the economy; if conceived of as an extra-market mechanism for redistributing income, research would focus on a determination of the political power of the various economic groups existing in the community as measured by their capacity to exact transfers of income from their fellow citizens or, alternatively, the consensus existing in the community as to what the appropriate distribution of income consists in. On either assumption, government would have little use for optimal intervention strategies developed by economists: in the first case, because such strategies already would be known to them; in the second, because in a world consisting of groups that are exclusively concerned with their own economic welfare, aggregate concepts such as potential welfare would have little relevance.

The pertinency of the theory of distortions critically depends on whether the use of aggregate concepts of economic well-being is acceptable to the community-at-large. Indeed the concept of optimality itself is defined in such terms. An optimal production tax, for example, maximizes the potential welfare of the community given its productive factors and technology, but may very well decrease the real income of one of the groups in the community. Surely to that group the tax is not optimal, nor can it be so considered by the group that gains since, most likely, further gains for that group would be possible from further tax changes. It is only from the perspective of maximizing the utility level of one group while that of the second group is held constant—an aggregate criterion—that the tax or subsidy arrangement can be said to be optimal.

Even if one were to insure the relevance of the analysis by assuming a liberal government subscribing to and interested in potential welfare maximization, but who is ill-informed as to how to achieve it, the applicability of the theory of distortions to the 'real world' is likely to be hampered by a variety of complicating factors. For one, there is the identification problem. The government must be able to identify distortions in the economy and to accurately specify their *quantitative* extent. The optimal tariff argument, for example, calls for the imposition of a tariff at the correct *ad valorem* rate. Too low a rate will increase potential welfare but not to the maximum extent, while too high a rate may even imply a level of potential welfare below that obtaining under free trade (this explains the general predisposition of economists for low tariff rates even when the existence of monopoly-monopsony power in international markets is strongly suspected). Second, the theory abstracts from the matter of administrative costs by assuming that government intervention is a costless operation—that is, that there is no cost attached to the choice between a tax and a subsidy. This assumption ignores the empirical consideration, frequently introduced into arguments about protection, that poor countries have considerably greater difficulties in levying taxes to finance subsidies than they have in levying tariffs on imports. Thirdly, there is the problem of political constraints. Experience has taught us that politicians of developed as well as less-developed countries prefer subsidizing local enterprise through tariff protection rather than a direct subsidy precisely because of the indirect and thus less obvious nature of the former; furthermore, it may be less embarrassing and politically more acceptable to use a tariff to subsidize an industry and blame the need of such subsidization on alleged unfair methods used by foreigners than to use a direct subsidy financed by internal taxation and implicitly accept the blame oneself. Finally, international treaty obligations—the GATT for example—might arbitrarily prohibit certain forms of industrial assistance to the benefit of other forms whose effect on the favoured industry can be more or less the same. Any or all of these factors—the identification problem, administrative costs and political constraints—can prevent a welfare-oriented government from applying an optimal intervention strategy, and the latter two in particular can make such a government more receptive to the use of a tariff even in circumstances where a purely domestic intervention mechanism is called for by optimal intervention strategy.

Solution of the identification problem awaits the development of more refined techniques of empirical investigation and thus for the moment at least represents a formidable obstacle to the applicability of optimal intervention analysis. Administrative and political costs, on the other hand, pose no such problems for they can be incorporated into the welfare calculus along with the potential welfare effects of the alternative methods of promoting favoured industries in determining the optimal strategy in any given situation unless, of course, such costs are deemed to be infinite, in which case certain forms of support can be ruled out by assumption and the focus of the problem reoriented to a determination of the optimal intervention strategy subject to the postulated constraint. As mentioned above, such interventions are known as 'second-best' policies, and are considered in the latter part of this chapter.

IV DISTORTIONS IN COMMODITY MARKETS; 'FIRST-BEST' POLICIES

The first type of distortion to be discussed is that existing in the domestic market for commodities which has the effect of creating a divergence between the marginal rate of substitution between goods in consumption and their marginal rate of transformation in production. One possible source of such divergence is the presence of externalities in consumption which prevents the identification of the marginal *social* rate of substitution between goods in consumption with their relative price ratio; another is the presence of externalities in production which prevents the identification of the marginal *social* rate of transformation between the goods in production with their relative price ratio; and the third the presence of monopoly or oligopoly conditions in the production of a good, which has the effect of raising the price to consumers above their marginal cost of production. The latter two types of distortions are similar in that both cause a divergence between market price and social opportunity cost with price being equal to marginal social value; while market price and social opportunity cost are equal with the first type of distortion, but price does not reflect marginal social value.

If a closed economy is assumed, the problem of the 'first-best' intervention in the presence of a distortion in domestic commodity markets is greatly simplified since a tax (subsidy) on production is equivalent in effect to a tax (subsidy) on consumption and *vice versa*. Both tend to reduce (increase) consumption and production of the taxed (subsidized) good. Hence, a marginal subsidy is warranted on either the consumption or production of a good that yields external economies in either consumption or production, as well as on a good whose price is greater than marginal cost because of imperfect competition or taxation; while a tax is required in the opposite circumstance. Furthermore, since in the two-sector model a tax on one good is equivalent to a subsidy on the other, and *vice versa*, a tax on the good not subject to the distortion would be an optimal intervention in the first case, and so on.

Allowing for international trade enriches the analysis not only because it distinguishes the effect of a domestic production tax from one on domestic consumption, but also because explicit consideration of the foreign trade sector permits the introduction of taxes on trade—export and import taxes—as distinct from taxes on domestic production and consumption that do not discriminate between foreign and domestic sectors. The rules for optimal intervention, however, become more complex.

For example, in the case where externalities in consumption make the marginal social rate of substitution diverge from the private, a tax or subsidy on consumption is required rather than a production tax or subsidy since the latter breaks the equality between domestic and foreign rates of transformation without restoring the equality between the marginal social rate of substitution in consumption and the common transformation rates in production. Similarly, a consumption subsidy only makes matters worse when either external economies in production or monopoly power exists since a consumption subsidy creates a distortion in consumption without eliminating the pre-existing production distortion. Finally, and probably empirically the most important, in neither of the above cases will the tariff be the optimal intervention mechanism for, as noted above, the tariff only can remove the inequality related to the initial distortion by introducing a new inequality in the process.

The 'first-best' policy in the presence of a distortion related to domestic production, that has the effect of raising the market price of the commodity in which the country has a comparative advantage above its social opportunity cost is illustrated in Figures 8.1 and 8.2. If good Y is assumed to be the export good, the commodity market distortion raises the price of Y above its social opportunity cost which in the diagram is reflected by the fact that the market price ratio at which a particular combination of X and Y is produced is less steep with reference to the horizontal than the slope of transformation curve at the production point. In the absence of the opportunity to trade, the country will produce more X and less Y than would be socially optimal; the closed-economy equilibrium is represented in Figure 8.1 by the point P, C, the slope of MM corresponding to the market price ratio, and that of RR to the true comparative cost ratio or marginal social opportunity cost. The opening of trade at an international price ratio indicating that the country's true comparative advantage lies in Y has two alternative possible results, according to the relation between the international price ratio and the closed-economy market price ratio. This relation may indicate either an apparent comparative advantage in X, in which case the country specializes in the wrong direction, or an apparent comparative advantage in Y corresponding to the country's true comparative advantage, in which case the country specializes in the right direction but to a suboptimal extent.

The first case is represented in Figure 8.1 by the international price ratio II, which leads the country to the production equilibrium

259

P' and the consumption equilibrium C', involving the export of X, in which the country is at a true comparative disadvantage. The point P' necessarily represents a lower value of output at the international price ratio than the closed-economy production point P; but C' may lie on either a lower indifference curve than the closed-economy consumption point C, or a higher one, the latter possibility

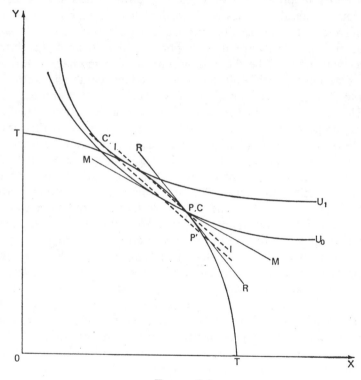

FIGURE 8.1

being illustrated in the diagram. In other words, trade leads to a production loss and a consumption gain, and the latter may or may not offset the former.

The argument for protecting by a tariff in this case is that the country will gain by imposing a tariff on imports to raise their price to consumers above the world price, compensating for the distortion that makes the apparent cost of domestically produced importables exceed their true social cost. (Alternatively, the country could levy a tax on exports to compensate for the distortion that makes their true social cost exceed their apparent cost.) Since the country's true comparative advantage lies in the good it imports, the imposition of an import tariff (or an export duty) at a rate just sufficient to compensate for the distortion would effect a return to self-sufficiency at the production and consumption equilibrium P,C, since a tax on trade cannot reverse the direction of trade. The effect of the tariff would be to increase the value of the country's output at the international price ratio, but, as the diagram exemplifies, the resulting pattern of consumption might yield a lower level of economic welfare than would be attained in the absence of protection. In short, the imposition of the tariff to correct the distortion of domestic prices from opportunity costs achieves a production gain at the expense of a consumption loss, and the net effect may be a gain or a loss, by comparison with free trade. Thus free trade in the wrong direction may be superior to protection designed to correct a distortion of domestic market prices; which policy is actually superior depends on the magnitudes of the distortion of domestic prices from opportunity costs and the difference between the closed-economy exchange ratio and the international exchange ratio, and the shape of the community's preference system. The optimal intervention in this case would be a production subsidy to Y effectuated either directly or indirectly by taxing the production of X, until the slope of the international terms-of-trade line is tangent to the economy's transformation curve.

The second case is illustrated in Figure 8.2 where at the international price ratio II the country's apparent comparative advantage lies in the commodity in which it has a true comparative advantage, and the opportunity to trade leads to the production equilibrium P' and consumption equilibrium C', involving the export of commodity Y. P' necessarily represents a higher value of national output at the international exchange ratio than the closed-economy production point P, so that the country enjoys both a consumption gain and a production gain from trade; but the volume of international trade falls short of the optimum level, owing to the excess of the price of Y over its comparative cost.

In this case, the arguments for intervention in international trade to correct the distortion of domestic prices would indicate an export subsidy on Y (or import subsidy on X). The same policy might be recommended to overcome the inability of the tariff to promote exports in the circumstances of the case previously considered. (In either case, to be effectively a subsidy on trade rather than on production, the export subsidy would have to be accompanied by measures preventing re-importation.) The introduction of such a

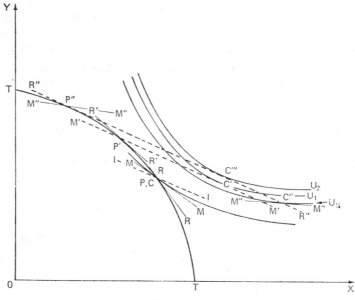

FIGURE 8.2

subsidy at a rate just sufficient to offset the distortion would lead to the production equilibrium P'' and the consumption equilibrium C'' shown in Figure 8.2 the new domestic price ratio being represented by $M''M''$. The subsidy would necessarily raise the value of output at the international exchange ratio above what it would be under free trade, but, as the diagram illustrates, it might nevertheless lead to a consumption pattern yielding a lower level of welfare than that enjoyed under free trade, owing to the consumption loss induced by the effect of the subsidy in raising the domestic relative price of the exported good Y above the world market price. In order to achieve the maximum attainable economic welfare (C'' in Figure

8.2), the country should subsidize production of Y (or tax production of X) at a rate sufficient to compensate for the domestic distortion, without discriminating between domestic and foreign consumers by a tax (in the first case) or subsidy (in the second case) on international trade.

The foregoing analysis lumps together distortions originating in external economies and diseconomies, and distortions originating in imperfectly competitive market organization; and it assumes that the distortions are independent of the governmental intervention, so that intervention can be designed to offset them. This assumption is legitimate for the first type of distortion, but of doubtful validity for the second. Monopolistic practices are generally intimately interrelated with commercial policy, and there is reason to believe that producers often collude to exploit the profit opportunities created by protection. Where this is so, the attempt to offset monopolistic distortions by protective interventions in trade (taxes or subsidies on trade) may well be offset by increased distortions, so that interventions generates a consumption loss without a countervailing production gain; the same reaction could render nugatory the attempt to employ optimal intervention in the form of production taxes or subsidies. In these circumstances, the only effective means of achieving maximum economic welfare would be a direct attack on the source of the distortion, through trust-bursting policies, although it is worth noting that genuine free trade may be the most effective policy for controlling monopoly.

To this point attention has focused on distortions related to domestic production, that have the effect of raising the market price of a good above its social opportunity cost, in which case the economy is constrained to a sub-optimal production point under free trade conditions. The alternate situation of externalities in consumption also is worth considering both because it is likely to have considerable empirical significance and for analytical completeness. This case is illustrated in Figure 8.3 where at the international terms-of-trade given by the slope of II the production point is P and the consumption point C on U_2. However, because of external diseconomies associated with the consumption of the import good X, the marginal social rate of substitution in consumption is less than the marginal private rate; hence point C does not represent the optimal consumption point on terms-of-trade line II. Geometrically,

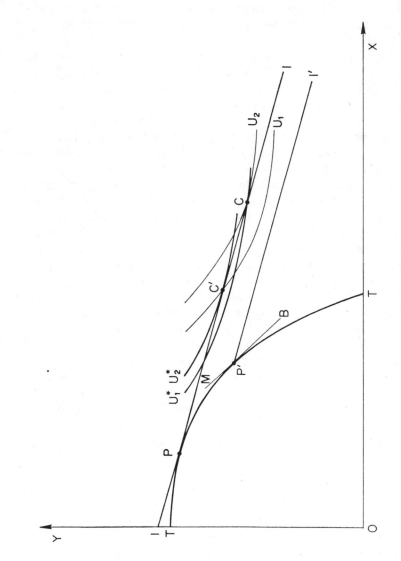

FIGURE 8.3

264

the diverence between the social and private evaluation of the various consumption bundles can be expressed by drawing the community indifference curve U_1^* through point C with a less steep slope than U_2 at that and every other point. U_1^* is one contour of the community indifference map $U_1^*, U_2^*, \ldots$, etc. that represents the real rather than the apparent potential welfare of the community. It is clear that from the perspective of the former point C' not C is the optimal consumption point for the economy on II. To achieve this point, the relative price of X must be increased to the slope of the apparent community indifference curve U_1 at point C'. A domestic consumption tax imposed at a proper rate is sufficient for this purpose and does not alter the production point P. A tariff, on the other hand, that increases the relative price of X paid by consumers to the slope of MB also raises the domestic price of import-substitutes to producers; hence the production point shifts to P'. There is a consumption gain and a production loss with the tariff in this case, corresponding to its consumption tax and production subsidy components, and which effect dominates cannot be determined on the basis of *a priori* reasoning alone—that is, without the relevant empirical data. In Figure 8.3, for example, it is clear that the economy will be better off with free trade than with a tariff that raises the relative price of imports to the slope of MB, since the consumption possibility line in this case lies everywhere below U_1^*, the real potential welfare level obtainable under free trade. But the economy might be better off with a tariff than with free trade if the tariff were imposed at a lower *ad valorem* rate.

In summation, let us now generalize the above results concerning domestic commodity market distortions and the optimal intervention mechanism. If in an open economy there exists a distortion such that two of the variables DRS, DRT and FRT are equal while the third has a different value under free trade, the policy geared to equate the three—the 'first-best' policy—will be to intervene with a tax or subsidy precisely at the point at which the distortion occurs. In domestic commodity markets, should a distortion exist with respect to the domestic consumption or production of commodities, such as $DRS \neq DRT$ either because of consumption externalities ($DRS \neq FRT = DRT$) or production externalities and monopolistic practices ($DRS = FRT \neq DRT$), the first-best policy in the first case is to impose a consumption tax or subsidy that does not discriminate between imports and domestically produced goods, while a domestic production tax or subsidy is required in the second case. On the other hand, should the distortion exist only with respect to the domestic consumption and production of importables—that is, in the foreign trade sector—, so that $DRS = DRT \neq FRT$, the tariff is the first-best solution.

V. FACTOR MARKET DISTORTIONS

The argument so far has been concerned with the rules of optimal intervention in the presence of domestic distortions in commodity markets. The problem, however, often is more complex than presented, since a distortion that makes the market price of a good greater than its social opportunity cost may not originate in the commodity market, but may be a reflection of a distortion existing in domestic factor markets that makes the price of a factor of production greater than its social opportunity cost to the economy. Such a distortion, which creates a divergence between relative factor prices in the different industries in the economy, may be due to the exercise of market power through unionism, factor taxation or social regulations that differs by industry (e.g. minimum-wage laws). It is one of three possible types of factor market distortions, each to be discussed in turn. The other two types are factor immobility and factor price rigidity.

1. *Factor Price Differentials*

The effect of the factor price differentials type of factor market distortion is twofold: first, it makes the allocation of factors between industries inefficient, so that production is below the maximum attainable—in terms of the two-sector model, the transformation curve is pulled in toward the origin, except at the extreme points of specialization on one or the other commodity. Second, it will normally cause the market exchange ratio between the commodities to differ from the social opportunity cost ratio, the only exception occurring when a distortion in the market for one factor is exactly offset by an opposite distortion in the market for the others. Specifically, if the marginal productivity of one factor in one industry exceeds its marginal productivity in the other industry, the price of

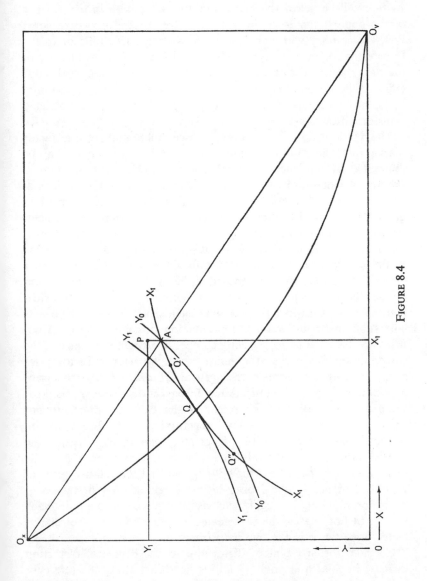

FIGURE 8.4

267

the commodity produced by the former industry must exceed its opportunity cost. Consequently, in this case, the country's economic welfare will be below the maximum attainable both in the absence of the opportunity to trade and under free trade for two reasons: first, the country will be on a transformation curve inferior to the transformation curve that would be available to it in the absence of the distortion in the factor market; and second, owing to the discrepancy between the commodity price ratio and social opportunity costs, the country will choose a suboptimal position on that restricted transformation curve.

The relationship between a factor price differentials type of factor market distortion and the shape of the transformation curve can be illustrated by reference to the Edgeworth-Bowley box diagram in Figure 8.4 where units of labour are represented on the horizontal axis and units of capital on the vertical, the origin with respect to good X in the northwest corner of the box, that with respect to good Y in the southeast corner, the contract curve southwest of the diagonal (X being capital-intensive, Y labour-intensive), and the transformation curve with reference to the origin in the southwest corner of the box consequently northeast of the diagonal. For every point on the efficiency locus, there is a corresponding point of the transformation curve. Consider point Q on the efficiency locus which has its corresponding point P on the production possibility curve. Since firms are assumed to be perfectly competitive profit maximizers, the slopes of the isoquants at Q must equal the relative factor price ratio, i.e. with reference to the vertical, $dL/dK = P_k/P_L$ (the price of capital in terms of labour). A factor market distortion exists if for some reason relative factor prices in the two industries are not equal, i.e. $P_k/P_{L_x} \neq P_k/P_{L_y}$. Two general types of distortions are possible; the first when P_k/P_{L_x} is greater than P_k/P_{L_y}, so that the relative price of capital is higher in the capital-intensive sector; the second when P_k/P_{L_x} is less than P_k/P_{L_y}, so that the relative price of capital is higher in the labour-intensive sector. The first type of distortion moves Q to a point such as Q', the second to a point such as Q''. In both cases, the tax creates a wedge between the relative factor price ratios in the two industries.

Consider the first type of distortion. As the degree of distortion increase in this case, point Q moves northeast along the reference isoquant X_1X_1 forcing P down the vertical PX_1. With the price of capital increased in industry X by the tax, efforts to substitute labour for capital in that industry require that the relative price of capital fall in both industries and hence a decrease in the *difference* between factor intensity ratios in the two industries. The capital-intensive industry X becomes less capital-intensive and the labour-intensive industry Y becomes less labour-intensive. There is some degree of distortion—in this case given by the ratio of the slopes of the isoquants $x_1 x_1$ and $y_0 y_0$ at point A—which will cause P and Q to coincide. Furthermore, because of the assumed homogeneous nature of the production functions, a degree of distortion that places one point of the contract curve on the diagonal will do so for all points, and therefore for all points on the corresponding transformation curve as well. Both the contract curve and the production possibility curve become contiguous with the diagonal in this case, and the factor intensity ratios are equalized in the two industries. Should there be any further increase in the degree of distortion, the contract curve swings over northeast of the diagonal and the transformation curve becomes concave outward. Factor intensities reverse as commodity X becomes labour-intensive and commodity Y capital-intensive. Thus, the existence of a factor market distortion may cause industry X to use physically more labour-intensive techniques than industry Y even if, in the absence of distortions, it would be the capital-intensive industry.

Let us now assume a closed economy and that the initial factor market distortion raises the relative price of labour in the labour-intensive sector (Y) of the economy; hence, the relative price of good Y is greater than its social opportunity cost. The distortion itself is assumed to either be a tax on the use of labour in Y only or a tax on the income of labour in Y only. Table 8.1 (i) lists the effects of various interventions in commodity and factor markets on efficient factor allocation and efficient consumption given the tax on labour in Y. Appropriate interventions in the commodity market can maximize the level of economic welfare attainable from the distorted transformation curve but do nothing to expand the transformation curve to the maximum level obtainable with the economy's given supply of productive factors and the state of the technical arts. A tax on good X or a subsidy to good Y can remove the excess burden in commodity markets if levied at the appropriate rate, but have no effect on efficient factor allocation since the commodity market intervention attacks the symptom of the factor market distortion but not the distortion itself.

There are four ways in which efficient factor use can be achieved in this situation. Either the factor subject to the distortion (labour in industry Y) can be subsidized in the industry in which the distortion occurs, or that factor can be taxed in the other industry (a tax on labour in industry X); or the other factor can be taxed in the industry in which the distortion occurs (a tax on capital in Y), or the other factor can be subsidized in the other industry (a subsidy to capital in X) to the extent necessary to restore the equality between the relative factor price ratios in the two industries. Of these, only the first two simultaneously eliminate the associated distortion of commodity prices from opportunity costs; the others accentuate the distortion in commodity markets (with both a tax on capital in Y and a subsidy to capital in X, the divergence between the price of Y and its social opportunity cost increases). Accordingly, two 'first-best' solutions to the problem of an initial distortion in factor markets which makes the price of labour in industry Y higher than its social opportunity cost are subsidization of labour in industry Y and taxation of labour in industry X.

There are, however, more than two 'first-best' solutions to the problem in this circumstance. If the tax on capital in Y were combined either with a tax on commodity X or a subsidy to commodity Y, and if a subsidy to capital in X were combined either with a tax on commodity X or a subsidy to commodity Y, Pareto optimality would obtain in both factor and commodity markets even though each of the measures in themselves would not have the desired effect. Six optimal *combinations* are possible in all. These are listed in column (a) of Table 8.1 which when added to column (b), the tax on labour in industry Y (T_{Ly}), gives the neutral taxes in column (c). $[S_{Ly} + T_{Ly}]$ and $[T_{Ky} + S_y + T_{Ly}]$ both are equivalent to no tax; $[T_{Lx} + T_{Ly}]$ and $[S_{Kx} + T_x + T_{Ly}]$ to an income tax on labour; $[T_{Ky} + T_x + T_{Ly}]$ to a general commodity tax; and $[S_{Kx} + S_y + T_{Ly}]$ to an income subsidy to capital. All taxes and subsidies within a bracket are of equal *ad valorem* rate.

The case where a factor price differentials type of factor market distortions exists in the context of an open economy can now be investigated. Given the existence of a distortion in the market for a factor requiring its marginal productivity to be higher in the

TABLE 8.1 *The Welfare Effect of Commodity and Factor Interventions Given a Tax on Labour in Industry Y*

(i)

	(a) Effect on Efficient Factor Allocation	(b) Effect on Efficient Consumption	(c) Overall Effect of Change
$T_x = S_y$	No	Optimum	Improvement but less than optimum
$T_y = S_x$	No	Worse	Deterioration
T_{Ky}	Optimum	Worse	*A priori* indeterminate but less than optimum
S_{Ly}	Optimum	Optimum	Optimum
T_{Lx}	Optimum	Optimum	Optimum
S_{Kx}	Optimum	Worse	*A priori* indeterminate but less than optimum
T_{Kx}	Worse	Optimum	*A priori* indeterminate but less than optimum
S_{Lx}	Worse	Worse	Deterioration

(ii)

'First Best' Combinations

(a)		(b)		(c)
S_{Ly}	+	T_{Ly}	=	no tax
T_{Lx}	+	T_{Ly}	=	income tax on labour
$[T_{Ky} + T_x]$	+	T_{Ly}	=	general commodity tax
$[T_{Ky} + S_y]$	+	T_{Ly}	=	no tax
$[S_{Kx} + T_x]$	+	T_{Ly}	=	income tax on labour
$[S_{Kx} + S_y]$	+	T_{Ly}	=	income subsidy to capital

industry in which the country has a comparative advantage, the opportunity to trade may have either of the two consequences analysed in connection with distortions in the commodity markets; and, as demonstrated in that analysis, the protectionist policy of remedying the effects of the distortion by an export or import duty (if the country specializes on the commodity in which it has a comparative disadvantage) or an export or import subsidy (if the country specializes on the commodity in which it has a comparative

271

advantage) may make the country either worse off or better off than it would be under free trade. A policy of subsidization of production of the commodity overpriced by the distortion, or of taxation of production of the other commodity, would maximize the economic welfare attainable from the restricted transformation curve. The important point, however, is that all of these policies aimed at offsetting the distortion by operating on the prices received by producers of commodities would leave the country on a transformation curve restricted by the inefficiency of factor use induced by the factor market distortion. As in a closed economy, this particular cause of suboptimal economic welfare could be eliminated in four different ways—by a tax on the use in one industry or subsidy on the use in the other of either factor, the rate of tax or subsidy being chosen to exactly offset the distortion. But only two of these—a subsidy on the use of the factor subject to distortion in the industry in which its marginal productivity is required to be higher, or a tax on its use in the other industry—would simultaneously eliminate the associated distortion of commodity prices from opportunity costs, the other two accentuating the distortion in the commodity market. If combinations of taxes, and taxes and subsidies, are allowed, six 'first-best' combinations are possible, as listed in Table 8.1. If not, the attainment of maximum economic welfare requires subsidization or taxation of the use of the factor subject to distortion; taxation or subsidization of commodity production can maximize welfare subject to the inefficiency of factor use but cannot correct that inefficiency; taxation or subsidization of commodity trade not only fails to eliminate inefficiency in factor allocation but may even reduce welfare, given the inefficiency of factor allocation, below what it would be under free trade.

2. *Factor Immobility and Factor Price Rigidity*

For the analysis of arguments for protection by a tariff derived from immobility of factors and downward rigidity of factor prices, it is convenient to pose the problem in terms of whether the opening of the opportunity to trade make a country worse off when these conditions exist, so that a prohibitive tariff would secure a higher level of welfare than could be attained under free trade, even though in reality the argument for protection on these grounds usually arises when trade is already established and the international price of imports suddenly falls. The difference of assumptions merely simplifies the problem without altering the conclusions.

As Haberler in his classic article 'Some Problems In The Pure Theory of International Trade' has shown, there is a fundamental difference between the effects of immobility of factors, combined with flexibility of factor prices, and of downward rigidity of factor prices, whether combined with immobility or not. As the analysis of the standard model of trade shows, the country would enjoy a consumption or exchange gain from trade even if production remained at the closed-economy equilibrium point. Production would remain at that point if factors were completely immobile but their prices were perfectly flexible; if factors were partially mobile, production would shift to some point within the transformation curve but necessarily entailing a higher value of production at world market prices, that is, yielding some production or specialization gain. It follows that so long as factor prices are flexible, immobility of factors cannot prevent the country from being better off under free trade than with protection. The fundamental reason for this is that immobility does not by itself entail a distortion of the first-order conditions of Pareto optimality. So long as factor prices are flexible, and immobility is taken as an immutable fact of life factor prices will reflect the alternative opportunity costs of factors to the economy; hence there is no domestic distortion to be offset by protection, and protection will simply introduce a distortion of the marginal conditions for optimality in foreign trade.

Downward rigidity of factor prices does introduce a distortion, if such rigidity does not reflect a perfectly elastic supply of the factor in question (derived, for example, from an infinite elasticity of substitution between leisure and consumption) but instead reflects institutional limitations on voluntary choice (imposed, for example, by conventional pricing of labour services or collective bargaining). Analysis of the effects of downward rigidity of factor prices requires definition of the terms in which factor prices are rigid downwards, since factor prices may be rigid in terms of one commodity or the other or of the utility level enjoyed, and consideration of various possible combinations of downward price rigidity and immobility.

If factor prices are rigid in terms of X and both factors are immobile, production will remain where it was in the absence of

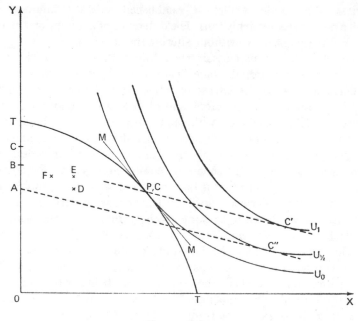

FIGURE 8.5

trade (at point *P* in Figure 8.5). The result will be the same as with factor price flexibility, since the marginal productivities of the factors in the *X* industry in terms of *X* are unchanged, while the marginal productivities of the factors in the *Y* industry are unchanged in terms of *Y* but greater in terms of *X*, because the price of *X* in terms of *Y* has fallen as a result of trade. If both factor prices are rigid in terms of *Y* or of constant-utility combinations of *X* and *Y*, and both factors are immobile, production of *X* will cease, and both factors used in producing *X* will become wholly unemployed (the economy will produce at point *A* in Figure 8.5, level with *P*,*C*). This result follows from the fact that the marginal productivities of the factors in the *X* industry will be unchanged in terms of *X* but lower in terms of *Y* or any combination of *X* and *Y*, because the price of *X* in terms of *Y* has decreased as a result of trade. Since the value of each factor's marginal product is now below its price when the factors are combined in the ratio optimal at these factor prices, and

274

since neither factor price can fall to induce factor substitution and raise the marginal productivity of the other factor, the cost of production X must exceed its price at any positive level of output.

If both factor prices are rigid (in terms of X or of Y or of a constant-utility combination of X and Y), and both factors are perfectly mobile, production of X will cease and factors will be transferred into production of Y. Some of the factor used intensively in producing X must, however, become unemployed, so that production of Y will be less than the maximum possible production shown by the transformation curve, since full employment of both factors necessitates a reduction of the price of that factor in terms of both commodities, according to the well-known Stolper-Samuelson analysis. The amount of unemployment of the factor in question will be greater, and the increase in production of Y less, if factor prices are rigid in terms of Y than if they are rigid in terms of X, since a given factor price expressed in Y now buys more X, and the marginal productivity of the surplus factor in the Y industry can fall if factor prices are rigid in terms of X but not if they are rigid in terms of Y. (The extremes are represented for illustrative purposes by points B and C in Figure 8.5; if factor prices are rigid in terms of utility, production of Y will fall somewhere between these points.)

If both factors are immobile but the price of one of them is flexible, whereas the price of the other is rigid in terms of Y or of a constant-utility combination of X and Y, production of X will not cease altogether; instead, enough of the rigid-priced factor in that industry will become unemployed to lower its ratio to the other factor to what is consistent with its rigid price. Obviously, the unemployment of that factor and the decrease in production of X will be greater if that factor's price is rigid in terms of Y than if it is rigid in terms of a constant-utility combination of X and Y, and in the latter case will be less the less important is Y in the factor's consumption. (This case is represented in Figure 8.5 by the single point D, in the same horizontal line as A and P,C.) If one of the factors is mobile, and its price is rigid in terms of X or of a constant-utility combination of X and Y, whereas the other factor is immobile and flexible-priced, some of the rigid-priced factor will transfer to the Y industry, increasing output there. The transfer will proceed to the point where its effect in raising the ratio of the mobile factor to the other in the Y industry lower the marginal productivity of the mobile factor in the Y industry to the level set by its price-rigidity. (This case is represented by point E in Figure 8.5; E may be vertically above D as in the diagram or to the left of it, and must correspond to a higher value of output at world prices than D.) If one of the factors is mobile and flexible-priced, whereas the other factor is immobile and its price is rigid in terms of X or of Y or of a constant-utility combination of X and Y, production of Y will increase and of X decrease as compared with the case of immobility of both factors; production of X may or may not cease entirely depending on the elasticities of substitution between the factors in the two industries and on the terms in which the immobile factor's price is rigid. (This case is represented by point F in the diagram, and may or may not correspond to a higher value of output than at D.)

Whatever the combination of factor immobility and factor price rigidity assumed, production will be altered to some point in the interior of the transformation curve corresponding to production of less X and possibly no more Y than in the closed-economy equilibirum (except for the extreme case of complete immobility and factor price rigidity in terms of X already noted). This does not, however, necessarily imply that free trade makes the country worse off than it would be under the self-sufficiency obtainable by a prohibitive tariff. It may, or it may not. Figure 8.5 illustrates the possibility of the country's being better off with free trade than with a prohibitive tariff even in the extreme case in which production of X ceases altogether, with no consequent increase in the production of Y, owing to a combination of complete factor immobility with factor price rigidity. In this case, as the diagram shows, the country could be made still better off than under free trade by subsidizing production of the initial output of X sufficiently to permit the factors being paid the minimum prices they demand, but trading at the international exchange ratio. In the less extreme cases, more complex forms of subsidy may be necessary to achieve the ouput combination that has the highest value at the international exchange ratio attainable under the relevant restrictions on factor mobility.

VI. 'SECOND-BEST' POLICIES

The analysis to this point has been concerned with policies that are designed to completely offset an assumed distortion in the economy and thus maximize potential welfare subject to the economy's fixed factor endowment and technology. These are the so-called 'first-best' policies. There can be expected to be situations, however, when 'first-best' policies are ruled out—for example, when with fixed terms-of-trade and a domestic consumption or production distortion, the policy-maker is confined to the use of tariffs; or when with variable terms-of-trade, tariffs or their equivalent are prohibited to the policy-maker, so that he is confined to the use of either domestic consumption taxes or domestic production subsidies. In both cases it can be shown that, in general, it will be possible to improve on the level of economic welfare attainable under free trade by the imposition of a tax on international trade in the first case, and a tax on domestic consumption or a subsidy on domestic production in the second; but the welfare-maximizing rate of tax or subsidy in either case will not correspond to the degree of the given distortion. Unlike 'first-best policies, 'second-best' ones cannot completely offset the distortion and thus make good the total potential welfare loss due to the distortion.

The economic effects of the application of tariffs to correct distortions in the domestic economy can be analysed with the assistance of Figure 8.6 The diagram depicts the demand and supply conditions of a good which is obtainable through importation at the price P_f, and is produced domestically subject to a distortion which makes the private cost of production and thus the supply curve in monetary terms $S_M S_M$ greater than the true domestic supply curve reflecting real costs of production $S_R S_R$ by a proportioned d of the latter.

Under free trade and in the absence of government intervention the economy will produce Oq, and import $q_1 q_4$ of the good. Because of the distortion that causes $S_R S_R$ to lie below $S_M S_M$, the country is over-trading, producing too little of the import substitute and by implication too much of the export good. It could thus replace $q_1 q_2$ of imports by additional domestic production at a saving real cost equal to the area A, which area represents the reduction of real income below the attainable maximum due to the distortion. In order to achieve this result, the government should give a subsidy on production at the rate d, the proportional excess of the private over the real social cost at Oq_2. But this 'first-best' policy is ruled out by assumption. If instead the government levies a tariff on imports at the rate d, it will obtain the cost saving A, but it will also restrict total consumption by the amount of q_3q_4, and this will entail a loss of consumer's surplus equal to the area B. Area B may be greater or less than the area A, depending approximately on whether q_3q_4 is greater or less than q_1q_2, that is, on whether the demand curve is less or more steep than the supply curve. If area B is greater than area A, the correction of the domestic distortion by the impo-

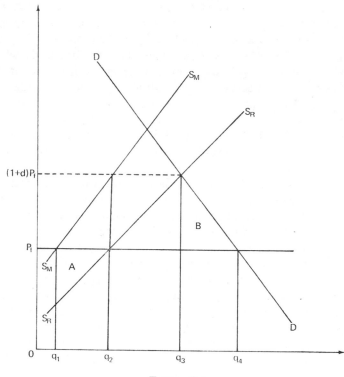

FIGURE 8.6

sition of the tariff results in a net economic loss by comparison with the situation under free trade. But it can be demonstrated that even in the case where area B is greater than area A, it will in general be possible, through the use of the tariff, to increase the level of potential welfare by comparison with its free trade level if the choice open to policy-makers is between no tariff and some tariff. In other words, there will always be a positive tariff between zero and the distortion rate that gives us a 'second-best' welfare optimum.

Consider a marginal increment of the tariff over its zero level. The consequent production gain to the economy is equal to the difference between the fixed terms of trade and the real costs of producing the import substitute, that is, between P_f and $S_R S_R$; while the consumption loss is equal to the difference between the fixed terms of trade and marginal rate of substitution is consumption given by the difference between the demand curve and P_f. It is clear from the diagram that the former distance becomes smaller and smaller as the tariff increases by marginal increments and is zero when the rate of the tariff is equal to the rate of distortion; while the latter distance becomes greater and greater as the tariff increases. Since the marginal production gain from tariff increments is a decreasing function of these increments, while the marginal consumption loss is an increasing function of tariff increments, there must exist a positive rate of tariff between zero (where marginal gain is greater than marginal loss) and the rate of distortion (where marginal gain is less than marginal loss) that equates marginal production gain with marginal consumption loss. The imposition of this positive rate of tariff is the 'second-best' policy, and by necessity must be less than d the degree of domestic distortion.

The case where the terms of trade are variable but the assumed prohibition on the use of tariffs confines the policy-maker to the use of a domestic consumption tax is considered next. In this circumstance, it is useful to compare the efficient consumption possibility frontier under two conditions; (1) that where the home country through its monopoly power is able to equate the domestic marginal rate of transformation between goods with the marginal rate of transformation through trade, and (2) that where the country is constrained to equate its marginal rate of transformation at home with the world terms of trade, as must be the case when the terms of trade are fixed. The use of a tariff is required to achieve a desired position on the former frontier; the use of a domestic consumption tax, a desired position on the latter. Since it can be demonstrated that the efficient consumption locus obtainable with a tariff lies everywhere outside that obtainable with a domestic consumption tax, use of the latter can only be considered as a 'second-best' policy. Still the level of potential welfare attainable with a domestic consumption tax will be greater than that obtainable under free trade with no taxes given that the terms of trade are assumed to be variable.

The construction of the efficient consumption locus when the home country is assumed to be able to equate its domestic marginal rate of transformation with the marginal rate of transformation through foreign trade is illustrated in Figure 8.7. Consider the

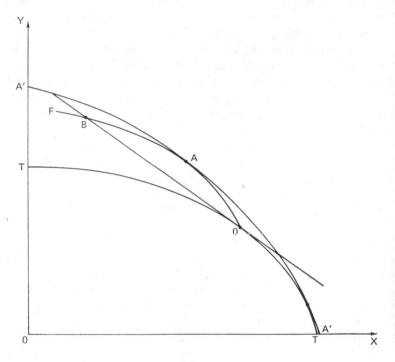

FIGURE 8.7

arbitrarily determined point O on the domestic transformation curve TT. Place the origin of the foreign offer curve OF at this point and determine the point A where the slope of the foreign offer curve (the marginal transformation rate through trade) is equal to the slope of TT at O (the domestic marginal transformation rate). This point must lie on the efficient consumption locus, since it represents the maximum amount of Y consumption possible for a given amount of X consumption, given the home transformation and the foreign offer curve. The locus of such points, known as the Baldwin envelope curve, is derived by moving the origin of the foreign offer curve along *TT*, keeping its axes parallel to those of the transformation curve; and is represented in Figure 8.7 by the curve *A'A'*.

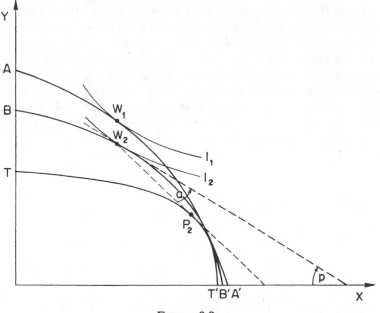

FIGURE 8.8

The efficient consumption locus under the free trade conditions that the domestic marginal rate of transformation be equal to the world's terms of trade must lie inside the efficient locus *A'A'*. Consider the situation in Figure 8.7 when the origin of the foreign offer curve is put at point *O* on *TT*. The point *B* at which the tangent line *OB* intersects the foreign offer curve indicates a point on the free-trade efficiency locus. It is clear from the Figure that there exists several points on *A'A'* that are superior to *B* in the sense that they involve either a greater amount of consumption of one good for a given amount of consumption of the other, or greater consumption of both goods. By moving the foreign offer curve northwest along *TT*, the locus of *B* consumption points can be traced out, lying everywhere inside *A'A'*.

Given the efficient consumption loci $A'A'$ and $B'B'$ in Figure 8.8, the optimal consumption points W_1 and W_2 are determined by the community's indifference map. W_1 represents the 'first-best' solution in this case, but it requires the use of a tariff which by assumption is denied the policy maker. W_2 is the 'second-best' solution and requires the use of a domestic consumption tax, since the slope of the indifference curve at W_2 is flatter than the only price ratio (terms of trade) W_2P_2 consistent with the attainment of this point. The wedge a between the domestic price ratio p (the slope of the indifference curve at W_2) and the world terms of trade W_2P_2 is equal to the necessary rate of tax. Point W_2 clearly is superior to the no-tax free-trade point, which would have to lie northwest of W_2 on $B'B'$, since the no-tax terms-of-trade line must be flatter than W_2P_2 and thus the production point northwest of P_2.

CHAPTER 9

Exogenous Change in an Open Economy

The analysis of the present chapter is an extension of that of Chapter 3 to an open economy. Changes in a country's demand preferences, factor endowment and technology all are considered under conditions of free trade, where instead of investigating the effect of such change on the excess demand and supply of commodities in domestic markets at constant commodity (and factor) prices, using the assumption of stability of equilibrium to predict the direction of the price change required to restore equilibrium, the effect of parametric change on the excess demand and supply of commodities in international markets (demand for imports and supply of exports) is taken at constant terms-of-trade, using the assumption of stability of equilibrium in international markets and the constancy of the foreign offer curve to predict the direction of the change in the terms and volume of trade required to restore equilibrium. The two analyses differ in the respect that while excess demand and supply must result in, and be adjusted by, a change in the commodity price ratio in a closed economy, changes in the volume of imports and exports can fully absorb changes in the demand for imports and exports in an open economy without the benefit of a terms-of-trade adjustment if the country in question is assumed to be too small to affect the prices it pays for imports and receives for exports in world markets. The analytical method of considering the effect of parametric change on the domestic country's demand for imports at constant terms-of-trade thus allows both for the isolation of the effects of parametric change and the development of concepts for the analysis of these effects, concepts which are directly applicable to economies whose terms-of-trade are fixed by the world market and, if the foreign offer curve is unchanged, a determination of the direction of change of the terms and volume of trade when variable terms-of-trade can be assumed.

I. THE SYMMETRY BETWEEN THE CLOSED AND OPEN ECONOMY ANALYSIS OF PARAMETRIC CHANGE

As in the case of a closed economy, three types of exogenous change are considered: changes in demand preference, factor accumulation and technical change. The closed and open economy analyses of demand preference change are compared in Figure 9.1 where the change specified is such that, at constant commodity prices, labour consumes more Y, the good that uses labour relatively intensively in its production, than X. $M_L M_L$ and $M_c M_c$ represent the respective initial budget constraints of labour and capital and C_L and C_c their initial consumption points, which by the principles of vector addition must sum to the aggregate consumption point C. Point P, the initial aggregate production point, coincides with C in closed economy equilibrium, in which case the economy's transformation curve is tangent to the national income line MM at point C. The aggregate production and consumption points diverge in an open economy, however; in Figure 9.1 point P represents the initial aggregate production point and point C the economy's initial consumption point, so that the economy exports PQ of good Y in exchange for QC of good X at the terms-of-trade given by the slope of MM.

The specified change in labour's utility function requires that labour's consumption point shift northwest along $M_L M_L$ inducing a northwest shift in the aggregate consumption point along MM. The effect of such change in an open economy is to reduce the excess demand for X and excess supply of Y at constant terms-of-trade, just as in a closed economy, illustrated in Figure 3.1, the effect is to create an excess demand for Y and excess supply of X at constant commodity prices. In a closed economy this impact effect is adjusted by a rise in the relative price of good Y, a shift in production towards Y and away from X, and a rise in the absolute (and relative) price and marginal product of labour combined with a fall in the price and marginal product of capital. An identical adjustment takes place if the terms-of-trade in an open economy are variable: since

Y is the export good the terms-of-trade shift in favour of the domestic country, the output of Y increases and that of X decreases, and labour enjoys an increase in both its absolute and relative price and marginal product while capital suffers a decrease in its price and marginal product (had Y been the import good, a terms-of-trade deterioration

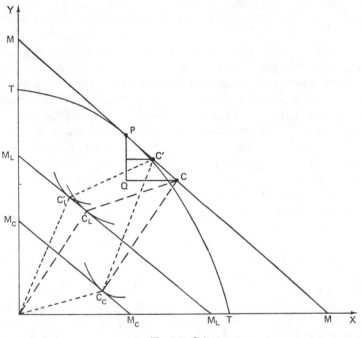

FIGURE 9.1

would have increased the price of labour and decreased that of capital). Thus in a closed economy and an open economy with variable terms of trade, capital unambiguously loses both in terms of numéraire income and utility (capital remains unaffected by the change in open economy with fixed terms of trade); but while labour registers a corresponding gain in terms of numéraire income in these cases, the effect of the preference change on its utility level is *a priori* indeterminate unless labour's old and new utility functions can be commonly indexed. Similarly, the effect of the preference change on the community's potential welfare is *a priori* indeterminate if an aggregate evaluation perspective is adopted.

285

A similar result obtains, that the adjustment to the impact of parametric change is not affected by the allowance for international trade, if such change is assumed to consist in factor accumulation rather than a shift in demand preference. In this case the main question that arises from the disaggregative point of view is whether the conclusion of both the closed economy one-sector Hicksian model and the two-sector model of general equilibrium continues to hold, that an increase in the quantity of a factor must lower its price and raise that of the other factor, when the economy engages in international trade. The answer is that it does provided that the terms-of-trade are variable. As the analysis of Figure 3.5 demonstrates, an increase in the stock of a productive factor taken at constant commodity prices in a closed economy creates an excess supply of the commodity that uses that factor intensively, and an excess demand for the other good, because on the one hand the demand for both goods increases if neither good is inferior in consumption, while on the other the output of the good that uses the accumulating factor intensively in its production rises and that of the other good falls (the Rybczynski Theorem). An excess supply of the commodity that uses the accumulating factor intensively consequently requires a fall in the relative price of that commodity, and therefore in the relative price, and the marginal product in terms of both commodities, of the factor whose quantity has increased.

In the context of an open economy, factor accumulation reduces the supply of exports and demand for imports at constant terms-of-trade if the country imports the commodity that uses the accumulating factor intensively in its production, and increases the supply of exports and demand for imports if the country exports that commodity. In either event, the effect of factor accumulation in an open economy with variable terms-of-trade will be to lower the price of the commodity that uses the accumulating factor intensively in its production—in the first case because it reduces the demand for imports, in the second because it increases the supply of exports of that commodity at constant terms-of-trade—and thus reduce the absolute and relative price and marginal product of the factor whose quantity has been increased, and increase the price and marginal product of the other factor.

The analysis of factor accumulation in the context of an open

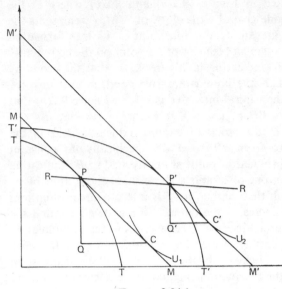

FIGURE 9.2(a)

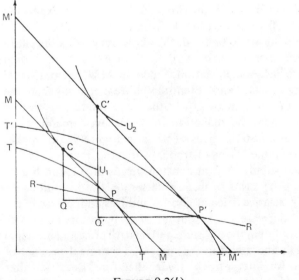

FIGURE 9.2(b)

economy is illustrated in Figures 9.2(*a*) and 9.2(*b*) where at the constant terms-of-trade given by the slope of *MM*, *P* represents the economy's initial aggregate production point on its transformation curve *TT*, and *C* its aggregate consumption point on the community indifference curve U_1, indicating in Figure 9.2(*a*) that the economy exports *PQ* of good *Y*, the labour-intensive good, in exchange for imports *QC* of *X*, the capital-intensive good; in Figure 9.2(*b*) that the economy exports *PQ* of good *X* in exchange for imports *QC* of *Y*. An increase in the stock of capital induces a shift in the transformation curve from *TT* to *T'T'*; specifically, at constant terms-of-trade, the production point shifts from *P* to *P'*, indicating an increase in the output of *X* and a decrease in the output of *Y*. Given the assumption that neither good is inferior in consumption, factor accumulation increases the demand for both goods, and the entire increase in national income *MM'* accrues to the accumulating factor. An increase in the demand for both goods on the consumption side, and an increase in the output of *X* and decrease in the output of *Y* on the production side, combine to imply in Figure 9.2(*a*) a *reduction* in the demand for imports and supply of exports at constant terms-of-trade, and in Figure 9.2(*b*) an *increase* in the demand for imports and supply of exports at constant terms-of-trade. The former is reflected by a reduction, the latter by an expansion of the dimensions of the trade triangle from *PQC* to *P'Q'C'*.

Should the terms-of-trade be fixed, the above represents the entire adjustment to the increase in capital in both cases, with capital gaining the entire increase in national income *MM'*, labour's real income remaining constant and potential welfare increasing from the level indicated by U_1 to that by U_2. In the more interesting case of variable terms-of-trade, the reduction in the excess demand for *X* and supply of *Y* at constant terms-of-trade in Figure 9.2(*a*) implies an improvement in the terms-of-trade, while the increase in the demand for *Y* and supply of *X* at constant terms-of-trade in Figure 9.2(*b*) implies that the terms-of-trade deteriorate. But in both cases, the increase in the relative price of good *Y* induces an increase in the output of *Y* and decrease in the output of *X* by comparison with point *P'*, and thus a fall in the absolute and relative price and marginal product of capital, and a rise in the price and marginal product of labour. Allowing for international trade, therefore, does not alter the result obtained when factor accumulation is assumed to take

288

place within the context of a closed economy, at least if variable terms-of-trade are assumed. An interesting by-product of this analysis is the clear demonstration it gives of the efficacy of simplifying assumptions: abstracting from international trade and demand considerations in no way alters the conclusion of the one-sector Hicksian model, that an increase in the quantity of a factor must lower its price and raise that of the other factor.

But while the adjustment to the impact of parametric change implies an increase in the price of labour and decrease in the price of capital regardless of whether the economy exports or imports the commodity that uses the accumulating factor (capital) intensively in its production, the potential welfare effect of change will be different in the two cases. This is because the terms-of-trade improve in Figure 9.2(a) and deteriorate in Figure 9.2(b). If an initial equal increase in potential welfare due to capital accumulation at constant terms-of-trade is assumed in the two cases, this implies that the increase in potential welfare will be greater when the accumulating factor is intensive in the production of the import by comparison with the export good, and it is even possible in the latter circumstance (consistent with the stability conditions) that the country in question can be made absolutely worse off in terms of potential welfare as a result of factor accumulation (in this case, gainers could not compensate losers for their losses without becoming losers themselves.) This will be the case if the potential welfare decreasing effect of the deterioration of the terms-of-trade dominates the welfare increasing effect of factor accumulation taken at constant terms-of-trade, what Jagdish Bhagwati has described as 'immiserizing growth'. (The analogy between this case and that when the accumulating factor loses in a closed economy should be noted.)

Finally, the case of technical improvement must be considered in the context of an open economy. Similar to other types of parametric change, allowance for international trade simply transfers the changes in the demand and supply of commodities induced by technical improvement from the domestic to the international market. If, for simplicity, technical improvement is assumed to take place in one industry alone, on the production side of the analysis, technical progress that is neutral or saves the factor that is intensive in the production of the good in which it occurs must increase the output of that good, and reduces that of the other good, at constant *commodity* prices, though it is *possible* for technical progress to reduce the output of the good in which it takes place if it sufficiently saves the factor that is unintensive in the production of that good (labour-saving technical change in the capital-intensive good or capital-saving technical progress in the labour-intensive good). With respect to consumption, the restoration of the initial relative cost ratio originally altered by technical change involves lowering the relative price of the factor used less intensively in the industry where progress takes place, and raising the price of the other factor. Thus more than the whole of the increase in national income due to progress at constant commodity prices goes to that factor which is used intensively in the industry in which the progress has occurred. In consequence, the proportion of expenditure out of national income on the good for which this factor's marginal propensity to consume is relatively high rises, and it is even possible that total expenditure on the good preferred by the factor from which income is redistributed will fall; it will do so if the reduction in consumption due to straight income redistribution exceeds the increase in consumption due to the *net* increase in national income which accrues to the favoured factor. But it seems permissible to exclude this possibility, along with that of technical progress that reduces the output of the good in which it occurs, as exceptional ones; hence, at constant commodity prices, technical progress can be considered to create an excess demand for the commodity not subject to technical improvement, and an excess supply of the other good.

In the context of an open economy technical progress in one industry implies either an increased or decreased dependence on foreign trade according to whether such change occurs in the import or export commodity. Should the export commodity be that subject to technical change, the country's supply of exports and demand for imports increases at constant terms-of-trade, while the opposite occurs when technical change takes place in the import good. In either event (assuming variable terms-of-trade), as in the case of the closed economy (illustrated by Figure 3.10), the adjustment to the impact of technical change implies a fall (rise) in the price of the commodity subject (not subject) to technical change, a decrease (increase) in its output, and a fall (rise) in the price of the factor intensive in its production which serves to offset to some extent the rise (fall) in the price of that factor necessary for taking the effect of technical change at constant commodity prices. But as in the case of factor accumulation, though the adjustment to the impact of technical change is invariant to whether such change takes place in the import or export commodity, the evaluation of the adjustment from the aggregate perspective of potential welfare differs. The increase in potential welfare due to technical change at constant commodity prices will be augmented by an improvement in the terms-of-trade should technical change take place in the import commodity, and diminished should the export commodity experience technical improvement, in which case 'immiserizing growth' due to technical progress also is possible.

II. THE EFFECT OF ECONOMIC GROWTH ON INTERNATIONAL TRADE

The analysis of parametric change in an open economy has an important application to a problem of considerable past and present —the effect of economic growth on international trade. The central question of economic interest is whether growth will increase the demand for imports, taken at constant terms-of-trade, more than proportionally to the increase in the value of national product, also measured at constant terms-of-trade, in the same proportion as, or less than proportionally to the increase in the value of the national product. From the growing country's point of view, the question is whether growth makes the country relatively less self-sufficient, no more or less dependent on trade, or relatively more self-sufficient. From the point of view of the foreign country, the question is whether the market for its exports expands more than proportionally to, at the same rate as, or less than proportionally to the growth of this country. The three possibilities can be conceptualized in terms of three types of growth: pro-trade-biased growth, which increases the country's demand for imports and supply of exports more than proportionally to output; 'neutral' or unbiased growth, which increases the country's demand for imports and supply of exports in proportion to output; and anti-trade-biased growth, which increases the country's demand for imports and supply of exports less than proportionally to output, all taken at constant terms of trade. Figure 9.3 represents a particular type of unbiased growth, in which

291

production and consumption of each of the two goods, and therefore exports and imports, expand proportionally with income at constant terms of trade—as shown by the fact that $M'M$, $C'C$, and $P'P$ all meet in the origin. In addition to the three general types of growth, two extreme cases can be distinguished: ultra-pro-trade-biased growth, in which more than the whole increase in national

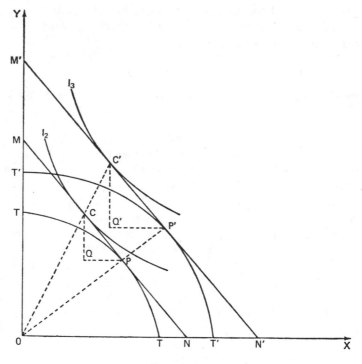

FIGURE 9.3

income is devoted to the purchase of imports so that the demand for home-produced goods actually falls and the country becomes absolutely less self-sufficient at constant terms of trade; and ultra-anti-trade-biased growth, in which more than the whole increase in national income is devoted to the purchase of home-produced goods, so that the demand for imports actually falls and the country becomes absolutely more self-sufficient at constant terms of trade. Given the assumption of the stability of international equilibrium and the constancy of the foreign offer curve, the growing country experiences a deterioration in its terms-of-trade which offsets to some extent the increase in potential welfare resulting from economic growth at constant terms-of-trade in all the above cases with the exception of ultra-anti-trade-biased growth, in which case the fall in the demand for imports implies a terms-of-trade improvement.

Unless complete specialization in production is assumed, the effect of growth on the demand for imports depends on the combined behaviour of both consumption and production. For analytical purposes it is convenient to consider separately the effects on the country's self-sufficiency of the consumption and production shifts associated with growth, before considering their combined effect. The behaviour of the consumption of importables as national product rises formally can be related to the 'output-elasticity of demand for

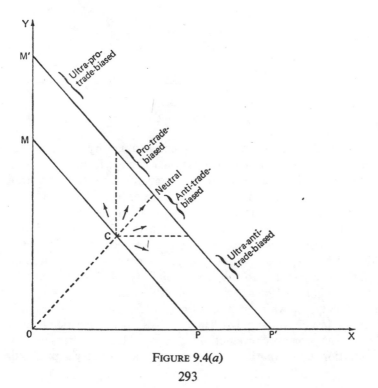

FIGURE 9.4(a)

293

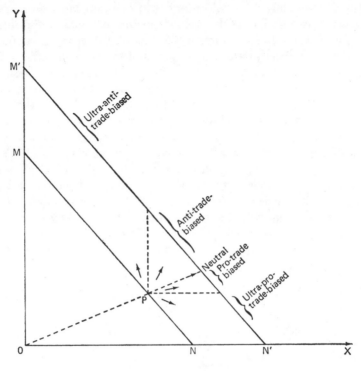

FIGURE 9.4(*b*)

importables'—the proportional change in quantity of importables demanded, divided by the proportional change in national output which causes the change in import demand: growth is pro-trade-biased, neutral, or anti-trade-biased according as this elasticity exceeds, equals, or falls short of one, ultra-anti-trade-biased if the elasticity exceeds the original ratio of national income to imports (an alternative way of expressing a negative output-elasticity of demand for exportables). The ranges of shift of the consumption point corrresponding to the five possible types of growth are illustrated in Figure 9.4(*a*). The production shift can similarly be classified into five types, which can be formally described in terms of an 'output-elasticity of supply of importables'. If this elasticity exceeds one, so that domestic production of importables increases more than proportionally to national income and the country's production pattern becomes more self-sufficient, growth is anti-trade-biased; if the elasticity is negative, so that domestic production of importables falls, growth is ultra-pro-trade-biased; and so on. The ranges of shift of the production point corresponding to these types are shown in Figure 9.4(*b*).

The effect of growth on the demand for imports is the combined result of its effects on consumption demand and domestic supply;

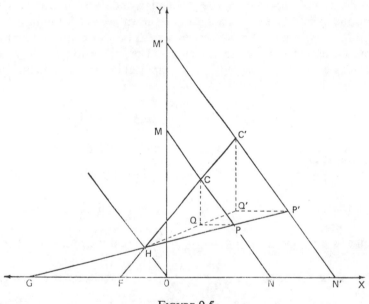

FIGURE 9.5

and the addition of the effects of the consumption and production shifts is complicated. If both shifts are biased in the same direction, or one is neutral, the combined effect is clearly pro-trade-biased or anti-trade-biased. If, however, the two shifts are biased in opposite directions, the net effect cannot be simply assessed. Because consumption of imports initially exceeds domestic production of them, biases of the same degree (as measured by the deviation from unit output-elasticity) but in opposite directions will not cancel out; instead, the bias on the consumption side will dominate unless the production shift is sufficiently more biased than the consumption shift. In other words, the degrees of bias must be compared. But where there is ultra-bias in the production shift and the possibility of contrary ultra-bias in the consumption shift is ruled out, some simplification is possible: ultra-anti-trade-bias in the production shift is sufficient to make the effect of growth ultra-anti-trade-biased, and ultra-pro-trade-bias in the production shift is sufficient to prevent growth being ultra-anti-trade-biased on balance.

The relation between the output-elasticities of consumption and production of importables, the production and consumption biases, and the overall bias of growth can be shown geometrically in terms of Figure 9.5 which reproduces Figure 9.3 but for clarity omits the transformation and indifference curves. The proportional changes in aggregate output, consumption of importables and production of importables are respectively:

$$\frac{MM'}{OM} = \frac{NN'}{ON}, \frac{CC'}{FC} = \frac{NN'}{FN}, \text{ and } \frac{PP'}{GP} = \frac{NN'}{GN}$$

Hence the output-elasticity of consumption of importables is $\frac{CC'}{FC} - \frac{MM'}{OM} = \frac{ON}{FN}$, and the output elasticity of production of importables is $\frac{PP'}{GP} - \frac{MM'}{OM} = \frac{ON}{GN}$. The proportional change in demand for imports is $\frac{CC'}{HC} = \frac{PP'}{HP} = \frac{QQ'}{HQ}$, and the output-elasticity of demand for imports is $\frac{CC'}{HC} - \frac{NN'}{ON}$. The magnitude of the latter, and hence the overall bias of growth, can be determined simply by comparing the slopes of OH and MN. If OH and MN are parallel, as in Figure 9.5 $\frac{C'C}{HC} = \frac{NN'}{ON}$, the output-elasticity of demand for imports is unity and growth is neutral; if OH lies to the right of a line through O parallel to MN, $\frac{C'C}{HC} \frac{NN'}{ON}$, the elasticity exceeds unity, and growth is pro-trade-biased; conversely, if OH lies to the left of the line through O parallel to MN, the elasticity is less than unity and growth is anti-trade-biased. By extension, if $C'C$ and $P'P$ meet in H at an obtuse angle growth is ultra-pro-trade-biased, while if H lies to the right of MN growth is ultra-anti-trade-biased. The

296

bias of the consumption shift can be measured by the excess of the output-elasticity of consumption of importables over unity, and the production shift by the excess of unity over the output-elasticity of production of importables (so that pro-trade-bias is positive and anti-trade-bias negative in each case). On these definitions the consumption bias is represented in Figure 9.5 by $\frac{FO}{FN}$ and the production bias by $\frac{GO}{GN}$; $\frac{GO}{GN}$ is larger than $\frac{FO}{FN}$, thus demonstrating the point previously stated that where the biases are opposed the production bias must be larger than the consumption bias if the latter is not to predominate.

The concepts of neutral, pro-trade-biased, anti-trade-biased, and ultra-pro- and ultra-anti-trade-biased growth, together with the distinction between the consumption, the production, and the overall effect of growth, must now be applied to analysing the effects of different types of growth. Following convention, we shall be concerned with three types of economic growth—technical progress, population increase, and capital accumulation—which are assumed to be analytically separable. And we shall consider their effects in two types of economy, one which exports manufactured goods in exchange for foodstuffs—a 'manufacturing country'—and one which exports foodstuffs in exchange for manufactured goods—an 'agricultural country'. Both countries are assumed to be only partially specialized—this is the more interesting case, and can readily be adapted to the case of complete specialization.

To make the analysis more concrete, it is assumed that food is labour-intensive in production and a necessary good in consumption, while manufactures are capital-intensive in production and a luxury good in consumption. Further, it is assumed that capital is better off than labour, so that the average and marginal propensities to consume manufactures are higher for capital than for labour, and the average and marginal propensities to consume food are higher for labour than for capital.

In considering the effects of growth, it is convenient to distinguish between technical progress, which alters the production functions of the economy, and population increase and capital accumulation, which increase the quantity of a productive factor without altering the production function. The effects of factor accumulation are the simplest to deal with, and will therefore be discussed first. For reasons which will become clear in the course of the argument, it is necessary to consider the production effects before the consumption effects.

The production effect of factor accumulation is given by the familiar Rybczynski theorem; if the terms-of-trade are constant, and one factor accumulates, there will be an absolute reduction in the production of the good which uses that factor less intensively, and the production of the good using that factor more intensively will increase by more than the value of the total increase in output. Given the assumption that food is labour-intensive and manufacturing capital-intensive, it implies in the present instance that capital accumulation will reduce agricultural production and increase manufacturing production at constant terms of trade. Capital accumulation in the manufacturing country will therefore have an ultra-pro-trade-biased production effect; whereas capital accumulation in the agricultural country will have an ultra-anti-trade-biased production effect. Conversely, population growth will reduce manufacturing output and increase agricultural output; thus the production effect of population growth will be ultra-anti-trade-biased in the agricultural country.

It also follows from the previous argument that, at constant terms-of-trade (and so long as the country remains incompletely specialized), all of the increase in output goes as income to the factor which is accumulating. On our assumption of differing marginal and average propensities to consume the goods, capital accumulation will increase the average proportion of income spent on manufacturers in the community, and population growth will increase the average proportion of income spent on food. Hence the consumption effect of capital accumulation will be anti-trade-biased in the manufacturing country and pro-trade-biased in the agricultural country, while the consumption effect of population growth will be the reverse in the two countries. As explained earlier, an ultra-anti-trade-biased production effect will dominate the consumption effect while an ultra-pro-trade-biased production effect will rule out an ultra-anti-trade-biased total effect. Hence capital accumulation in the agricultural country and population growth in the manufacturing country will be ultra-anti-trade-biased, while the opposite type of factor accumulation in each country may be anything from ultra-pro-trade-biased to anti-trade-biased, but will not be ultra-anti-trade-biased.

Let us now turn to the effects of technical progress. Following Hicks' definition according to which neutrality is defined in terms of a fixed capital-labour ratio, at constant factor prices, neutral technical progress in an industry leads to expansion of the output of that industry at the expense of the other, at given terms-of-trade; in other words, neutral progress is ultra-biased. It follows that neutral progress in manufacturing has an ultra-pro-trade-biased production effect in the manufacturing country, and an ultra-trade-biased production effect in the agricultural country; while the effects of neutral progress in agriculture are exactly the reverse.

Now consider technical progress which is biased, in the sense that it alters the optimum ratio of one factor to the other employed at the initial factor prices in the industry in which progress occurs. Such progress may be described as saving the factor whose optimum ratio to the other is reduced. As described in Chapter 3 if progress is labour-saving, the capital-labour ratio rises; if capital-saving, the optimum ratio falls. Assume that the biased progress occurs in the manufacturing industry. To maintain the constant commodity price ratio between manufactures and foodstuffs in this instance, resources relocate from the latter to the former necessitating an increase in the relative price of capital, the intensive factor in manufactures. With a higher price of capital, labour will be substituted for capital in both industries, which results in an unambiguous drop in the capital-labour ratio in the static sector. If progress in manufacturing is capital-saving, neutral, or slightly labour-saving, the capital-labour ratio in manufactures also will be lower than originally. In this case, with a constant factor endowment ratio and lower capital-output ratios in both industries, resources must flow from the labour to the capital-intensive sector if full employment is to be maintained; and technical progress will be ultra-biased towards the production of manufactures.

But if progress is sufficiently strongly labour-saving to offset the substitution effect of cheaper labour, the new capital : labour ratio in manufactures will be higher than the original. And with a higher capital : labour ratio in the one industry and a lower ratio in the other, the overall endowment ratio might have been maintained by a shift of resources in either direction (and to any extent) between the industries. Thus in this case the effect of technical progress in manufacturing may lie anywhere between the extremes of ultra-bias towards production of manufactures, and ultra-bias towards production of foodstuffs.

What about the consumption effect of technical progress? The restoration of the initial relative cost ratio involves lowering the relative price of the factor used less intensively in the industry where progress has occurred, and raising the price of the other. If, however, the possibility of ultra-biased consumption effects through income-redistribution is excluded, it follows that progress in manufacturing, which reduces the income of labour and the proportional demand for food, will have an anti-biased-trade consumption effect in the manufacturing country and a pro-trade-biased consumption effect in the agricultural country; while the consumption effects of progress in agriculture will be the reverse.

Remembering that cases of ultra-anti-trade-biased and ultra-pro-trade-biased consumption effects have been excluded by assumption, the conclusions about the total effects of technical progress to which the foregoing analysis leads can be summarized as follows:

(a) The following types of progress will be ultra-anti-trade-biased:

(*i*) Neutral technical progress in agriculture in the manufacturing country;

(*ii*) Neutral technical progress in manufacturing in the agricultural country;

(*iii*) Capital-saving technical progress in manufacturing in the agricultural country;

(*iv*) Labour-saving technical progress in agriculture in the manufacturing country.

(b) The following types of progress will be ultra-pro-trade-biased to anti-trade-biased, but not ultra-anti-trade-biased:

(*i*) Neutral technical progress in manufacturing in the manufacturing country;

(*ii*) Neutral technical progress in agriculture in the agricultural country;

(*iii*) Capital-saving technical progress in manufacturing in the manufacturing country;

(*iv*) Labour-saving technical progress in agriculture in the agricultural country.

(c) The following types of progress can be biased in any way whatever from ultra-pro-trade-biased to ultra-anti-trade-biased:

(i) Capital-saving technical progress in agriculture in either country;

(ii) Labour-saving technical progress in manufacturing in either country.

In brief, progress which is neutral or saves the factor used relatively intensively in the industry in which it occurs will be ultra-anti-trade-biased if it occurs in a country's import-competing industry, and ultra-pro-trade-biased to anti-trade-biased but *not* ultra-anti-trade-biased if it occurs in a country's export industry; progress which saves the factor used relatively intensively in the other industry than that in which the progress occurs may have any effect whatsoever.

The production, consumption, and total effects of growth of the various types analysed in the argument so far on the growing country's demand for imports and supply of exports are summarized in Table 9.1. The results in many cases are rather indefinite. It should perhaps be remarked that the chief reason why this is so lies in our original assumption that each factor prefers to consume the product in which it is employed intensively so that progress in that product, by redistributing income towards that factor, increases the relative demand for the product. If each factor preferred the product in which it was used less intensively, the consumption and production effects of progress would work in the same direction in many cases, giving unambiguous results. This may be confirmed by scrutiny of the summary Table: if factors' preferences for goods were the opposite of those assumed, the effects of growth of the types discussed would be *either* ultra-anti-trade-biased, *or* pro-trade-biased to ultra-pro-trade-biased, except in cases of capital-saving progress in agriculture and labour-saving progress in manufactures.

The next step is to analyse the effects of growth in the two countries together, that is, of the growth of the world economy. If growth of the same type is going on in the two countries, conclusions about the movement of the terms of trade between them (i.e. between manufactures and food) can be drawn directly from the Table in many cases. For example, capital accumulation and neutral or capital-saving technical progress in manufactures turn the terms of trade in favour of the agricultural country, population growth and neutral or labour-saving technical progress in food turns the terms of trade in favour of the manufacturing country. But capital-saving progress in agriculture and labour-saving progress in manufactures may turn the terms of trade either way.

TABLE 9.1 *The Effects of Economic Growth*

Type of Growth	Manufacturing Country			Agricultural Country		
	Production Effect	Con-sumption Effect	Total Effect	Production Effect	Con-sumption Effect	Total Effect
Capital accumulation	UP	A	UP to A	UA	P	UA
Population Growth	UA	P	UA	UP	A	UP to A
Neutral technical progress						
(*a*) manufacturing	UP	A	UP to A	UA	P	UA
(*b*) agriculture	UA	P	UA	UP	A	UP to A
Capital-saving technical progress						
(*a*) manufacturing	UP	A	UP to A	UA	P	UA
(*b*) agriculture	UA to UP	P	UA to UP	UP to UA	A	UP to UA
Labour-saving technical progress						
(*a*) manufacturing	UP to UA	A	UP to UA	UA to UP	P	UA to UP
(*b*) agriculture	UA	P	UA	UP	A	UP to A

A: anti-trade-biased
P: pro-trade-biased
UA: ultra-anti-trade-biased
UP: ultra-pro-trade-biased

In the general case, with population increasing, capital accumulating, and technical progress being applied in both countries, the movement of the terms of trade will depend on the bias and the rate of growth in each country. This dependence can be expressed in the following formula:

$$R_{pm} = \frac{\varepsilon_a R_a - \varepsilon_m R_m}{\eta_a + \eta_m - 1},$$

where R_{pm} is the rate of increase (decrease if negative) of the relative price of manufactures, R_a is the rate of growth of output in the agricultural country and ε_a its output-elasticity of demand for imports, R_m and ε_m are the rate of growth and ouput-elasticity of demand for imports of the manufacturing country, η_a and η_m are the two countries' price-elasticities of demand for imports, and $\eta_a + \eta_m - 1$ is the 'elasticity factor' which determines the proportion of the initial value of trade by which a country's trade balance would improve if the price of its export good fell. The sense of the formula is that $\varepsilon_a R_a$ and $\varepsilon_m R_m$ are the rates of increase in the countries' demands for each other's goods; if these are unequal, equilibrium must be maintained by a relative price change whose magnitude will vary inversely with the elasticity factor.

In conclusion, some interpretive comments would appear to be in order. For one, the analysis clarifies the relationship between the effect of various forms of economic growth on international trade, and not the opposite. It tells, for example, how factor accumulation can affect the terms-of-trade but not the effects of changes in the terms-of-trade on factor accumulation. The perhaps more economically significant question of the causes of technical change, population growth and capital accumulation are left unexplained. Secondly, the analysis highlights those factors relevant to a determination of how economic growth affects international trade—e.g. whether the factor that accumulates is intensive in the production of the import or export commodity, whether technical change takes place in importables or exportables, etc.—by abstracting from a variety of complicating factors which are themselves established by this procedure as relevant factors though not thoroughly investigated. We refer here not only to those that have been explicitly mentioned—e.g. inferiority in consumption which allows for an ultra-trade-bias on the consumption side—but the abstraction from a third factor, land, which avoids the classical problem of diminishing returns, abstraction from a multiplicity of products, intermediate goods, and the presence of many countries; all being capable of altering the postulated effect parametric change can be expected to have on international trade. Such abstraction should not be taken as proof that the analysis is 'unrealistic', but rather as proof that these factors are potentially important to the question at hand.

Policy-Induced Change in a
Open Economy

The analysis of a change in budgetary scale in a closed economy where the real resource transfer to government is financed by a general tax—that is, a tax that does not alter commodity and factor prices at impact is reviewed to put the present analysis in perspective. If a general consumption tax is used for this purpose, each factor-owner bears the burden of the resource transfer in proportion to its contribution to national product if the government's marginal propensity to consume either good is equal to the average of the marginal propensities of both factors to consume that good (weighted by their incomes if tastes are not homothetic). Should government have a marginal preference for the labour-intensive (capital-intensive) good as compared with the (weighted) average of the private tax-paying community, on the other hand, the impact effect of the transfer creates an excess demand for that good at constant prices, whose adjustment requires an increase in the price and marginal product of labour (capital) and a decrease in the price and marginal product of capital (labour). Capital (labour) bears a more than proportionate and labour (capital) a less than proportionate part of the burden of the resource transfer to government by comparison with their contributions to national product, and it is even possible in this case for labour (capital) to gain in an absolute sense.

The extension of this analysis to an open economy requires an assumption be made concerning the terms of trade; specifically, whether such terms will be assumed to be fixed or variable. The former is the more relevant one in the case of a small country, and is convenient for the large country case as well, since the method used to analyse this case divides the total effect of the parametric change into two separate and distinct components; the impact or primary effect of the change taken at constant terms of trade, and the secondary or general equilibrium adjustment of the excess demand or supply created by the impact effect. The key difference between the two cases is that the entire adjustment to the impact effect in the small country case is through a change in the volume of trade while in the large country case the terms of trade change as well.

The extension of the closed economy analysis of a change in budgetary scale to that of an open economy is made convenient by the derivation of the function relating the consumption possibilities available to the private community consistent with a fixed amount of government utility, the economy's domestic transformation schedule and the fixed terms of trade. This is accomplished in Figure 9.A.1 where $T_d T_d$ represents the domestic transformation curve and TT the efficient consumption locus when the terms of trade are given by the slope of TT. The government's utility block is placed such that $\bar{U}_G$ the government indifference curve representing

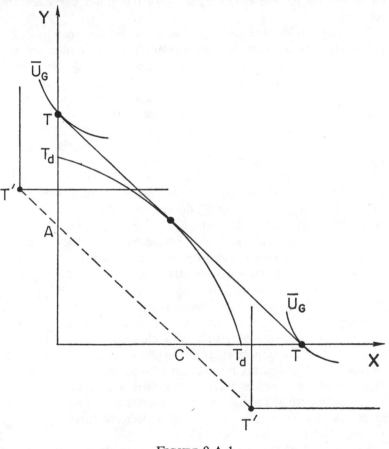

FIGURE 9.A.1

a given level of government utility is tangent to either point T or the locus TT, with its axes parallel to those of the transformation curve. Now run $\bar{U}_G$ along TT from one end point to the other, making certain that the two pairs of axes are kept parallel to one another. The resultant constant government utility 'net' consumption possibility curve $T'T'$ represents the set of efficient outputs available for private consumption from the economy's 'gross' set of efficient outputs consistent with the given level of government utility, whose slope is equal to the given terms of trade. Since negative consumption of a good is not possible, the segments $T'A$ and CT' of the 'net' curve and the corresponding segments of the 'gross' curve are not relevant.

The analysis of an increase in budgetary scale in an open economy is simplified by assuming zero government in initial equilibrium and then introducing a tax-financed budget consistent with the government utility level U_G. The case is illustrated in Figure 9.A.2 where P represents the initial production point and C the initial aggregate consumption point to which the individual consumption points C_C and C_L correspond. As in the case of a closed economy, the relationship between public tastes and income-distribution-weighted private tastes is crucial to whether the increase in budgetary scale creates an excess demand for the import good or export good at constant terms of trade. In the former case, the origin of the government's utility block falls northwest of C', the cum-transfer aggregate private consumption point, on AC (point B); in the latter it falls northeast of C' on AC (point B'). However, regardless of whether an excess demand for the import or export good is created at constant terms of trade, if these terms are fixed (the small country assumption), the final individual consumption points are C'_C for capital and C'_L for labour. Each factor bears the burden of the resource-transfer to government in proportion to its contribution to national product. This case is in contrast to that of a closed economy where the adjustment to the impact effect of an increase in budgetary scale financed by a general tax requires an increase in the output of the good for which an excess demand is created, and an increase in the price and marginal product of the factor that is used intensively in the production of that good, and a decrease in the price and marginal product of the other factor.

The case where the terms of trade are variable suggests a novel

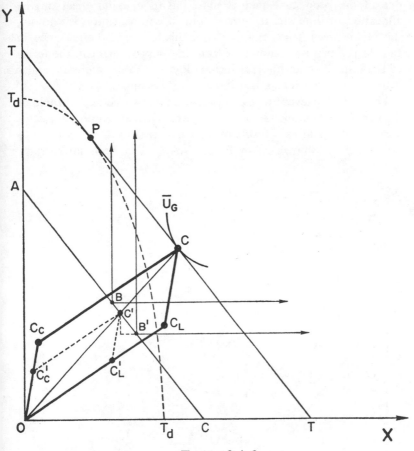

FIGURE 9.A.2.

possibility. In a closed economy it is possible for the absolute share of one factor to increase as a result of a tax-financed increase in budgetary scale, so that more than the entire burden of the resource transfer to government is shifted onto the other factor. In an open economy it is possible for both factors to gain in an absolute sense if the impact effect of the resource transfer to government creates an excess demand for the export good, and thus a terms of trade improvement, sufficient for this purpose. The improvement in the terms of trade necessarily implies that the actual absolute share of

307

one of the productive factors must fall (due to its effect on the allocation of domestic resources), but, if compensation is allowed, this factor nevertheless can gain. For this to occur, the real income gain to the private community from the improvement in the terms of trade must offset the real income loss to the private community from the government's absorbtion of real resources.

The factors relevant to a determination as to whether all three of the relevant economic factors—the government and both productive factors—can gain as a result of increased real resource transfer to government is illustrated in Figure 9.A.3. The economy's trans-

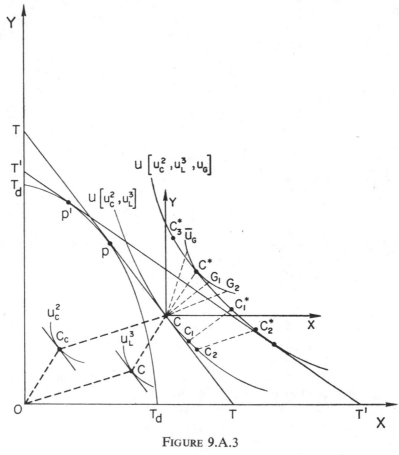

FIGURE 9.A.3

formation curve is $T_d T_d$ and $U[U_c^2,\ U_L^3]$ represents the private community's indifference contour corresponding to both capital's indifference contour U_c^2 and labour's indifference contour U_L^3, tangent to the initial terms of trade line TT at the initial consumption point C. It is desired to derive the *total* community indifference contour corresponding to the aggregate private contour $U[U_c^2,\ U_L^3]$ and the given government utility contour U_g. Place the origin of the $\bar{U}_g$ block at point C and determine the government consumption vectors associated with the slopes of the private indifference contour at different points. C^*C for example is the government consumption vector (assumed a straight line for simplicity) associated with the slope of the private contour at point C; CG_1 the vector associated with the slope of the private contour at C_1, etc. Such government consumption vectors can thus be added onto the corresponding private consumption points to form the curve $U[U_c^2,\ U_L^3,\ U_g]$ with $C_1 C_1^*$ parallel to CG_1, $C_2 C_2^*$ parallel to CG_2, . . ., etc. This curve shows the various aggregate consumption points consistent with the utility levels U_c^2, U_L^3 and U_g, whose slope at any point is equal to that of the individual utility contours at the corresponding points.

There are two relevant questions at this stage of the analysis. The first is whether there exists a positive terms of trade that is consistent both with the productive curve $T_d T_d$ and the consumption curve $U[U_c^2,\ U_L^3,\ U_g]$, as is for example $T'T'$ in Figure 9.A.3. Given $T_d T_d$, this clearly is a function of the extent of the government's absorbtion of real resources. The greater the absorbtion, the less likely that a terms of trade line with a negative slope exists that is both tangent to $T_d T_d$ (or consistent with complete specialization of the export good) and the relevant total community indifference curve contour. The existence of such terms of trade is a limiting case indicating that, through compensation, it would be impossible to finance the given amount of government utility without having one of the private factors suffer a deterioration in its utility position as a consequence. The second question, of course, is, given the existence of the requisite terms of trade, whether the change in the terms of trade generated by the real resource transfer to government in any particular case would be sufficient for this purpose. This change in the terms of trade depends on (i) the difference between the government's marginal propensity to consume imports and the income-distributed weighted private marginal propensity to do so, and (ii) on the shape of the foreign offer curve. The greater the difference between the relevant marginal propensities and the more inelastic the foreign offer curve in the neighbourhood of the initial terms of trade, the greater will be the change in the terms of trade.

The above analysis of an increase in budgetary scale in an open economy easily can be extended to that of differential tax incidence (a change in tax functions with budgetary scale and expenditure constant) and differential expenditure incidence (a change in expenditure functions with budgetary scale and tax functions constant), but the specifics of these analyses are left to the reader. In the case where one tax is substituted for another with budgetary scale and expenditure patterns constant, the direct effect of the tax substitution on the distribution of income will be the only relevant effect if the terms of trade are fixed; and if such terms are variable it also will be possible for both factors to increase their absolute share of national product with a sufficient terms of trade improvement. There will be no direct distributional effect if expenditure patterns change with budgetary scale and tax patterns constant (this assumes the utility of government is independent from that of private taxpayers; if not, the differential effect of the change in government expenditure on private citizens must be obtained), and no distributional effect at all if the terms of trade are fixed. Assuming that private demand functions are independent of that of the government, a change in government expenditure will improve or deteriorate the terms of trade depending upon whether the government's marginal preference for the import (export) good increases or decreases by comparison with its initial preference function.

CHAPTER 10

The Theory of Economic Growth

The two-sector model of production and distribution has been applied in previous chapters to the analysis of both exogenous and policy-induced change in the context of closed and open economics. Such analysis has been, technically, comparative static in nature, in that factor supplies and technology have been taken as exogenously given, or subject to exogenously given change. In this chapter the model is opened out into a dynamic model of economic growth, though to a limited extent only, by assuming that the stock of capital available to the economy is determined by the savings behaviour of the community. The model is not made fully dynamic, however, because it is assumed, first, that the rate of population growth is exogenously given, and second, that the rate of technical progress is not only exogenously given but takes a particular form, namely that of purely labour-augmenting or 'Harrod-neutral' technical progress. The model is considered first in the context of a closed economy but is later extended to allow for international trade.

I. A ONE-SECTOR GROWTH MODEL

As a prelude to the analysis of the two-sector model, it is useful to consider a one-sector growth model based on the Hicksian model of distribution discussed in Chapter 2. A comparative-statics model of distribution between capital and labour on the assumption of a constant returns to scale technology, the Hicksian model can be readily converted into a growth model by assuming, first, that either the working population grows at an exogenously given natural rate of increase, technology being given, or that the 'effective' working population grows at a rate given exogenously by the sum of the

311

natural rate of population increase and the rate of Harrod-neutral (purely labour-augmenting) technical progress; second, that the single output of the economy can be used either for consumption or for capital investment—in this connection, it simplifies the analysis, without loss of generality, to assume that capital equipment once installed lasts for ever, so that problems of depreciation can be ignored; and third, that the accumulation of capital is governed by the existence of a fixed ratio of savings to total income (or output).

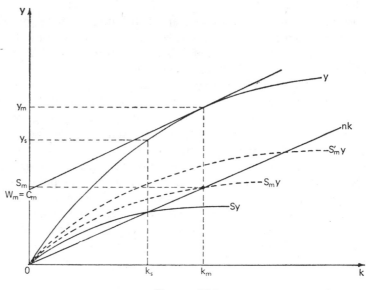

FIGURE 10.1

The one-sector model of economic growth is depicted in Figure 10.1, where Oy represents output per head of the effective labour force (assumed to increase at an exponential rate n as a result of the combined effects of population growth and Harrod-neutral technical progress) and $O.sy$ represents saving per head at different levels of output per head, determined by the fixed savings ratio s. The ray $O.nk$ represents what may be termed the capital or investment requirements of constant output per head: a proportion n of the existing stock of capital per head must be invested if capital per head (and therefore output per head) is to remain constant as the effective labour force grows over time.

Given the savings ratio, the economy will converge on a long-run equilibrium position (in *per capita* terms) determined by the inter-section of the savings curve and the capital requirements curve, with capital per head of the effective labour force k_s and output per head of the effective labour force y_s. The necessity of convergence on this equilibrium can be seen by considering any arbitrary initial level of capital per head. If the initial level is to the left of k_s, savings per head exceeds the investment required to keep capital per (effective) head constant, and the level of capital per head must grow over time; conversely, if the initial level of capital per head is to the right of k_s, the investment requirement exceeds saving per head and capital per head must shrink over time; the increase or decrease of capital per head will cease when savings per head become equal to the investment requirement.

Since the economy must converge on an equilibrium level of capital and output per (effective) head of population, with the aggregate growth rate determined by the rate of growth of the effective labour force, determined exogenously by the rates of natural increase and Harrod-neutral technical progress, the growth rate ceases to be of theoretical interest. This, incidentally, is an important point for economic policy. Much theory and policy-making in the past two decades has been devoted to methods of increasing the rate of economic growth; but the model demonstrates that policy-induced increases in the growth rate can only be transi-tional, unless policy is aimed either at increasing the rate of popula-tion growth—which virtually no one would regard as desirable—or at increasing the rate of technical progress—which is a more complex problem than altering savings and investment behaviour, which is the usual focus of growth-oriented economic policy.

In place of the growth rate, which is in the long run exogenously determined, economic interest centres on the characteristics of the steady-state growth path of the economy, and specifically on the level of consumption per head enjoyed in the course of long-run equilibrium growth. By assumption, as capital per head grows, so does output per head; but so also does the investment requirement. Moreover, the investment requirement grows proportionally with capital per head, whereas output per head grows less than proportionally with capital per head. The difference between output and the investment requirement is the level of consumption per head that can be maintained in perpetuity; and for the reasons just given it must first grow and then decline as capital per head increases, being subject to a technically determined maximum. (The determining factors are the technology that determines the shape of the relation between capital and output per head, and the exogenously given growth rate that determines the investment requirement.) The interesting theoretical question, therefore, concerns the conditions required for maximum 'permanent' consumption per head. This maximum is determined diagrammatically by parallelism of the tangent to the Oy curve with the investment requirements curve $O.nk$, yielding output per head Oy_m and requiring investment per head OS_m, corresponding to the savings ratio s_m with consumption per head $S_m y_m = Ow_m$. The slope of $O.nk$ is n, the rate of growth; and the slope of the Oy curve is the marginal product of capital, which, because output and capital are measured in the same units, and capital lasts for ever, is the rate of return on capital or the rate of interest. Hence one statement of the condition for maximization of consumption per head is that accumulation should be carried to the point where the rate of interest equals the (exogenously given) rate of growth of the economy. Another statement of the condition follows from the observation that $y_m w_m$ is the absolute share of capital per man in the total product per man (its marginal product multiplied by its quantity per man) and Ow_m the absolute share of labour per man; from this it follows that maximum consumption per head will be achieved if the share of labour is entirely consumed and the share of capital is entirely invested. This result will ensue automatically if, following the Marxist tradition, it is assumed that capitalists reinvest all their profits and workers consume all their wages; but the result could equally well be achieved by proper regulation of the total saving of the economy.

The conditions for maximum permanent consumption per head just developed are described in the literature as the 'golden rule' conditions (alternatively, as the 'neo-classical growth theorem'). But it is important to realize that they are technical conditions, and not normative rules or prescriptions. They have to be interpreted in the following sense. If an economy were to the right of the 'golden rule' capital per head level k_m, as with savings ratio S'_m, it could raise its consumption per head immediately and at all future points of time by reducing its savings ratio to the 'golden rule' ratio S_m; hence in this case the 'golden rule' is a normative prescription for increasing welfare, unless society is assumed to derive utility from the possession of property independently of its consumption goods yield. But if the economy is to the left of the 'golden rule' position, the increase in its savings ratio required to raise it in the long run to that position would entail a sacrifice of immediate consumption for the sake of higher future consumption; and this would involve an intertemporal choice between present and future consumption, the basis for which is not provided by the model. Since most societies can reasonably by assumed to fall short of the golden rule position— rates of return on capital typically exceed growth rates of gross national product—the 'golden rule' conditions provide no guidance to current economic policy.

The one-sector model of economic growth just analysed has the theoretical advantages that the rate of return on capital is a unique function of the stock of capital per head, and independent of the rate of current saving and investment, and that a given savings ratio applied to the output from a given stock of capital per head implies a unique rate of production of capital goods. In both cases, the reason is the fixed (unitary) rate of exchange between consumption goods and investment goods implicit in the aggregation of output into a single good. In the two-sector model of growth, to which attention is now turned, the (instantaneous) rate of return on capital depends on the allocation of production between investment and consumption, and the rate of production of investment goods is not uniquely determined by the savings ratio but depends also on the relative price of investment goods in terms of consumption goods, which in turn has to be determined by a general equilibrium adjustment process.

II. TWO-SECTOR GROWTH MODEL: CLOSED ECONOMY

The two-sector model of general equilibrium developed in the previous chapters can be converted into a growth model by assuming that the effective labour force grows at a constant rate (as a result of natural increase and Harrod-neutral technical progress[1]) and that

[1] Technical progress must be assumed not only to be Harrod-neutral, but to proceed at the same rate in the two industries.

capital accumulation is determined endogenously by a given savings ratio. It simplifies matters to assume the capital equipment is, besides being perfectly malleable (to allow for substitution between capital and labour), permanent in duration; permanent durability is not a significant restriction of the analysis, since replacement investment on any reasonable theory of depreciation can be included in the investment required to keep the capital stock *per capita* intact. As in the case of the other applications of the two-sector model it turns out that the alternative possible assumptions about the relative capital-intensities of the two sectors are crucial to the results of the analysis.

As with the one-sector model, the process of growth in a two-sector model is most conveniently approached in terms of variations in the stock of capital per head of the effective labour force. For any given stock of capital per head, there will be a *per capita* transforming curve between investment goods and consumption goods. The transformation curves for successively large stocks of capital per head will be outside one another, in such a fashion that, if a given price ratio between investment goods and consumption goods is selected, points on the successive transformation curves with a slope equal to that price ratio will lie along a straight line, the 'Rybczynski line' for that commodity-price ratio and the corresponding factor-price ratio. If the investment good is relatively capital-intensive in production, the Rybczynski line RR will slope upwards to the northwest as shown in Figure 10.2; if the investment good is relatively labour-intensive in production, the Rybczynski line will slope downwards to the southeast, as shown in Figure 10.3.

For the arbitrarily chosen price ratio between investment and consumption goods, there will be for each transformation curve a corresponding budget line representing the community's income, the terminal points of which represent the value in terms of the two goods respectively of the income producible with the stock of capital per head that determines the location of the transformation curve. These budget lines are represented in Figures 10.2 and 10.3 $M_{I_1}M_{c_1}$, $M_{I_2}M_{c_2}$, . . ., etc. On each such budget line there will be a point representing the quantity of investment goods that must be produced to keep the stock of capital per head constant over time; as in the one-sector model, this quantity will be the existing stock of capital per head multiplied by n, the rate of growth of the effective

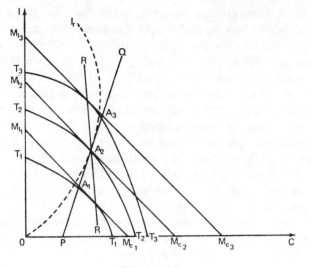

FIGURE 10.2

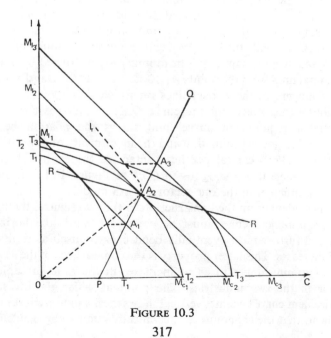

FIGURE 10.3

labour force. These points are represented in the Figures by A_1, A_2, A_3 Such points will lie along a straight-line locus PQ intersecting the horizontal axis to the right of the origin O. The locus is a straight line because, with a given commodity and factor-price ratio (and hence constant marginal product of capital) both income and the investment required to keep capital per head intact increase in proportion to the quantity of capital; it intersects the horizontal axis to the right of O because, again with fixed factor prices, a fixed part of income is attributable to the services of labour. This part is represented by the distance OP; it can be thought of as the output that labour alone would produce if it could hire capital at the rental price corresponding to the arbitrarily chosen commodity and factor-price ratio.

The budget lines $M_I M_c$, and the locus PQ, are constructed on the assumption of an arbitrary price ratio. PQ cannot, in fact, represent the combinations of investment and consumption goods the economy can in fact produce with different stocks of capital, subject to the condition of keeping capital per head intact, because these combinations must lie on the transformation curves corresponding to the different stocks of capital per head. Instead, PQ is merely a reference line, from which the locus of combinations of investment and consumption goods the economy will produce with different capital stocks and keeping capital per head intact is constructed by drawing horizontal lines from the points A_1, A_2, A_3, etc., to the transformation curves tangent to the budget lines on which these points lie. Such horizontal lines trace out the curve $O.A_2.I_r$, which is termed 'the investment requirement curve' and shows the relation between consumption goods production and the investment goods production required to keep capital per head intact as the capital stock per head increases. It is analogous to $O.nk$ in Figure 10.1, the investment requirement in the one-sector growth model.

As is evident from the construction in the two figures, the investment requirement curve must be concave towards the horizontal axis, and further must eventually bend back on itself as capital per head increases. This latter property is the consequence of the assumption of diminishing returns to increases in the ratio of capital to labour in the two industries. The point at which the investment requirement curve becomes vertical shows the maximum consumption per head that the economy can technically attain—the 'golden rule' position. At this point, the whole of the output of a marginal increment of capital is required to produce the additional investment goods required to keep capital per head intact. The marginal product of capital in producing investments goods is the own rate of return on capital or the rate of interest, while the increment in the capital requirement per unit increment of capital is n, the exogenously-given rate of increase of the effective labour force. Hence we derive the 'golden rule' condition for the maximization of consumption per head along the economy's equilibrium growth path, equality of the rate of interest with the exogenously-given steady-state equilibrium growth rate. Further, by multiplying both sides of the equation by the value of capital (measured in either investment goods or consumption goods) we obtain the alternative form of the condition, that aggregate saving and investment should equal the total income capital; and by then dividing each side by income (measured in the same units of investment or consumption goods) we obtain a third alternative formulation that the savings ratio should be equal to the share of capital in total income.

The investment requirement curve shows the long-run-equilibrium consumption-per-head possibilities open to the economy, and the corresponding levels of investment goods production necessary to sustain these possibilities. The position of steady-state equilibrium growth actually arrived at will be determined by the assumed fixed savings ratio of the community, in conjunction with the (derived) investment requirement locus OI_r. The fixed savings ratio must now be introduced into the diagram, in the form of an 'investment supply' locus OI_s. This poses the problem of taking account of the effect of variations in the relative price of investment goods in terms of consumption goods on the relative amounts of investment goods and consumption goods corresponding to the fixed savings ratio. The technique required for this is developed in Figures 10.4 and 10.5, which correspond to the contrasting assumption that investment goods are respectively capital-intensive and labour-intensive in production.

In Figures 10.4 and 10.5, the line OS on the left-hand side of the diagram is so drawn that, for any level of income OM_I measured in terms of the investment good, a line with a negative slope of 45° through M_I intersects OS at a point showing the level of saving and investment determined by the fixed saving ratio of the economy.

For any transformation curve corresponding to a given stock of capital per head, such as T_1T_1, general equilibrium of the economy requires that the production point B_1 be such that, when ouput is evaluated at the relative prices prevailing at that

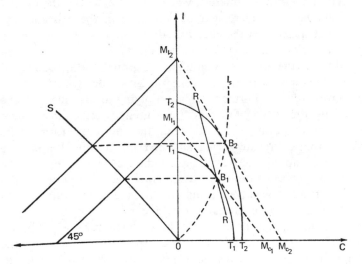

FIGURE 10.4

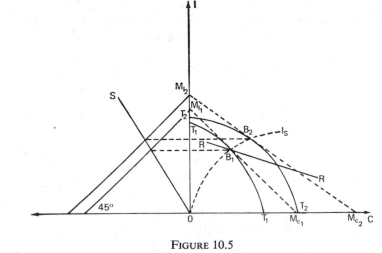

FIGURE 10.5

320

point, the resulting income measured in terms of the investment good, OM_{I_1}, when multiplied by the fixed savings ratio, results in a quantity of investment goods demanded equal to the ouput of these goods at the point B_1. The equilibrium quantities of investment goods demanded, as determined by the savings ratio, from the incomes producible with successively larger capital stocks per head trace out what may be termed 'the investment supply curve', OI_s. Every point on the investment supply curve represents a unique stable equilibrium, given the amount of capital per head, because a shift of production towards investment goods would raise the ratio of the value of investment goods production to the value of total output, while leaving the savings ratio unchanged, and vice versa.

If the investment good is capital-intensive as in Figure 10.4, an increase in income at constant prices would move the consumption and investment demand-equilibrium point of the economy outwards from B_1 along a vector OB, through the origin O, while it would move the consumption and investment production equilibrium point northwest along the Rybczynski line through B_1. To restore equilibrium between production and consumption, the quantity of investment goods produced must fall and demand must rise by comparison with these positions, implying both a more than proportional increase in income measured in investment goods to $OM_{I\cdot2}$ and a more than proportional increase in the equilibrium quantity of investment goods demanded and supplied to the equilibrium point B_2. Consequently in this case the investment supply curve must be concave towards the vertical axis. Conversely, if the investment good is labour-intensive, as in Figure 10.5, the investment supply curve must be convex to the vertical axis (concave to the horizontal axis).

The steady-state growth path equilibrium of the economy is determined by the intersection of the investment requirements curve and the investment supply curve, as indicated in Figures 10.6 and 10.7 for the two cases of capital-intensity and labour-intensity of the investment goods industry respectively. In the Diagrams, TT is the steady-state growth equilibrium transformation curve per capita, $M_I M_c$ the budget line depicting the value of income, and PQ the reference locus investment requirement curve at the equilibrium price ratio between investment and consumption goods. At points southwest of X along I_r, the supply of investment goods is greater

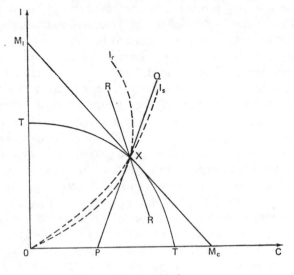

FIGURE 10.6

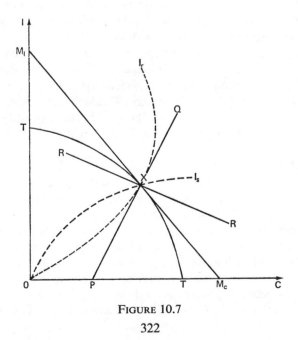

FIGURE 10.7

than the investment requirement; hence capital per head will increase and the transformation curve will move outward, and conversely for points northeast and northwest of A, B.

III. TWO-SECTOR GROWTH MODEL: OPEN ECONOMY

The diagrammatic apparatus just developed provides an interesting starting point for an analysis of the effect on the economy of the opening of the opportunity to trade internationally. For this purpose, trade is assumed to make available the opportunity to exchange the two goods at a different price ratio than the closed-economy equilibrium price ratio. To justify this assumption it must be assumed that the newly-opened economy is small in relation to the outside world; to validate that assumption in the context of economic growth, it is simplest to assume that the rest of the world is in growth equilibrium and is growing at the same exogenously-determined rate as the newly-opened economy.

There are two possibilities: that at the world price ratio the country has an (initial) comparative advantage in the production of consumption goods, and that it has an (initial) comparative advantage in the production of investment goods. In each case it is necessary to distinguish between the case in which investment goods are capital-intensive in production, and that in which they are labour-intensive in production.

The case of initial comparative advantage in consumption goods is analysed by means of Figure 10.8, showing the case where investment goods are capital-intensive in production and Figure 10.9 the case where they are labour-intensive in production. In each case, the more favourable price ratio for consumption goods leads the country initially to export those goods and import investment goods, its new production point being Y' and consumption point X'. The value of income in terms of investment goods rises from M_1 to M_1', increasing the amount of investment goods supplied by savers from that corresponding to X to that corresponding to X'; the economy's income-expansion line for saving rises from OI_s' (its position for the no-trade price ratio) to OI_s'' (its position for the world-trade price ratio). At the same time the investment requirement line rotates clockwise around the investment requirement

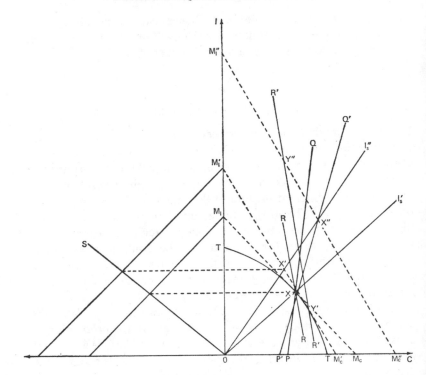

FIGURE 10.8

locus (not shown, for simplicity), from PQ to $P'Q'$, its position for
the initial stock of capital and corresponding capital requirement
lying horizontally to the right of X on the new budget line $M_I'M_C'$
reflecting the relatively lower price of capital goods in the world
market. The economy therefore begins to accumulate capital. As it
does so its production equilibrium point moves along the new
Rybczynski line through its new production point Y', to the northwest in Figure 10.8 and the southeast in Figure 10.9.

Assuming for simplicity that the economy remains incompletely
specialized in production, its new long-run growth equilibrium
position is established at the intersection of the new investment
supply locus OI_s'' and the new investment requirement line $P'Q'$,
with production equilibrium at Y'' and consumption-investment
equilibrium at X''. Where investment goods production is labour-

324

intensive, as shown in Figure 10.9, the initial comparative advantage in consumption-goods production must increase with growth and the country become increasingly specialized on consumption goods

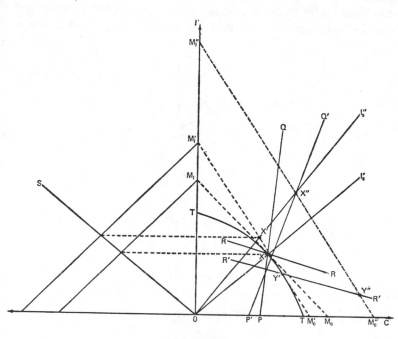

FIGURE 10.9

production. Where investment goods production is capital-intensive, growth reduces the initial comparative advantage in consumption goods production and may even reverse it. The latter possibility is shown in Figure 10.8.

Whether the investment goods industry is capital-intensive or labour-intensive, the accumulation of capital consequent on the relative price change favouring consumption goods introduced by the opportunity to trade implies that consumption per head must be higher in the long-run equilibrium growth position that it was with the initial stock of capital immediately after the opening of trade. (This proposition implicitly excludes as economically unrealistic and uninteresting the possibility that the initial no-trade equilibrium was characterized by a savings ratio higher than the golden rule level.) Since consumption per head must be greater after the opening of trade, with the given initial stock of capital, long-run growth equilibrium with trade must entail an increase in consumption per head as compared with the no-trade growth equilibrium position.

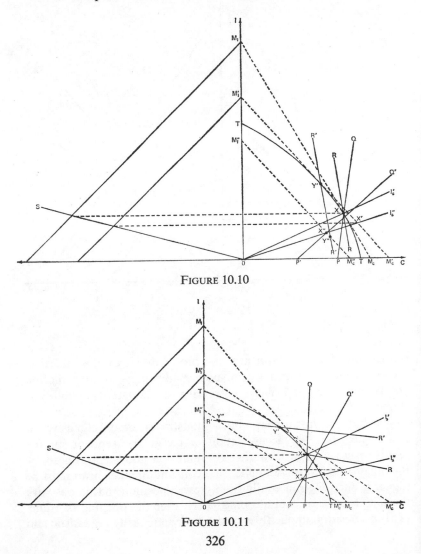

FIGURE 10.10

FIGURE 10.11

326

The opposite case of initial comparative advantage in the production of investment goods is analysed in Figure 10.10, again embodying the assumption that investment goods are relatively capital-intensive in production and Figure 10.11 the converse assumption. At the new international price ratio the value of income in terms of investment goods producible with the pre-trade capital stock falls, and saving is no longer sufficient to maintain capital per head intact. The investment requirement shifts right for the initial stock of capital and corresponding required investment *per capita* for the same reason as in the previous case. The economy begins to decumulate capital, shifting along its new Rybczynski line to the southeast (Figure 10.10) or to the northwest (Figure 10.11). As before, the economy may come into equilibrium before complete specialization occurs, the new equilibrium being determined by the intersection of the new investment requirement curve and the new investment supply curve. Where the investment good is labour-intensive in production (Figure 10.11) the final equilibrium production and investment-consumption points must entail increased specialization on the export of investment goods. Where the investment good is capital-intensive in production, the final equilibrium position may involve continued (but reduced) dependence on the export of investment goods, or conversion to the export of consumption goods (as shown in Figure 10.10). In either case, consumption per head must be reduced below the level achieved immediately after the opening of trade by use of the initial stock of capital per head, and could conceivably be reduced in the final equilibrium below the level enjoyed before the opening of trade.

Figures 10.8 and 10.10 illustrate the possibility of reversal of initial comparative advantage after the opening of international trade, as a result of growth in the former case and contraction in the latter case, when the investment goods industry is capital-intensive. However, this possibility can be excluded if the possibility of unstable and multiple equilibrium is excluded as unrealistic. The reason involves reversion to the analysis of long-run growth equilibrium in the closed economy. For that equilibrium to be unique, the investment supply curve reflecting savings behaviour must lie above the investment requirement curve for constant capital per head everywhere to the left of their intersection, and below it everywhere to the right of that intersection. Now, in Figures 10.8 and 10.10, the intersection of the new Rybczynski line $R'R'$ and the new investment supply curve OI_s'', where the reversal of comparative advantage occurs, must correspond to a point on the closed-economy investment supply curve; and if the investment requirements curve $P'Q'$ lies below that intersection in the economic expansion case of Figure 10.8 or above it in the economic contraction case of Figure 10.10, the afore-mentioned requirement for uniqueness of long-run growth equilibrium must be violated.

This analysis of the effects of the opening of international trade on the long-run growth equilibrium of an economy can readily be converted, on lines familiar in international trade theory, into an analysis of the effects of import duties on the equilibrium of the economy in a long-run equilibrium growth context. In general terms, Figures 10.9 and 10.8 suggest that, where under free trade the country exports consumption goods and imports investment goods, the imposition of a tariff on imports (of investment goods) will lead to a decumulation of capital, which must decrease the country's dependence on imported investment goods when these are labour-intensive in production and increase it when investment goods are capital-intensive in production. Conversely, Figures 10.11 and 10.10 suggest that where under free trade the country exports investment goods and imports consumption goods, the imposition of a tariff on imports (of consumption goods) will lead to an accumulation of capital which must decrease the country's dependence on imports when investment goods are labour-intensive in production and increase it if investment goods are capital-intensive in production. These propositions are obviously subject to the tariff being less than prohibitive with the transformation curve corresponding to the original stock of capital per head, and to the change in the stock of capital per head being insufficient to lead to self-sufficiency or complete specialization of the country in production.

Figures 10.12 and 10.13 illustrate the case in which under free trade the country would export consumption goods and import investment goods, on the alternative assumptions that investment goods are relatively capital-intensive and relatively labour-intensive in production, and the country imposes an initially non-prohibitory tariff on imports. Production moves initially from B to B'; the new consumption point C' must lie along a line through B', with a slope equal to the world (free trade) price ratio (including the tariff) the resulting national income M_I' measured in investment goods, multiplied by the community's savings ratio, must yield the amount of investment goods actually absorbed at C'. The effect of the tariff on imported consumption goods is to reduce national income measured in investment goods, reduce the savings supply curve from OS' to OS'', less than sufficient to maintain capital per head intact, and

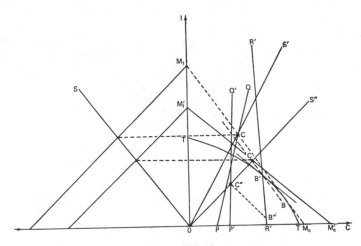

FIGURE 10.12

start the economy decumulating capital. Because of the production inefficiency introduced by the tariff, the investment requirement curve is shifted left for the initial stock of capital. As the economy decumulates capital, its production equilibrium point moves inwards along its Rybczynski line, southeast in the case of capital-intensiveness of investment goods production (Figure 10.12), northwest in the case of labour-intensiveness of investment goods production (Figure 10.13). Long-run growth equilibrium is restored at the intersection of the investment requirement and investment supply surves, providing that this intersection occurs with the country incompletely specialized and trading in the same direction as initially. As the Figures imply, such an equilibrium implies that the country becomes both absolutely and relatively more dependent on the export of consumption goods and import of investment goods in the case in which investment goods are relatively capital-intensive in produc-

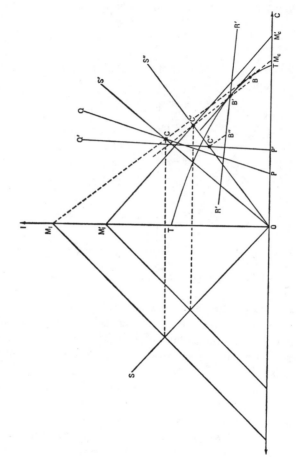

FIGURE 10.13

tion, as compared with the initial post-tariff situation; and both absolutely and relatively less dependent on the export of consumption goods and import of investment goods (as compared with the immediately post-tariff situation) in the case in which investment goods are relatively labour-intensive in production.

Figures 10.14 and 10.15 illustrate the case in which under free trade the country would export investment goods and import consumption goods, again on the alternative assumptions of relative capital-intensity and relative labour-intensity of investment goods production. The new consumption point C' in each case is related to the new production point B', as in the previous two cases, by the conditions that the slope of the line joining them must be the world price ratio and that the quantities consumed (invested) must be such that the given savings ratio applied to the total value of those quantities at domestic (tariff-inclusive) prices yields the amount of investment shown by the equilibrium consumption point. The imposition of the tariff increases the value of income, measured in terms of investment goods, generated by the initial capital per head and corresponding transformation curve, and so raises the investment supply curve from OS' to OS'', thus starting the economy accumulating capital; because of the production inefficiency generated by the tariff, the investment requirement curve shifts to the right for the initial stock of capital. As the economy accumulates capital it moves outwards along its Rybczynski line (northwest in Figure 10.14, southeast in Figure 10.15). Assuming that long-run growth equilibrium is restored while the country remains incompletely specialized and trading in the initial free trade direction, long-run growth equilibrium is restored at the intersection of the new investment requirement and investment supply curves. In the case of relative capital-intensiveness of investment goods production (Figure 10.14), the country becomes absolutely and relatively more dependent on the export of investment goods than in the immediate post-tariff situation. In the case of relative labour-intensiveness of investment goods production (Figure 10.15), the country becomes absolutely and relatively less dependent on the export of investment goods than in the immediate post-tariff situation.

The results just derived are extremely artificial and unrealistic, inasmuch as they rest on the highly indefensible assumption of the majority of contemporary growth models that society's proclivity to

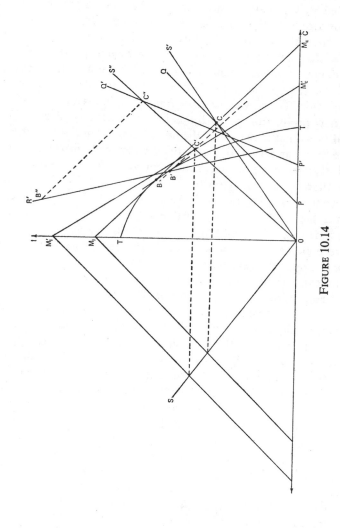

FIGURE 10.14

accumulate capital can be represented by a fixed savings ratio applied to income, rather than by considerations of prospective return, prospective family needs for future income, and so forth, and the mechanics by which they are derived essentially exploit the inverse relationship between the relative price of investment goods in terms of consumption goods and the amount of real investment (as

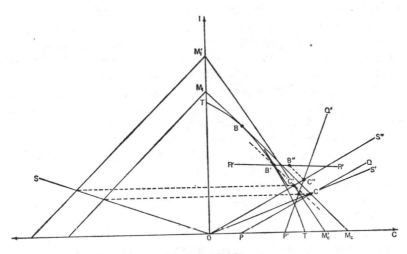

FIGURE 10.15

contrasted with its value) that a given savings ratio applied to a given total income implies. Nevertheless, they lend themselves to the kind of suggestive remarks about policy implications that general equilibrium theorists are occasionally addicted to making, often on the basis of models less rigorously specified than the present one.

Specifically, the results suggest that protection is a bad policy, in the sense of inhibiting the growth of output and consumption per head, in countries which export consumption goods and import investment goods, and a good policy for achieving the same objectives in countries which export investment goods and import consumption goods. (This generalization, however, has to be qualified by recognition of the possibilities implicit in Figures 10.12, 10.13, 10.14 and 10.15 respectively, that consumption per head may be

333

higher with protection and capital decumulation than under free trade in the first case, and lower with protection and capital accumulation than under free trade in the second case.) Since the less developed countries typically or 'stylistically' belong in the former category and the developed countries in the latter category, the happy conclusion suggests itself that free trade on both sides would tend to reduce inequalities of consumption per head (a different problem than the traditional problem of factor-price inequalities) between the two groups of countries. On a lower plane of generality, the analysis would generally support the practices of less developed countries in differentiating in their protective and subsidization policies between consumption and investment goods.

The analytical technique developed in this chapter has been based on the crudest of assumptions about savings behaviour—a fixed overall savings ratio—and applied only to the simplest of trading situations—the opening of the opportunity to trade at a fixed price ratio different from the closed-economy equilibrium price ratio. It is obvious, however, that it could easily be extended to incorporate more complex assumptions about savings behaviour and deal with more ambitious problems in trade theory.

Different savings proportions for capital and labour incomes could be readily (if cumbersomely) introduced by means of the apparatus for handling income distribution developed in Chapter 2. On the trade theory side, the determination of the 'trade triangle' for given terms of trade is only the first step in the determination of the offer curve. Provided that population growth (or population growth plus Harrod-neutral technical progress) is assumed to proceed at the same rate in both countries, an analysis of trade and growth equilibrium in a two-country world model economy could easily be developed by use of two sets of offer curves, one corresponding to the initial no-trade growth equilibrium stocks of capital in the two countries and determined by the associated transformation curves and savings ratios, and the other incorporating full adjustment of the national stocks of capital per head to alternative potential world commodity price ratios. The model could also be easily extended to deal with once-over changes in technology, of a neutral, labour-saving, or capital-saving kind.

Finally, it must be observed, however reluctantly, that by abstracting from those factors that determine the growth rate of the economy the analysis of this model—and others like it—fails to consider the very problem that appears to be of greatest interest to policymakers, at least in the less developed regions of the world economy, namely that of accelerating the rate of economic growth. As often has been stressed in this book, abstraction is an indispensable element of scientific investigation of economic problems, but what has been meant of course has been the abstraction from complicating or obfuscating elements related to the problem at hand, not abstraction from the problem itself. For this reason, in the context of present world interests, economic growth models of the vintage developed in this chapter are open to the charge of being irrelevant, though in defence of the analysis it can justifiably be said that the problem of maximising consumption per head on any given growth path is an important economic problem as is the effect of international trade on the growth path.

REFERENCES

CHAPTER 1

K. Arrow, *Social Choice and Individual Values* (New York: John Wiley and Sons, 1951).

R. H. Coase, 'The Problem of Social Cost', *Journal of Law and Economics*, Vol. 3 (1966), pp. 1–44.

M. Friedman, 'The Marshallian Demand Curve', *Journal of Political Economy*, Vol. LVII (December 1949), pp. 463–95

——, 'The Methodology of Positive Economics', *Essays in Positive Economics* (Chicago: University of Chicago Press, 1935), pp. 3–43.

J. R. Hicks, *Value and Capital* (Oxford: Clarendon Press, 1939).

——, *A Revision of Demand Theory* (Oxford: Clarendon Press, 1956).

A. Marshall, *Principles of Economics* (London: Macmillan for the Royal Economic Society, 1961, 9th edition).

L. Robbins, *The Nature and Significance of Economic Science* (New York: St Martin's Press, 1962, 2nd edition).

CHAPTER 2

J. R. Hicks, *The Theory of Wages* (London: Macmillan & Co., 1932).

H. G. Johnson, *The Two-Sector Model of General Equilibrium* (London: Allen & Unwin, 1971).

M. B. Krauss, H. G. Johnson and T. Skouras, 'On the Shape and Location of the Production Possibility Curve', *Economica*, Vol. XL, (August 1973).

—— and H. G. Johnson, 'The Theory of Tax Incidence: A Diagrammatic Analysis', *Economica*, Vol. XXXIX, No. 156 (November 1972), pp. 357–82.

J. R. Melvin, 'On the Derivation of the Production Possibility Curve', *Economica*, Vol. XXXVIII, No. 151 (August 1971), pp. 287–294.

K. M. Savosnick, 'The Box Diagram and the Production Possibility Curve', *Ekonomisk Tidsskrift*, Vol. LI (September 1958), pp. 183–97.

W. F. Stolper and P. A. Samuelson, 'Protection and Real Wages', *Revue of Economic Studies*, Vol. IX (November 1941), pp. 58–73.

CHAPTER 3

J. R. Hicks, *Value and Capital* (Oxford: Clarendon Press, 1939).

H. G. Johnson, *The Two-Sector Model of General Equilibrium* (London: Allen & Unwin, 1971).

T. M. Rybczynski, 'Factor Endowment and Relative Commodity Prices', *Economica*, Vol. XXII (November 1955), pp. 336–41.

REFERENCES

CHAPTER 4

J. M. Buchanan, 'The Pure Theory of Government Finance: A Suggested Approach', *Journal of Political Economy*, Vol. LVI (December 1949), pp. 496–505.

——, '"La Scienza Delle Finanze": The Italian Tradition in Fiscal Theory', *Fiscal Theory and Political Economy* (Chapel Hill: The University of North Carolina Press, 1960), pp. 24–74.

A. C. Harberger, 'The Incidence of the Corporation Income Tax', *Journal of Political Economy*, Vol. LXX (June 1962), pp. 215–40.

H. G. Johnson, 'A Comment on the General Equilibrium Analysis of Excise Taxes', American Economic Review, Vol. XLV (March 1956), pp. 151–6.

——, 'Minimum Wage Laws: A General Equilibrium Analysis', *The Canadian Journal of Economics*, Vol. II, No. 4 (November 1969), pp. 599–604.

—— and P. Mieszkowski, 'The Effects of Unionization on the Distribution of Income: A General Equilibrium Approach', *The Quarterly Journal of Economics*, Vol. XXXIV, no. 4 (November 1970), pp. 539–61.

M. B. Krauss and H. G. Johnson, 'The Theory of Tax Incidence: A Diagrammatic Analysis', *Economica*, Vol. XXXIX, no. 156 (November 1972), pp. 357–82.

——, 'On The Theory of The Incidence of Government Policy', mimeographed.

P. M. Mieszkowski, 'On The Theory of Tax Incidence', *Journal of Political Economy*, Vol. LXXV (June 1967), pp. 250–62.

R. A. Musgrave, *The Theory of Public Finance* (New York: McGraw-Hill Book Co., 1959).

CHAPTER 5

J. M. Buchanan, *Demand and Supply of Public Goods* (Chicago: Rand McNally & Co., 1968).

——, *Public Finance in Democratic Process* (Chapel Hill, N.C.: University of North Carolina Press, 1967).

J. G. Head, 'The Theory of Public Goods', *Revista di diritto finanziario e scienze delle finanze*, Vol. XXVII (June 1968), pp. 209–36.

P. A. Samuelson, 'The Pure Theory of Public Expenditures', *Review of Economics and Statistics*, Vol. XXXVI (November 1954), pp. 387–9.

CHAPTER 6

E. Heckscher, 'The Effect of Foreign Trade on the Distribution of Income', *Ekonomisk Tidskrift*, Vol. XXI (1919), pp. 497–512, reprinted in translation in *Readings in the Theory of International Trade* (Philadelphia: Blakiston, 1949), pp. 272–300.

H. G. Johnson. *Aspects of the Theory of Tariffs* (London: Allen & Unwin, 1971), Chapter 1.

——, 'Factor Endowments, International Trade and Factor Prices', *Manchester School*, Vol. XXV, no. 3 (September 1957), pp. 270–83.

J. E. Meade, *A Geometry of International Trade* (London: George Allen & Unwin, 1952).

——, *Trade and Welfare* (Fair Lawn, N.J.: Oxford University Press, 1955).

R. A. Mundell, 'International Trade and Factor Mobility', *American Economic Review*, Vol. XLVII, no. 3 (June 1957), pp. 321–35.

B. Ohlin, *Interregional and International Trade* (Cambridge: Harvard University Press, 1933).

P. A. Samuelson, 'International Trade and the Equalization of Factor Prices', *Economic Journal*, Vol. LVIII (June 1948), pp. 163–84.

——, 'International Factor-Price Equalization Once Again', *Economic Journal*, Vol. LIX (June 1949), pp. 181–97.

CHAPTER 7

H. G. Johnson, *Aspects of the Theory of Tariffs* (London: Allen & Unwin, 1971), Chapters 1, 2, 6, 8 and 9.

——, 'Optimum Tariffs and Retaliation', *Review of Economic Studies*, Vol. XXI (1953–4), pp. 142–53.

——, 'The Standard Theory of Tariffs', *The Canadian Journal of Economics*, Vol. II, no. 3 (August 1969), pp. 333–52.

A. P. Lerner, 'The Symmetry Between Import and Export Taxes', *Economica*, Vol. III, no. 11 (August 1936), p. 306–13, reprinted in *Readings in International Economics* (Homewood, Ill.: Richard D. Irwin, 1968), pp. 197–204.

L. A. Metzler, 'Tariffs, The Terms of Trade and the Distribution of National Income', *Journal of Political Economy*, Vol. LVII, no. 1 (February 1949), pp. 1–29.

W. F. Stolper and P. A. Samuelson, 'Protection and Real Wages', *Review of Economic Studies*, Vol. IX (November 1941), pp. 58–73.

CHAPTER 8

J. Bhagwati and V. K. Ramaswami, 'Domestic Distortions, Tariffs and The Theory of Optimum Subsidy', *Journal of Political Economy*, Vol. LXXI, no. 1 (February 1963), pp. 44–50.

A. Friedlaender and A. L. Vandendorpe, 'Excise Taxes and the Gains From Trade', *Journal of Political Economy*, Vol. 76 (September/October 1968), pp. 1058–68.

G. Haberler, 'Some Problems in the Pure Theory of International Trade', *Economic Journal*, Vol. LX, no. 2 (June 1950), pp. 223–40.

REFERENCES

H. G. Johnson, *Aspects of the Theory of Tariffs* (London: Allen & Unwin, 1971), Chapters 4–7.

R. G. Lipsey and K. Lancaster, 'The General Theory of the Second Best', *Review of Economic Studies*, Vol. XXIV, no. 63 (1956–7), pp. 11–32.

J. E. Meade, *Trade and Welfare* (London: Oxford University Press, 1955).

CHAPTER 9

J. Bhagwati, 'Immiserizing Growth: A Geometrical Note', *Review of Economic Studies*, Vol. XXV, no. 3 (June 1958), pp. 201–5.

W. M. Corden, 'Economic Expansion and International Trade: A Geometric Approach', *Oxford Economic Papers*, N.S., Vol. VIII, no. 2 (September 1956).

H. G. Johnson, *Aspects of the Theory of Tariffs* (London: Allen & Unwin, 1971). Chapter 7.

——, *Money, Trade and Economic Growth* (London: Allen & Unwin, 1962), Chapter VI.

CHAPTER 10

H. G. Johnson, *The Two-Sector Model of General Equilibrium* (London: Allen & Unwin, 1971), Chapter 3.

——, 'Trade and Growth: A Geometrical Exposition', *The Journal of International Economics*, Vol. I, no. 1 (February 1971), pp. 83–102.

SUBJECT INDEX

AUTHOR INDEX